Financial Planning for the Individual

A guide to investment and personal finance

ALAN KELLY FCA
Partner, Grant Thornton

Financial Times Business Information
in association with
The Institute of Chartered Accountants in England and Wales

Published in 1989 by FT Business Information Ltd
50-64 Broadway, London SW1H 0DB
Registered number 980896
First edition – February 1986
Second edition – October 1987
Third edition – October 1989

ISBN 1 85334 033 2

Typeset by York House Typographic, York Avenue, Hanwell, London W7 3HY.
Printed and bound in Great Britain by Camelot Press, Southampton.

Contents

Preface

In the previous editions of this book, I described its main purpose as being to state in a concise and easily readable form the main aspects involved in financial planning for individuals. The purpose of the third edition is precisely the same, with the book again aimed primarily at individuals wishing to make maximum use of their money. Hopefully, it should also be useful for professional advisers.

Since the second edition was published at the beginning of October 1987, there have been many fundamental changes both in legislation and in the market place, the most important of these being mainly as follows:

- the effects of the Financial Services Act 1986;
- the stock market crash of October 1987 (two weeks after the second edition was published);
- annual inflation having risen from 4.1% in May 1987 to 8% in May 1989;
- bank base rates having risen from 9% in May 1987 to 14% in May 1989;
- reduction in the top rate of income tax from 60% to 40%;
- increase in the top rate of capital gains tax from 30% to 40%;
- introduction of independent taxation of married couples to take effect from 6th April 1990;
- pension legislation having been made even more complex;
- assured tenancies being available under the Business Expansion Scheme;
- more generous rules for personal equity plans.

These and other changes have been taken into account in this third edition which has been written to reflect the 1989 Budget proposals (plus amendments in the 1989 Finance Bill up to the date of this Preface) on the basis that they will subsequently become law. The book also includes an additional chapter on trusts.

However, despite the crucial changes which have taken place, it should be remembered that the basic principles of planning one's financial affairs to maximum advantage have not really altered.

I am very grateful to all the persons who have assisted me in the preparation of this book. In particular, I should like to thank Tony Ede and Brian Laventure from my own firm (Grant Thornton), Michael Evans of NPI, Ian McIntosh of Standard Life, Brian Lawless of Sun Life, Andrew Peet and Derick Solt of Norwich Union, John Allsop of J.M. Finn & Co, and my secretary, Esther Holloway. I should also like to state my appreciation to my wife and children – Christine, Julian and Amanda – for their forbearance while I have been preparing this book.

Brighton
Sussex

ALAN KELLY
June 1989

1. Introduction

A definition of financial planning for the individual could be: 'Finding the best ways of utilising the financial facilities that exist in order to maximise personal wealth and minimise personal taxation'. This book is concerned with achieving that optimum state.

The range of knowledge required to manage one's own financial affairs successfully can be very wide, covering the whole field of savings, investments, pension arrangements, life assurance policies, mortgages, provision for school fees and tax avoidance measures. Under the heading 'investment' alone, the opportunities extend from the traditional areas of unit trusts, stocks and shares to the specialist investments such as art, stamps, forestry and even bloodstock. However, while many individuals will have little cause to venture into the less traditional fields, they will still be faced with a myriad of options in every aspect of financial planning.

The key to successful planning lies not just in making the right selection, but making the decision that best suits one's personal requirements. This involves striking the correct balance between savings and investments, ensuring that one has sufficient liquidity, and establishing that investments are tax efficient and provide the return at the right time.

The benefits of thorough forward planning of financial matters, both in the long and the short term, cannot be over-emphasised. To this end, this first chapter includes a comprehensive examination of how to recognise indicators which signal the need for financial action and how to establish the requirements of any individual.

For the purpose of convenience, the male gender has been generally used throughout the book. However, unless otherwise stated, the information applies equally to females.

Signposts for action

There are a number of circumstances that should signal that appropriate action may be necessary, including those as follows:

(a) substantial unearned income in respect of interest received from building societies and bank deposits;
(b) no life assurance premiums paid, indicating that life cover may be required;
(c) high rates of personal taxation;
(d) investment portfolio showing very small holdings in many individual companies with the resultant copius paperwork;
(e) substantial proportion of an estate in a marriage being in the husband's name;
(f) a higher rate taxpayer with large holdings in loan stocks or high yielding gilts;

(g) an individual with a potential tax repayment claim but all capital in building society accounts, bank deposit accounts, etc. where tax on interest received cannot be reclaimed;

(h) a higher rate taxpayer with a small mortgage or no mortgage;

(i) credit balances on directors' current accounts in private companies where the companies have substantial cash balances at the bank;

(j) no pension scheme contributions in the accounts of companies;

(k) no self-employed pension contributions or personal pension contributions paid where the individual is self-employed or in non-pensionable employment;

(l) an individual about to sell his business or property;

(m) no capital funding arrangements for share purchase or partnership purchase on death or retirement;

(n) an income which just exceeds the maximum for age allowance purposes;

(o) no will;

(p) an elderly person with grandchildren or nieces and nephews.

The types of action which may be taken in all of these circumstances are dealt with in depth in the subsequent chapters.

Recent major changes

A particular problem for both the individual and the professional adviser is the constantly changing financial environment resulting from new legislation and changes in economic and market conditions. Legislation enacted during the last three years has now been mainly implemented, and this has had a considerable impact on investment providers and intermediaries and in their dealings with clients.

The Financial Services Act 1986
The Financial Services Act 1986 which replaced the Prevention of Fraud (Investments) Act 1958 was introduced in order to provide greater protection for investors and has already had a significant effect on the activities of every person engaged in investment business. The Act has been implemented in stages since receiving Royal Assent in November 1986.

In order to carry on investment business, it is necessary for a person to be authorised to do so, unless exempt from the Act's provisions (conducting investment business without authorisation is a criminal offence). The three main routes by which a professional adviser may obtain authorisation are:

(a) by being a member of a self-regulatory organisation (SRO);

(b) by being a member of a recognised professional body (RPB);

(c) by direct authorisation by the Securities and Investment Board (SIB).

Under the polarisation rules, an intermediary involved in offering investment advice has a choice of two basic options. He can either choose total independence (an independent intermediary) or to be tied to one organisation (a tied agent or appointed representative).

An independent intermediary is a person (or firm or company) who has been authorised by one of the above bodies to advise on and/or arrange investments.

Where advice is being given, he is required, under the 'best advice' provisions (see below), to have knowledge of the investment market and the products offered, and to recommend those best suited to the particular individual.

An appointed representative is exempt from the requirements to be authorised since his investment activities are the responsibility of the single authorised business which appoints him and for which he is an agent. He can advise on and arrange only investment products provided by the business for which he is an agent. Disclosure of tied status is compulsory as independent impartial investment advice cannot be offered. (A further choice is available to those involved in arranging investment business and that is to be merely an introducer. An introducer must decide whether he will refer clients to one appointed representative or to independent intermediaries.)

The five broad categories of investment business defined in the Act are as follows:

(a) dealing in investments;
(b) arranging deals in investments through others;
(c) managing investments belonging to others;
(d) advising others on their investments (both general advice and in relation to specific investments);
(e) establishing, operating or winding up a collective investment scheme, such as a unit trust.

The adviser will have to comply with strict rules as regards his dealing in investments. The following requirements are of particular relevance.

'Know your customer'   This requirement includes a general provision that an adviser must take reasonable steps to ascertain details concerning the client's financial and personal situation which are relevant to the investment services to be provided. There are also specific requirements that the adviser should have reasonable grounds to assume that the client can meet the financial liabilities of the transaction and that he understands the risks involved.

'Best advice'   The best advice requirement follows on from the need to know the client. Therefore, an adviser must not make a specific recommendation to the client unless he knows it is suitable for him. Where a client requests a specific investment which the adviser believes is unsuitable, he must make that fact known (preferably in writing) to the client and only proceed if the client still insists. The appointed representative may only offer an investment provided by the business which has appointed him, whereas the independent adviser is required to offer those investments which are considered the best on the market and which meet the client's particular requirements.

Best advice also involves the adviser being satisfied that no other life assurance company or unit trust management group would offer more advantageous terms to the client concerned. For example, the adviser should keep himself informed as to the current terms in the market for a particular product, especially if these can be readily ascertained, e.g. annuities, term assurance, etc. For other products, the adviser must make regular surveys of the market. In assessing the products available, he must include those of a non-commission paying office.

In addition to direct monetary comparisons, the adviser should take into account such factors as the life assurance company underwriting requirements, past investment performance, standards of service and the financial strength of each company.

'Best execution'   This requirement again involves the adviser in establishing that the life assurance company, unit trust management group, etc. carries out the transaction on the best terms available. This will include price, charges and any other advantages to the client.

Customer agreement.   A further requirement is that an adviser will not be permitted to enter into a transaction with a client unless it is in accordance with the terms of a written agreement. Although the format for the agreement is not laid down, the regulatory bodies do list a substantial number of items to which it must refer. These include a statement of the basis on which the adviser is to be paid, a statement of the client's objectives and any restrictions on the type of investments which he wishes to make, details of termination procedures and of the client's cancellation rights, if any.

Cancellation rules   The cancellation rules of the SIB apply to investment agreements in respect of regular premium life assurance policies and personal pension contracts. Subject to certain exceptions, where the rights of customers are already adequately safeguarded, these rules also apply to single premium life assurance policies and unit trust schemes.

Record keeping   In order for the best advice and best execution rules to be adequately policed, there are strict requirements for the adviser's records to show the reasons for any particular recommendation. Accordingly, all instructions received from a client should be fully recorded. After the instructions have been carried out, the adviser must send the client a statement giving full details of the transaction.

Clients' money   This must be held on trust for the client and held in a separate bank account from the adviser's own monies.

Financial resources   These rules lay down the financial resources that must be maintained at all times and vary according to the size, nature and type of investment business and the associated risks involved.

'Big Bang'
'Big Bang' took effect on the London Stock Exchange on 27th October 1986 with the resultant changes:

(a) abolition of single capacity status of stockbrokers and jobbers, i.e. the convention that stockbrokers could not make a market in stocks and shares and that jobbers could not deal with the public was abolished;
(b) abolition of minimum stock exchange commissions;
(c) abolition of restrictions on outside ownership of member firms;
(d) introduction of new and sophisticated electronic dealing systems.

The Social Security Act 1986
The long awaited reform of pension provision was enacted in the form of the Social Security Act 1986. This legislation, together with other regulations, has become a landmark in the evolution of pensions in this country. Every employer

and employee is affected as part of a move towards greater flexibility in the creation of retirement benefits. The main provisions of the Act are considered in Chapter 7, 'Personal Pensions'.

The Building Societies Act 1986

On 1st January 1987, the main parts of the Building Societies Act 1986 came into force allowing building societies to offer a far wider range of retail financial services. Until that time, building societies were mainly confined to two principal functions — accepting deposits and providing loans for house purchase. The result of the new legislation is more choice for the consumer — both borrower and investor. The Act removes some of the restrictions formerly separating societies from banks and allows greater competition between individual societies and between societies and banks.

Societies are now able to offer the following services which were previously the preserve of other institutions: housing, estate agency, insurance, banking and investment. However, their main activity must remain mortgage lending.

Building societies may now convert themselves from mutual status to that of a limited company. This can only be effected with the consent of a substantial majority of the members voting on specific proposals for that purpose.

Independent taxation

The Finance Act 1988 introduced the principle of independent taxation, which is due to come into effect on 6th April 1990. From that date, married couples will be taxed separately. The main effect will be that married women will be taxed for the first time as individuals, with their own allowances and with responsibility for the payment of tax on their income and capital gains.

Apart from the aspects of privacy and independence, it is possible for married couples to reduce their joint tax bills by appropriate distribution of assets (and, consequently, income) between them. This requires tax planning in advance and is discussed in Chapter 10.

Professional advice

For some individuals, impartial professional advice will be essential at the outset, often because they do not have the time to devote to assessing their best course of action. However, for those who undertake their own financial planning, their approach should be as thorough as a professional adviser's should be. Despite this, it is almost inevitable that at some stage specialist advice will be required.

Obtaining professional advice involves its own selection process. Apart from the requirements of the Financial Services Act, it would be useful to examine the main criteria which should indicate that the professional adviser is providing a thorough and competent service.

(a) The adviser should consider all aspects of the client's affairs without restricting himself to particular areas.
(b) A positive service should be provided, with the adviser approaching the client where appropriate.
(c) Regular reviews of the client's affairs should be carried out.
(d) The adviser should recommend non-commission paying contracts and investments if they are most suitable for the client.

(e) Where a fee basis operates, any commissions received should be declared to the client and taken into account against the fee (alternatively, commissions may be used to obtain better terms for the client).
(f) The adviser should have a good technical knowledge and should often have an appropriate professional qualification.
(g) The adviser should carry an appropriate level of professional indemnity insurance.
(h) If the adviser has been recommended by a person who has already used his services, this would be clearly advantageous.

Ascertaining client requirements

In order to meet the 'know your customer' requirements included in the Financial Services Act, it is essential for the adviser to ascertain the circumstances of the client, together with his personal and financial requirements. To do this, the adviser should normally meet the client at least once and often several times before final advice can be given.

At the first meeting, the adviser will need to obtain certain necessary information. Appendix 1 is an in-depth questionnaire of a type which a professional adviser might employ and will provide a guide as to where action needs to be taken.

Reports

Once the requirements are established, the adviser will usually make a report covering proposals for a course of action to be taken, but it will be up to the client to decide whether to proceed with them or not. It is preferable that the proposals are made in writing to avoid any misunderstandings that could subsequently arise.

There is no set form of report as this will mainly depend upon the particular case as well as personal style. However, it is often useful for supporting statements to be prepared showing the capital and net spendable income position both under the present situation and that immediately afterwards if the proposed course of action is taken.

Reviews

Even after a client has acted upon the adviser's proposals, he will still need an ongoing service as far as regular reviews are concerned. In most cases an annual review should be sufficient but this will depend on whether the client's own circumstances have changed, e.g. inheritance of a capital sum, change of job, etc., or whether there have been external changes which require more immediate attention, e.g. new legislation, or major changes in economic and market conditions.

2. Investment planning

Once the individual's personal circumstances and financial requirements have been established as outlined in the previous chapter, consideration can be given to appropriate investment planning.

Investment considerations

The following specific information should be settled at the outset before a decision is taken regarding particular investments:

(a) the amount of capital available for investment;
(b) precise details of existing investments;
(c) the ages of the individual and his dependants;
(d) the degree of risk the individual is prepared to take, bearing in mind there is often a close correlation between risk and reward;
(e) the period of time for which the investments can be made before access to the capital is required;
(f) the current and likely future tax position of the individual;
(g) the income required from the investments;
(h) whether the main requirement is capital growth, income, or a combination of the two;
(i) whether the investments are to be made within any particular constraints, e.g. as trustee investments;
(j) the degree of involvement which the individual may wish to have in arranging and managing the investments;
(k) details of any anticipated capital receivable in the short term, e.g. proceeds from a life policy or an inheritance;
(l) details of any significant liabilities or personal expenses likely to arise in the near future, e.g. tax liabilities, purchase of new car, etc.;
(m) whether there are any personal priorities, e.g. school fees provision;
(n) whether adequate arrangements have already been made in respect of the following:
  (i) permanent health insurance;
  (ii) sufficient life cover to protect the family in the event of early death;
  (iii) house purchase (consideration should be given to repaying any mortgage or loan where tax relief is not obtained on the interest payable);
  (iv) pension provision;
  (v) wills and inheritance tax planning.

Having ascertained the above information, it should be possible to prepare a broad investment structure. For this purpose, capital should normally be invested in three categories in the following order, with the exact proportion in each category based on the individual circumstances.

(a) The first part of the capital should be in an emergency fund for complete security and immediate access, e.g. a building society account.
(b) The second part of the capital should be in low risk investments with guaranteed returns, e.g. short dated gilt-edged securities. Such investments can usually be realised at short notice. A higher net investment return (capital gains plus income) can often be provided from this part of the capital than from the emergency fund.
(c) The third part of the capital should be in higher risk/higher reward investments with the aim of providing a higher net return than the rate of inflation, or from fixed interest investments, e.g. carefully selected stocks and shares or unit trusts. (This part of the capital may also be used for the purposes of house purchase and pension provision.) The investments in this category should normally be considered as longer term investments, i.e. with a view to being held for a minimum period of four to five years.

Notes:
(a) For people who have retired or who will retire shortly, a greater percentage of capital should normally be invested in the first and second parts since they would usually be less able to make good any capital loss from future income.
(b) In considering the proportion of capital to be invested in the third part, the effect of inflation and normal life expectancy should be borne in mind. These are illustrated in the following tables.

The effect of inflation
£1,000 in today's money will be worth the amount stated at the end of the period shown if the annual rate of inflation over the period is as indicated.

Period years	4% inflation £	7% inflation £	10% inflation £
1	962	935	909
2	925	873	826
3	889	816	751
4	855	763	683
5	822	713	621
10	676	508	386
15	555	362	239
20	456	258	149
25	375	184	92
30	308	131	57
35	253	94	36
40	208	67	22
45	171	48	14
50	141	34	9

Normal life expectancy
The normal life expectancy of a person is as shown below.

Present age	Male years	Female years
50	25½	29½
55	21½	25½
60	17½	21
65	14	17
70	11	13½
75	8	10½
80	6	7½
85	4	5½
90	3	4
95	2	2½

When the general structure for the capital has been decided, the various types of investments can then be considered. These may be divided into the two main categories of (a) fixed investments; and (b) variable investments.

Fixed investments

The principal feature of fixed investments is that either the capital and/or the income therefrom is determined from the outset and guaranteed while the investment is held. These investments will form the first and second parts of capital (in some cases, they may also be included within the third part).

The specific choice of investment will depend on the exact circumstances of the individual and on the returns available from the various investments at the particular time together with the current and prospective levels of interest rates in general. The investment yields mentioned in this chapter are those available in April 1989 and are shown net of basic rate tax unless otherwise stated.

The more usual types of fixed investments are as follows:

(a) bank accounts;
(b) money market funds;
(c) building society accounts;
(d) National Savings investments;
(e) guaranteed income and guaranteed growth bonds;
(f) gilt-edged securities;
(g) eurobonds;
(h) local authority loans;
(i) company debentures and unsecured loan stocks;
(j) preference shares;
(k) purchased life annuities.

Bank accounts
Until recently, only deposit accounts could be considered as investments in the sense of paying interest. However, competition from building societies and within the banks themselves has led to interest-bearing current accounts being made generally available.

Since 6th April 1985, banks pay a composite rate of tax (21.75% in the current tax year) on interest paid on behalf of individuals resident in the UK who are then deemed to have received this net of basic rate tax. For a person not liable to income tax, no repayment claim can be made in respect of the tax suffered. (In these cases, the individual can choose to open a bank deposit account offshore with the result that gross interest would be paid.) Persons liable to income tax at higher rates would currently be assessed on £100 for every £75 of net interest received.

Current accounts   Traditionally, bank current accounts have provided a means of handling an individual's cash flow in a secure and manageable form by the provision of cheque books, standing orders, etc. and overdraft facilities. Most of the high street banks now offer interest on current accounts, the rates being mainly dependent upon:

(a) the general level of interest rates;
(b) the daily balance of the account;
(c) the charges made for services offered.

At the present time, the interest payable on current accounts varies generally between 5% and 8%.

Deposit accounts   Bank deposit accounts may be considered as an investment for emergency funds when the interest rates offered are competitive (although other factors should be taken into account, such as convenience, demonstration of financial status, etc).

At the present time, the interest payable on seven days' notice accounts is approximately 4.5% pa. However, for accounts with balances of £500 and over, it is possible to obtain a higher rate of interest depending on the amount of the balance (currently a rate of 9% is available for a minimum deposit of £10,000). In addition, instant withdrawals without loss of interest are often permitted.

Money market funds
These funds fall broadly into two main categories, (a) money market deposit accounts, and (b) high interest cheque accounts.

Money market deposit accounts   There are two basic types of money market deposit funds, fixed accounts and notice accounts, both of which are usually subject to a minimum investment of £10,000.

Fixed accounts are similar to ordinary term deposit accounts whereby a sum of money is invested for a fixed period, during which time investors do not have access to the money invested. This term can vary from overnight to five years.

Notice accounts require an investor to give a set period of notice on withdrawals while allowing him to leave the balance on deposit for an unlimited period. Similarly, the bank must give the investor the same period of notice of a change of interest rates. A typical period of notice is from seven days to six months.

The interest paid on both fixed accounts and notice accounts is calculated on a daily basis and credited at regular intervals, or at the end of the investment period if earlier. The rate payable reflects current money market interest rates and varies according to the amount invested and either the investment period or notice required on withdrawal. Like traditional bank deposit accounts, interest is effectively normally paid net of basic rate tax (the main exception to this is for investments of £50,000 or more for a fixed period of at least seven days where the interest is paid gross).

At the present time, amounts between £10,000 and £24,999 inclusive on seven days' notice attract interest of approximately 8.6% pa, while for an amount on one month's notice, a rate of 9% pa is offered.

For fixed terms, the following rates are currently payable by one of the major banks for amounts between £10,000 and £24,999 inclusive:

one month	—	9.00%
three months	—	9.25%
six months	—	9.25%
one year	—	9.13%

Money market deposit accounts may be suitable for individuals with very large amounts as a short term home until they commit their money on a longer term basis. An example of this could be where a person intends to invest on the stock market when he considers the time is opportune. For smaller amounts, it is likely that the National Savings Investment Account would be more suitable for non-taxpayers, and a building society account for other individuals.

High interest cheque accounts These accounts provide an individual with immediate access to his funds without loss of interest but with money market interest rates payable. Other services are also frequently offered such as a cheque guarantee card, standing orders, direct debits and an overdraft facility.

The main features of high interest cheque accounts, where interest rates at the present time usually vary between 8% and 10%, are as follows:

(a) a high minimum balance is required (this normally varies from £1,000 to £2,500) and if the balance falls below the stated minimum, either no interest or a reduced rate is payable;
(b) several accounts set a minimum level for further deposits and/or withdrawals of approximately £200 per transaction;
(c) most accounts pay different levels of interest, depending on the amount in the account, so that when the balance falls/rises beyond a certain point, the rate of interest changes accordingly;
(d) interest is generally calculated on a daily basis and credited to the account at the end of the month or quarter;
(e) although charges are not usually made provided the minimum balance is maintained, some accounts only allow a limited number of cheques to be drawn on a free basis;
(f) interest is paid net of basic rate tax;
(g) high interest cheque accounts are available from at least one unit trust management company with 1% discount being offered on units purchased through the account.

The main drawbacks to most high interest cheque accounts are the high minimum balance required, the minimum level set for further deposits and withdrawals, and the restriction on the number of cheques which can be drawn if charges are to be avoided. Consequently, these accounts will mainly be suitable for individuals with large temporary balances who do not write many cheques, e.g. for holding cash pending investment.

Building society accounts
Like bank deposit accounts, building society accounts can be very useful as a home for emergency funds subject to the level of the interest rates offered being competitive. (In addition, an investment in a building society account can assist in obtaining a mortgage when the funds available for lending are scarce.) Building societies also pay a composite rate of tax of currently 21.75% on interest paid on behalf of individuals who are then treated as having received this net of basic rate tax. A person not liable to income tax is unable to make a repayment claim in respect of the tax suffered. Higher rate taxpayers would currently be assessed on £100 for every £75 of net interest received.

At the present time, ordinary share accounts generally offer a rate of 6% pa and regular savings accounts 7%. However, for larger investments, the following rates are available, with instant withdrawals permitted without loss of interest and a monthly income facility being provided for investments of £5,000 and over:

for a minimum investment of £   500   —   8.00%
for a minimum investment of £ 2,000   —   8.25%
for a minimum investment of £ 5,000   —   8.75%
for a minimum investment of £10,000   —   9.00%

Accounts invested on a longer term basis and those requiring a greater period of notice of withdrawals or a loss of interest in lieu are also available (the requirement for notice of withdrawals or loss of interest in lieu is waived on some accounts, subject to the balance remaining in the account after withdrawal being not less than £5,000 or £10,000). Although these accounts often provide a higher rate of interest than accounts where no notice is required, they do not necessarily serve the same purpose. An investment without immediate access (or where loss of interest is suffered in order to obtain immediate access) should generally only be made after an emergency fund has been provided.

National Savings investments
There are various types of National Savings investments available with the purpose of appealing to investors with different requirements and tax rates. The following National Savings investments are offered at the present time:

(a) National Savings Certificates — 34th Issue;
(b) National Savings Index-Linked Certificates — 4th Issue;
(c) National Savings Ordinary Account;
(d) National Savings Investment Account;
(e) National Savings Income Bonds;
(f) National Savings Capital Bonds;
(g) National Savings Premium Bonds;
(h) National Savings Yearly Plan.

National Savings Certificates — 34th Issue This issue offers a guaranteed tax free return of 7.5% pa compound if held for the full five-year period. The minimum holding per individual is £25 and the normal maximum holding is £1,000 but holders of matured issues of certificates may purchase up to £10,000 of 34th Issue 'reinvestment certificates' in addition to the general £1,000 limit. If the certificates were encashed within five years, the return provided would be lower and would depend on the length of time that the certificates were held. Certificates held beyond the maturity date will continue to earn interest at the 'General Extension Rate' (currently 5.01%).

Even if the certificates were held to maturity, the net return provided is not particularly attractive at the present time compared to other investments available except for relatively small sums and for higher rate taxpayers.

National Savings Index-Linked Certificates — 4th Issue   The return offered by these certificates is based on the change in the Retail Price Index (RPI) over a period of five years together with predetermined rates of annual interest. Index-linking and interest are capitalised on each anniversary so that subsequent growth is based on the value at the beginning of the year. Early encashment, after the first year, will provide index-linking and interest additions up to the month of withdrawal. The minimum holding per individual in the 4th Issue of National Savings Index-Linked Certificates is £25 and the maximum holding £5,000.

If the certificates were held for the full five-year period, a tax free return of 4.04% pa compound would be provided on top of the rate of inflation during the period. However, like the 34th Issue of National Savings Certificates, if they were encashed within five years, the return provided would be lower and would depend on the number of years that the certificates were held.

Certificates held beyond the maturity date will continue to be index-linked and to earn interest (at a rate to be determined).

Whether National Savings Index-Linked Certificates prove to be a worthwhile investment will mainly depend on the future level of inflation. However, at the present time, they provide a better return for basic rate taxpayers compared to index-linked gilts with a similar maturity date (index-linked gilts are considered later in this chapter). For higher rate taxpayers, Index-Linked Savings Certificates are even more advantageous compared to index-linked gilts. Accordingly, for investors who require a guaranteed real return and are unlikely to require access to their capital for five years, National Savings Index-Linked Certificates have definite attractions.

National Savings Ordinary Account The rate of interest offered under this account is 5% pa for each complete calendar month where the balance is £500 or more, provided the account is open for the whole of 1989. The rate received on other balances is 2.5% pa. The minimum deposit per individual is £5 and the maximum deposit £10,000. Interest of up to £70 pa (£140 pa if the account is held jointly by husband and wife) can be received tax free.

Except for higher rate taxpayers maintaining a balance of not less than £500 nor more than £1,400 (the amount on which £70 pa tax free interest is receivable), the National Savings Ordinary Account is unlikely to be attractive compared to other investments available.

National Savings Investment Account This account credits interest on 31st December each year at a rate of currently 10.75% pa calculated on a daily basis. The interest is taxable, but is paid without any deduction being made at source. The minimum deposit per individual is £5 and the maximum deposit £100,000 but this can be exceeded by interest credited to the account. Withdrawals are subject to one month's notice.

A deposit in the National Savings Investment Account can be a worthwhile investment for an individual not liable to tax, particularly as there is no need for a tax repayment claim to be made.

National Savings Income Bonds The interest rate on this investment is currently 11.5% pa payable monthly on the fifth day of each month. The minimum holding per individual is £2,000 and the maximum holding £100,000. Although the interest is paid gross, it is subject to tax.

The main disadvantage with National Savings Income Bonds is that if the interest is to be paid in full, three months' notice of withdrawal is required and the bonds must be held for a minimum period of one year (if the bonds are encashed earlier, half the normal rate of interest is payable). Consequently, this investment is likely to be more attractive to non-taxpayers who require a monthly income and are in a position to give the required period of notice for withdrawals.

National Savings Capital Bonds This plan offers a return of 12% pa compound if held for the full five-year period. Although the interest is earned gross, it is subject to tax (see below). If the bonds were encashed within five years, the return provided would be lower and would depend on the length of time the bonds were held. The minimum investment is £100 and at present there is no maximum. There is no provision for the bond to earn interest after the maturity date.

The bondholder is liable to income tax on the interest added each year even though it is not actually paid to him. The real net return to a taxpayer at maturity is difficult to determine, due to the payment of tax in advance of receiving the proceeds and the uncertainty of future income tax rates.

Capital bonds are most attractive to individuals not liable to income tax who require guaranteed capital growth over a five-year period.

National Savings Premium Bonds Instead of bondholders receiving interest from their Premium Bonds, the interest is used to provide prizes for a limited number of holders. Weekly and monthly prize draws take place with the maximum prize in a weekly draw being £100,000 and in a monthly draw, £250,000. The prize fund represents approximately 6.5% pa of the total value of eligible bonds and all prizes (currently over 190,000 each month) are received free of tax. Bonds are not eligible for inclusion in the prize draws for the first three calendar months following their month of purchase. The minimum initial holding of Premium Bonds is £100 per individual (reduced to £10 for bonds bought on behalf of a child under 16) and the maximum holding £10,000.

Premium Bonds cannot strictly be classified as investments as the only return provided depends on 'the luck of the draw'. However, it is only the interest which is at stake with the return of the capital guaranteed. Consequently, this will be satisfactory for those persons who are prepared to forgo the interest on their Premium Bonds in order to obtain the chance of receiving a large, tax free windfall without risk of loss to their capital, except that imposed by inflation.

National Savings Yearly Plan Under the National Savings Yearly Plan, individuals are able to invest a minimum of £20 and a maximum of £200 per month for one year. At the end of the year, a Yearly Plan Certificate is issued with a value equivalent to the total monthly payments made plus the interest earned in the year. The interest offered for the following four years would be in accordance with a scale fixed at the outset of the Plan.

At the present time, a tax free return of 7.5% pa compound is provided over the five-year period, i.e. the certificates are held for the four years following the savings year. If the certificates were held for less than four years, the return obtained would be lower. The return offered to new investors may vary with market interest rates, but this will not affect existing investors.

For higher rate taxpayers who wish to build up a capital sum with the rate of interest fixed from the outset of the contract, the National Savings Yearly Plan is likely to be an attractive investment. However, for those investors who do not consider a fixed return to be important, a building society monthly savings account may be more advantageous, especially if access to the capital may be required before the end of the five-year period.

Guaranteed income and guaranteed growth bonds
The purpose of guaranteed bonds is to provide a fixed rate of income or growth over a preselected term in addition to the return of the original capital sum at the end of that period.

There are four main types of guaranteed bonds, all issued by life assurance companies. These bonds, which have different structures and accordingly are taxed in different ways, are as follows:

(a) a combination of temporary and deferred annuities;
(b) single premium endowment policies (this is the most usual type of bond);
(c) a series of single premium endowment policies;
(d) a series of single premium endowment policies plus term assurance.

The following are the principal considerations relating to guaranteed income and guaranteed growth bonds.

(a) The rate of income or growth shown is net of basic rate tax, but subject to higher rate tax at the time of payment of the income or at maturity. On income bonds, there may in addition be a potential higher rate tax charge on the return of capital (where deferred annuities are included as part of the income bonds, a charge to basic rate tax will also arise).
(b) Income payments are generally made annually, although sometimes half-yearly.
(c) If the individual should die during the term of the bond, the amount of the investment is returned (any accrued income to the date of death will sometimes also be paid).
(d) Surrender values, where allowed, are not normally guaranteed and will generally depend on financial conditions at the time.
(e) The returns are fixed. Therefore, before an investor becomes locked in at a fixed rate of interest, he should take the view that interest rates are unlikely to rise. However, if he considers that higher rates are likely, it may be appropriate for him to invest in a variable interest investment, e.g. a building society account on a temporary basis and then reinvest in guaranteed bonds at a later date if he proves to be correct.
(f) Since guaranteed bonds are frequently offered by less established insurance companies, potential investors should ensure as far as possible that the financial position of the company concerned is soundly based.
(g) If a person normally qualifies for age allowance, it should be remembered that his position could be affected by the taxation treatment of the guaranteed bonds.
(h) The rates of interest provided under guaranteed income and guaranteed growth bonds tend to lag behind general market interest rates. Therefore, potential investors should be prepared to act quickly when market rates have

fallen, but before this is reflected in the rates offered by the guaranteed bonds.

At the present time, returns of approximately 8.25% to 9.25% pa net of basic rate tax can be obtained.

Gilt-edged securities

Gilt-edged securities are issued by the British Government in the form of loans in order to finance its expenditure. Since the loans are Government-backed, their repayment on the relevant maturity dates is assured, although in the interim, prices will fluctuate according to market forces. The following are some of the more important characteristics of the gilt-edged market for the private investor (the tax treatment of income and capital gains is discussed in Chapter 10).

(a) Due to the very wide choice of the different gilt-edged securities offered, it is usually possible to select a particular gilt to fit the circumstances of most investors. The various types of gilts available are as follows:
(i)   short dated gilts (with maturity dates within five years);
(ii) medium dated gilts (with maturity dates after five years but within fifteen years);
(iii) long dated gilts (with maturity dates after fifteen years);
(iv) undated gilts (with no maturity dates);
(v)   convertible gilts (gilts with an option for the holder to switch into a longer dated gilt at a series of fixed dates, typically six months apart, in the original stock's life);
(vi) index-linked gilts (where both capital growth and income are based on changes in the RPI. See (f) below).

Dated gilts (other than index-linked gilts) can be further divided into low, medium and high coupon stocks. Coupons range from 2½% to 15½%. Normally, high coupon stocks will be more suitable for pension funds, charities and individuals not liable to tax, while low coupon issues will be more appropriate for individuals paying tax at the higher rate due to the greater potential for tax free capital growth.

(b) At maturity, £100 nominal stock will be redeemed for £100 except in the case of index-linked stocks.

(c) The volatility of the price of a gilt will mainly depend on the nominal rate of the coupon and the length of the period until the redemption date. Low coupon and long dated stocks will generally be more volatile than high coupon and short dated stocks.

(d) The shape of the yield curve, which plots the current redemption yields of different gilts against their periods to maturity, will normally indicate general expectations for movements in interest rates and the outlook for inflation. Short dated gilts generally reflect interest rates while other gilts also reflect inflation. At the present time, the redemption yields on very short dated gilts are generally very high to reflect current interest rates. However, in the case of long dated gilts, the redemption yields are much lower, partly as a consequence of acquiring a scarcity value due to the Government surplus (as a result of the surplus, the Government has been buying in gilts rather than issuing them to fund its liabilities).

(e) Price anomalies can arise in the gilt-edged market, and by being alert, it is possible for an investor to obtain considerable benefit from them. These anomalies usually occur due to there being a shortage or excess of a particular stock at a particular time.

(f) Index-linked gilts, whereby both the capital and interest exactly reflect the change in the RPI, were first issued in March 1981 and subsequently became available to private investors in March 1982. As a result, an individual was able for the first time to obtain a guaranteed real rate of return on his investments. (The change in the RPI is measured over the period from eight months before the issue date of a gilt to eight months before its redemption date.)

   However, in order for this return to be guaranteed, the gilt must be held until redemption since its price in the interim will be mainly determined by the following factors:
   (i)   the supply and demand position;
   (ii)   the current level and outlook for interest rates;
   (iii)   the yields offered by conventional gilts;
   (iv)   the rate of inflation which has occurred for the period from eight months before the issue date to the present time;
   (v)   the outlook for inflation from the present time until eight months before the redemption date.

Currently, investors can obtain a real rate of return to redemption before tax, based on projected inflation of 7% pa, from 3.15% for Treasury 2% Index-Linked Stock 1992 to 3.56% for Treasury 2½% Index-Linked Stock 2009. At the same projected rate of inflation, the following net redemption yields would be provided.

	Treasury 2% *I–L Stock 1992*	*Treasury 2½%* *I-L Stock 2009*
For a 25% rate taxpayer	9.64% pa	9.87% pa
For a 40% rate taxpayer	9.33% pa	9.46% pa

If future inflation should average less than 7% pa, the above returns would also be less. However, if the average inflation rate should be more than 7% pa, the above returns would be correspondingly greater.

   Based on current prices and the outlook for inflation, index-linked gilts appear to be a worthwhile investment for those investors wishing to obtain a guaranteed real return from part of their capital. This particularly applies to individuals paying tax at the higher rate. (Where a gilt is unlikely to be held until its redemption date, it should be remembered that as in the case of conventional gilts, the stocks with the earlier maturity dates will carry less risk.)

(g) Where gilt-edged securities are purchased via the National Savings Stock Register rather than through a stockbroker, the following advantages are provided:
   (i)   dealing costs are lower, especially for smaller bargains;
   (ii)   interest payments are made without deduction of tax, thereby avoiding the need for a non-taxpayer to make a repayment claim and also providing a person who is liable to tax with a cash flow advantage until the tax is paid.

However, by dealing in gilts via the National Savings Stock Register, the following disadvantages arise:
   (i)   a maximum investment is permitted in any one stock of only £10,000 per day (this does not apply to sales);

(ii)   it is not possible to specify either a date or a price at which a stock should be purchased or sold;

(iii)   approximately 36% of the gilts in issue cannot be dealt in via the Register.

Whether it is worthwhile to use the Register instead of a stockbroker will depend on the exact circumstances. However, in general, it will normally be advantageous to use the stockbroker for larger transactions, but the Register for smaller bargains.

Eurobonds

Eurobonds are bonds, usually issued in a foreign currency, which are traded internationally. Interest is normally paid gross on an annual basis. Although marketability is usually good in high quality bonds (Triple A bonds), an investment of less than £20,000 is not practical.

Due to the complexity of settlement and the variety of bonds available, professional advice is generally necessary when making an investment.

Local authority loans

Local authorities raise loans in order to assist in financing their expenditure. Although the security provided is generally of a high order, these loans do not have the same backing as gilt-edged securities, or the same marketability. As a result, the yields from local authority loans are usually greater than those available from comparable gilts.

There are three main types of local authority loans.

(a)   Fixed term unquoted corporation loans. These loans are normally issued at par and usually become repayable within three years also at par. Consequently, the return provided will be in the form of interest only and this will be based on general market rates at the time the loans are raised. Since fixed term unquoted corporation loans do not have quotations, an individual is unable to obtain the repayment of his investment until maturity (or death if earlier).

(b)   Quoted corporation loans. These loans have many of the features of gilt-edged securities, including a wide range of coupons and maturity dates. However, the market is often small and consequently it is not always possible to buy in reasonable amounts, with £1,000 or £2,000 sometimes being difficult.

(c)   Local authority yearling bonds. These loans are similar to fixed term unquoted corporation loans in that they are generally issued and redeemed at par, with the interest rate offered being in line with market rates at the time the loans are made. The loans are generally issued each Tuesday, paid for on the following day and redeemed on Wednesday, one year and six days later. However, the main practical difference between local authority yearling bonds and fixed term unquoted corporation loans is that the former can be bought and sold at any time from the date of issue until the redemption date.

The tax treatment with regard to an individual investing in local authority bonds is discussed in Chapter 10.

Company debentures and unsecured loan stocks

These loans which are normally raised by companies to provide, e.g., working capital, are often traded on the Stock Exchange. In the case of company debentures, the loans are secured on particular company assets, or a floating charge is made on the assets generally. However, no specific security is provided with unsecured loan stocks.

Company debentures and unsecured loan stocks can be issued in convertible or non-convertible form. When issued in convertible form, stockholders would be provided with the option to convert their investments into the ordinary shares of the company at fixed dates on stated terms. The market value of these 'convertibles' would then reflect the value of the company's ordinary shares in addition to the general level of interest rates and the status of the company concerned.

A major disadvantage of some company debentures and loan stocks is that the market for them is often narrow, with the result that deals cannot always be transacted. Even where they can be arranged, it is not unusual for there to be a wide margin between the bid and offer prices.

Mainly due to the greater risks involved and their inferior marketability, higher yields are available from non-convertible company debentures and loan stocks than from comparable gilt-edged securities. However, from the point of view of security, gilts would still generally be more suitable for most investors.

The tax treatment with regard to an individual investing in company debentures and unsecured loan stocks is discussed in Chapter 10.

Preference shares
Preference shares rank after debentures and unsecured loan stocks in order of security (in the event of the company being wound up, the holders of preference shares would not receive payment until after the loans had first been repaid). Therefore, higher yields would normally be expected from preference shares due to the greater risk involved.

However, there are additional factors which may affect yields on preference shares including, for example, the dividends paid being treated as franked income in a company's hands, whereas interest from debentures and unsecured loan stocks is treated as unfranked income. Since this makes preference shares more attractive to companies, reduced yields are generally offered. Other factors would be the particular terms offered by the preference shares, e.g. whether cumulative or non-cumulative (cumulative means if a dividend is missed, it accumulates for later payment), participating rights, voting rights, redemption dates, etc., which could result in lower yields being available.

Like debentures and loan stocks, the higher yields usually offered by preference shares would not generally provide sufficient compensation for most private investors for the greater security and marketability of gilt-edged securities. Furthermore, capital gains arising from preference shares would be subject to capital gains tax (this is not the case for gilt-edged securities).

It is now also possible to purchase convertible preference shares which are treated as wider-range investments. These are convertible into the ordinary shares at fixed dates on stated terms in a similar way to convertible debentures and unsecured loan stocks.

Purchased life annuities
Although there are several different types of purchased life annuities (including immediate annuities which commence immediately and deferred annuities which commence at a future date), the following features are held in common.

(a) For a lump sum payment, annuity instalments will be received at regular intervals by the individual, either for the remainder of his life or for a preselected term. The annuity can be arranged on a joint life and last survivor basis so that, if required, a guaranteed income can be provided for the annuitant and his wife during their lifetimes. The annuity can also be arranged to increase each year on a preselected fixed basis or in line with a preselected index (see (b) below).

(b) The annuity payments may be fixed or variable on one of the following bases:
   (i)   without profits level annuity, where the gross payment is determined at the outset and will not change;
   (ii) without profits increasing annuity, where the gross payment increases by a fixed percentage each year (usually between 3% and 10%);
   (iii) without profits index-linked annuity, where the gross payment is fixed for the first year and thereafter varies in line with an index (usually the RPI);
   (iv) with profits annuities, where part of the gross payment is guaranteed, and annual bonuses are declared to increase the payment. Bonuses, once declared, become part of the guaranteed payment;
   (v)   unit-linked annuities, where the gross payment is linked to the investment performance of a selected fund.

   The gross annuity is the sum of the capital and income elements before deduction of tax (see (c) below).

(c) The annuity paid consists of a capital element and an income element. The capital element represents a partial return of the original investment and would accordingly be tax free. The income element would be subject to taxation in the normal way. (Where an annuity is subject to guaranteed escalations, the capital content rises pro rata with the gross payments. This is unlike the other forms of annuity described above where the capital content remains the same as at the outset so that any increase in the annuity is subject to income tax.)

(d) The returns provided by annuities will usually be very high and will be mainly determined by the following factors:
   (i)   the type of annuity;
   (ii) the general level of interest rates;
   (iii) the age and sex of the individual (or individuals in the case of a joint life and last survivor annuity — with this type of annuity, it is the age and sex of the younger person which will have considerably more importance);
   (iv) the guarantee period (if any) for which the annuity is to be paid;
   (v)   the basis of annuity (see (b) above);
   (vi) the frequency of payment;
   (vii) the rates offered by individual insurance companies at the particular time, remembering that there are often significant differences between them. It is therefore worthwhile for several quotations to be obtained.

(e) Since annuity rates are constantly changing, an individual should take immediate action if he wishes to purchase an annuity at a time of falling interest rates.

The main disadvantage of purchased life annuities is that there is no access to the capital sum paid. In addition, in the event of the individual's death soon after arranging the annuity, there would be no return to his estate unless the annuity was effected with a guaranteed minimum period of payment or on a capital protected basis. (Under a capital protected annuity, the insurance company guarantees in the event of early death to return any excess of the purchase consideration over the total of the gross instalments paid.) Also, unless the annuity is arranged on an increasing or an indexed basis, there is no hedge against the effects of inflation.

A purchased life annuity will be mainly suitable in the circumstances outlined below.

(a) For individuals normally with a minimum age of, say, 75 who wish to increase their net spendable income, but who will not require the return of their capital. This situation could arise when the annuity is included as part of a package. Examples of this would be:
  (i) in a 'home income plan' where an annuity is combined with a loan to provide additional income for an elderly homeowner (see Chapter 11); or
  (ii) in a back to back arrangement, where an annuity is combined with a whole life policy to provide additional income for an elderly individual and an increase in the portion of his eventual estate passed on to the beneficiaries (see Chapter 9).
(b) For funding purposes at any age, e.g. a nine-year temporary annuity to provide the premiums for a qualifying life policy (in this case, the first premium would be paid directly out of capital).
(c) For inheritance tax purposes, an annuity may be effected to reduce the individual's estate, while at the same time securing a high income for life. This action may also make it possible for other assets to be disposed of during the individual's lifetime, which would otherwise have been retained to produce income.

Variable investments

Unlike fixed investments where either the capital and/or the income therefrom remains fixed once the investment has been made, in the case of variable investments both the capital and income can vary. Therefore, they should only be considered in forming the third part of the capital, i.e. higher risk/higher reward investments (this was considered earlier on page 8).

Shown below are the main characteristics and some timing indicators with regard to variable investments. Also discussed in this chapter are some particular types of investment (unit trusts, investment bonds, investment trusts, investments under the Business Expansion Scheme and personal equity plans are dealt with in later chapters).

Main characteristics
Although there are many different types of variable investments, they are all governed by the following common rules.

(a) Since an individual can obtain a guaranteed real return from his capital against inflation by investing in index-linked gilts, he should normally only invest in variable investments if he considers it likely that they will provide a higher return.

(b) Due to their particular nature, an individual should only invest the proportion of his capital in variable investments which he is prepared to put at risk with the objective of obtaining an above average return.
(c) Variable investments should usually be considered to be made on a medium to long term basis with the actual period depending on the particular type of investment.

Timing indicators
Timing is of the utmost importance with many investments, especially when those of a higher risk/higher reward nature are concerned. It is often more likely that an investor will make a profit from a poor investment in a rising market than he will from a quality investment in a falling market.

Although timing is often the most difficult aspect of investment — there is no automatic way of knowing when is the right time to buy or to sell — the indicators shown below, which particularly relate to stock market investments, frequently apply.

(a) It is often best to take a contrarian view to the general consensus, especially where a longer term approach can be taken.
(b) An opportune time to make an investment is often when both the relevant market and the investment under consideration have shown major falls. Although it may be worthwhile to wait until the market has steadied, if investment is delayed too long until the outlook has clearly improved, the market is likely to have already shown a substantial rise.
(c) When bad news is out and widely known, this is frequently a favourable time to invest. When eventually the news does improve, the stock market is likely to rise.
(d) After a period of general gloom, the institutions, which generally have a large positive cash flow, will normally have a substantial amount of money waiting for investment. When they do invest (and no advance notice is given of this), the weight of money will often cause the stock market to show a sharp rise over a very short period.
(e) A suitable time to sell an investment is often when both the investment concerned and the underlying market have shown considerable rises but have since started to decline.
(f) An indication that a stock market rise may be coming to an end is when there is a large number of rights issues from companies and new launches from unit trusts.
(g) The trend of the movement in interest rates will often indicate the direction of the stock market. If the trend appears to be upwards, this is likely to have a depressing effect on the market, whereas if the trend is downwards, the reverse would generally apply. (A rise in interest rates is often preceded by the economy beginning to overheat, with industry working close to full capacity, bottlenecks appearing, wages starting to accelerate, and inflation rising. As a result, the government of the day may feel obliged to impose a credit squeeze, including an increase in interest rates.)

Ordinary stocks and shares (equities)
Unless an individual has the time, the knowledge and the inclination to manage his own investments, he will usually benefit if his investments are handled instead by suitable professionals, e.g. by a stockbroker specialising in private portfolio management. However, if the investor does satisfy the above

requirements, he will often produce superior results to a stockbroker or other discretionary portfolio management service due to the personal attention he is able to provide. (It should also be remembered that in addition to any financial benefit, an individual may also obtain considerable satisfaction by choosing his own investments.)

Where an individual does decide to manage his own investments, these should be spread sufficiently in order to avoid undue risks. (It is mainly for this reason that direct investment in stocks and shares is more appropriate for larger investors.)

Offshore funds

Although offshore funds are usually more suitable for expatriate investors due to their special tax position, these funds are also generally available to UK residents to whom they can be attractive in appropriate circumstances (see page 25).

Offshore funds operate in a similar way to unit trusts with many of the same characteristics, e.g. full-time professional management, a wide investment spread, the price of the shares being directly related to the value of the underlying assets, etc. However, as offshore funds are not registered in the UK, the following special considerations apply.

(a) At the present time, few offshore funds are recognised by the Securities and Investments Board (SIB), with the result that there may not be the same level of protection for an investor as that provided by onshore funds if the offshore company should find itself in financial trouble. Consequently, it is of the utmost importance that the credentials of the company are investigated before an investment is made in any of its funds.

(b) The taxation position of UK investors in respect of offshore funds is as follows.

   (i) The offshore fund itself is generally exempt from taxation apart from perhaps a small amount of corporation tax and in some cases a withholding tax.

   (ii) As a result of legislation in the 1984 Finance Act, UK residents are liable to income tax, rather than capital gains tax, on any realised gains from 1st January 1984 unless the particular fund has obtained distributor status. (Unrealised gains which accrued to 31st December 1983 will, however, be subject only to capital gains tax on encashment.)

   (iii) To achieve distributor status, the main condition is that at least 85% of the income arising in the fund must be distributed and not accumulated (since distributor status is not granted by the Inland Revenue until after the end of each tax year, this cannot be guaranteed at the time the investment is made).

   (iv) Where a fund does not obtain distributor status and the income is accumulated within the fund, no tax liability will arise until the investment is sold, when the whole gain (capital gain plus undistributed income) will be taxed as income in the year of disposal. This can be very advantageous where the investment is sold in a tax year when the individual's income is low, e.g. at retirement, during a period of employment overseas, etc.

   (v) The income distributed to investors is payable gross. Investors will then be personally subject to tax thereon. Consequently, this would produce a cash flow advantage until the tax due was paid.

In the case of a non-taxpayer, the need to make a repayment claim may be avoided.

(c) If UK exchange controls were to be reintroduced, both existing and potential investments in offshore funds might be affected, but this would depend on the exact form of the legislation. (For very large investors who are concerned about the possible reintroduction of exchange controls, it may be appropriate to consider setting up an overseas trust. However, these trusts generally lack flexibility and are only appropriate for large amounts with a normal minimum of approximately £200,000.)

(d) Offshore funds are permitted to invest in a wider range of assets than unit trusts. Accordingly, if an individual wishes to invest, say, in currency funds, or directly in commodities, only offshore funds would be suitable.

(e) Several offshore funds (generally known as 'umbrella' funds) are available which effectively allow an investor to switch between a wide range of currency, equity and fixed-interest sub-funds with a limited number of switches often being permitted each year without charge. The basis for umbrella funds is that they are investment vehicles with a range of separate classes of shares but having a single embracing structure — hence the term 'umbrella'. Investors can buy shares in one or more of these classes of shares, or sub-funds, and can then switch (or convert) from one class to another.

One of the main reasons for forming umbrella funds was to postpone the payment of capital gains tax, as conversions within the fund were not deemed to constitute a sale and purchase. However, as provided in the 1989 Budget, such conversions are now regarded as disposals and are therefore chargeable to income tax or capital gains tax as discussed earlier (paragraph (b) above). Consequently, umbrella funds would now appear to offer little attraction apart from ease of administration on converting and enabling an investor to receive interest or dividends gross.

Even if an investor still finds an umbrella fund attractive despite the loss of the previous capital gains tax advantage, the following matters should be borne in mind.

(i) A larger commitment may be made to one particular group than would usually be the case on normal investment grounds. Only a small minority of groups have been able to produce a good past performance record across the whole range of their funds.

(ii) The timing of the switches between the sub-funds is vital. Therefore, unless this is mainly accurate, a well-managed general fund is likely to produce superior results.

(iii) If the Inland Revenue considers that there has been an unacceptably high level of trading, distributor status may not be granted. This is particularly relevant when actively managed sub-funds are included such as managed currency funds or bond funds.

(f) Unlike unit trusts, few offshore funds at the present time are authorised to advertise for direct subscription in the UK, except during the initial offer of shares through a filed prospectus (offshore funds can, under the Financial Services Act, seek authorisation direct from the SIB although the process is complex).

Mainly due to the greater protection provided, onshore funds would usually be more suitable for UK investors than offshore funds except in the following circumstances:

(a) where the possible reintroduction of exchange controls is of major concern to the investor;
(b) where the investor is a non-taxpayer (this applies particularly to a high yielding fund such as a sterling deposit fund or a gilt income fund);
(c) where the type of investment fund required is not available onshore, e.g. currency funds;
(d) where there is no intention for the fund selected to seek distributor status and the investor plans to sell his investment in a tax year when his income is low (this is particularly relevant to the current tax year in cases where deferment of income into the tax year 1990/91 or later is likely to result in a lower tax liability through the independent taxation of husband and wife (see Chapters 1 and 10)).

Currency funds
Currency funds are a particular type of offshore fund and consequently the considerations discussed above will also apply to them. The two main types of currency funds which are considered below are (a) deposit funds denominated in a single currency; and (b) managed currency funds.

Deposit funds For an investment other than in a sterling fund, it will be necessary for a view to be taken of the likely movement in the particular currency relative to sterling. The result of the investment will then depend on the amount of the currency gain (or loss) and the interest received on the chosen fund.

Managed currency funds The main considerations with regard to managed currency funds are as follows.

(a) As in the case of all managed investments, the expertise of the investment managers is of paramount importance.
(b) Movements in currencies are often more difficult to predict than movements in stock markets.
(c) Since the rules of most managed currency funds require the managers to invest in a minimum number of different currencies, the relative strength of the pound sterling will have a major influence on the result of the investment. Accordingly, if it is considered that sterling will be generally weak against most foreign currencies, an investment in a managed currency fund should appreciate. However, if sterling should be relatively strong against other currencies, the reverse is likely to apply.
(d) In choosing a specific fund, it is important to compare 'like with like' as far as possible.

Note: A direct equity investment or via a fund in an overseas stock market will take account of both stock market and currency movements (unless, in the case of a fund, the managers have taken action to reduce exposure to movements in the particular currency). Accordingly, if the investment being considered is to be made on a long term basis, a carefully chosen equity fund investing overseas may be a more suitable alternative to the currency fund alone, unless the investor does not wish to take a position in the stock market concerned.

Non-traditional investments
These investments (also often known as alternative investments) cover many areas including antiques, krugerrands, stamps, etc. The following considerations should be borne in mind before an individual invests in a non-traditional investment.

(a) Unless the individual himself has the necessary knowledge and expertise with regard to the investment concerned, appropriate advice from reputable specialists should be obtained.
(b) Due to the wide range of types of investment which can be classified under non-traditional investments, different criteria will often apply. Some of the more important matters which should be specifically considered before an investment is made include:
    (i)   whether the supply of assets is fixed or limited;
    (ii)   whether the assets are portable or easily managed;
    (iii) whether there are high costs of ownership in the form of insurance, protection against burglary, storage, maintenance, etc.
    (iv) whether the assets are readily marketable;
    (v)   whether there is a consistent means of determining the value of the assets;
    (vi) whether there is an advantageous tax effect of ownership;
    (vii) whether there is a disciplined and well-regulated market which provides legal protection for the investor.
(c) In the acquisition of a non-traditional investment, it is often necessary for large initial charges to be incurred with the result that there will usually be a wide margin between the buying and selling prices. Consequently, non-traditional investments should generally only be made on a long term basis.
(d) If an investor wishes to dispose of his investment at short notice, it may be necessary for him to accept a relatively poor price. Therefore, where possible, he should be prepared to wait until an opportune time arises for the sale to be made.
(e) It is often an added bonus that an individual can enjoy his asset in addition to regarding it from an investment viewpoint.
(f) For most individuals, non-traditional investments should only be considered after the more conventional investments have been made.

Construction of an investment portfolio

The following examples illustrate broad investment portfolios for two men aged 30 and 50 respectively based on their individual circumstances.

Example 1

A man aged 30 requires advice on a capital sum of £50,000 which he has available for investment. His main personal particulars and requirements are as below.

(a) He is married with two young children but does not wish to educate them privately.
(b) He is employed by a company and is a member of their pension scheme. His wife has earnings of £3,000 pa.
(c) He pays tax at the basic rate but is not liable to higher rate tax.
(d) He is buying a house with the assistance of a low cost endowment mortgage.
(e) He has already effected the permanent health and life assurance protection policies which he considers necessary.
(f) His principal requirements for the capital are as follows:
    (i)   a combination of income and growth;

(ii)   the capital should be easily accessible;
(iii)   £25,000 of the capital can be invested on a long term basis. He is prepared to take some risk with this part of the capital.

Since the permanent health, life cover, house purchase and pension requirements have all been considered, the entire £50,000 can be used solely for investment purposes. A suitable arrangement could be as follows:

	£	£
First part of capital		
Building society account with immediate access without loss of interest and/or National Savings Investment Account if to be in the name of the wife (see note (ii) below)		10,000
Second part of capital		
1 short dated, medium coupon gilt-edged security	5,000	
Treasury 2% Index-Linked Stock 1992	5,000	
Guaranteed income bond	5,000	
		15,000
Third part of capital		
1 UK equity income unit trust with the objective of providing an increasing income with potential for capital growth	5,200	
2 personal equity plans of £2,400 invested in equity income unit trusts in the names of each of the husband and wife	4,800	
1 UK growth unit trust with the objective of providing capital growth	5,000	
2 international growth unit trusts of £5,000 each with a wide overseas investment spread with the objective of providing capital growth	10,000	25,000
		£50,000

Notes:
(a) For the purpose of this example, it is assumed that there is no existing investment in a building society account or similar type of investment.
(b) With the introduction of separate taxation for married couples in 1990/91, consideration should be given to investing part of the capital sum in the wife's name, despite her having sufficient earnings to absorb her personal allowance.

Example 2

A man aged 50 inherits £150,000 from his mother and asks for investment advice with regard to this amount. His main personal particulars and requirements are as follows.

(a)   He is married with three children who have all left home and are in paid employment.
(b)   He is self-employed and is providing for his retirement mainly through personal pension policies. He would like to retire at age 60. His wife does not have any earnings.
(c)   He is already subject to a marginal rate of income tax at 40% before his inheritance is taken into account.
(d)   His house is jointly owned with his wife and the mortgage has been repaid.

(e) He has effected appropriate life assurance policies to fund for inheritance tax.
(f) Amongst his assets, he already has a portfolio of equities managed by his stockbroker. His wife has relatively few investments.
(g) His principal requirements for the £150,000 inherited are:
   (i)   to have access to one-third of the capital at short notice;
   (ii)   to supplement his existing pension benefits;
   (iii)   to achieve capital growth during the next ten years, but with risk being kept to a realistic minimum;
   (iv)   to purchase a country cottage;
   (v)   to use a relatively small amount of the inheritance to acquire some antique furniture for his house.

The above requirements could be met by the following arrangement:

	£	£
First part of capital		
Building society account with immediate access without loss of interest and/or National Savings Investment Account if to be in the name of the wife (see note (ii) below)		10,000
Second part of capital		
2 short dated, low coupon gilt-edged securities	16,000	
4th Issue Index-Linked National Savings Certificates	5,000	
Treasury 2% Index-Linked Stock 1992	12,000	
Treasury 2% Index-Linked Stock 1994	7,000	
		40,000
Third part of capital		
Additional personal pension contributions paid under the unused relief provisions (this is discussed in Chapter 7)	20,000	
Temporary annuity to fund an endowment with profits policy over ten years	15,000	
2 personal equity plans of £2,400 invested in equity income unit trusts in the names of each of the husband and wife	4,800	
1 international growth unit trust with a wide overseas investment spread with the objective of providing capital growth	5,200	
Country cottage	50,000	
Antique furniture	5,000	
		100,000
		£150,000

Notes:
(a) For the purpose of this example, it is assumed that there is no existing investment in a building society account or similar type of investment.
(b) With the introduction of separate taxation for married couples in 1990/91, consideration should be given to investing part of the capital sum in appropriate income producing investments in the name of the wife, as her investment income is only relatively low. In this way, her personal allowance may be fully absorbed and her basic rate tax band partially so. In addition, there may be capital gains tax advantages by suitable investments being made in her name.

3. Unit trusts, investment bonds and investment trusts

The purpose of this chapter is to consider the main characteristics and principal differences between unit trusts, investment bonds and investment trusts. In order to achieve this, unit trusts and investment bonds are first considered together. Then, at the end of the chapter, a comparison is made between unit trusts and investment trusts. Throughout the book, unless otherwise stated, unit trusts should be taken to mean authorised unit trusts.

Advantages of unit trusts and investment bonds

Unit trusts and investment bonds both enable individual investors to pool their resources, providing advantages when compared to investing directly in stock exchange securities as listed below.

(a) Full-time professional management on a day-to-day basis can be obtained. However, the investment expertise of the different fund managers varies considerably and this is likely to be reflected in the results of the investments concerned.
(b) As a result of the wide investment spread, the impact of disappointing results from individual investments is reduced. In addition, a spread of management can be obtained by investing in a number of different unit trusts or bonds, thereby further reducing risk. However, set against these advantages is that the likelihood of making exceptional gains is also reduced.
(c) Due to the large number of different types of unit trusts available, both by country and sector, the exact equity investment requirements of most individuals can usually be met by a careful selection of trusts.
(d) There is a considerable saving in paperwork for the investor, as dealing with scrip issues, rights issues, take-over bids, etc. is avoided. In addition, the preparation of tax returns is normally simplified.
(e) Both unit trusts and investment bonds are tax efficient when properly used. Unit trusts are exempt from capital gains tax on their realised gains, with the result that a fund manager is not inhibited in his investment decisions by tax considerations, and holders of investment bonds have a 20-year 5% pa tax deferred withdrawals facility. As far as the unit trust investor is concerned, no capital gains tax liability can arise until the units are sold. This can provide an important cash flow advantage compared to a direct investment in equities which are actively managed.
(f) Investment bonds provide a convenient method of investing in direct assets such as properties, particularly for relatively small amounts.

(g) Unit trusts and investment bonds provide an easy and convenient way of investing in overseas equities. This method is often adopted by stockbrokers to obtain overseas exposure for their private clients.

(h) Investment bonds generally provide a switching facility between funds at very low cost with no tax being payable by the bondholder on the exercise of this facility.

(i) Since the size of the bargains carried out by unit trusts and investment bonds is usually relatively large, an active investment policy can be undertaken less expensively than by the individual investor himself.

Advantages of management by stockbrokers

The main advantages of investing directly in stock exchange securities using the management services of stockbrokers compared to indirect investment through unit trusts and investment bonds are as follows.

(a) A more personal service is offered with the investor normally receiving a half-yearly valuation and report on his own portfolio. Capital gains tax calculations are also usually provided.

(b) Since it is usual for only a comparatively small number of investments to be held in a portfolio, the investor may consequently find this more exciting.

(c) For very large investors, a stockbroker service may be more advantageous through having direct holdings in companies rather than a much broader spread of indirect holdings within the unit trust or investment bond.

Direct stock exchange investment may also be appropriate where an individual has the time and inclination to make his own investment decisions. Many investors gain considerable personal satisfaction by choosing their own investments, with or without the assistance of a stockbroker, and following their progress in newspapers, etc. on a regular basis.

Basic constitution

Unit trusts
A unit trust is constituted by a trust deed which is an agreement between the trustees and the managers of the fund. The trust deed covers the main aspects of the running of the trust and is subject to approval by the Securities and Investments Board (SIB). The essential characteristics of the deed are that it lays down:

(a) the rights and responsibilities of all concerned;
(b) provisions enabling new members to join;
(c) the maximum charges that can be made by the managers for administering the fund;
(d) provision for calculating the buying (offer) and selling (bid) prices of units;
(e) types of investment permitted.

The role of the trustee, whose appointment is subject to approval by the SIB, is that of a watchdog. Its main duties are to ensure that the terms of the trust deed are strictly observed and to hold the cash and securities belonging to the fund. The responsibility for the choice of investments lies with the managers, although the trustee retains the right of veto.

Investment bonds
An investment bond is a non-qualifying single premium life assurance policy. The investments of the bond fund form part of the main assets of the life assurance company and the bondholder has no prior charge on the fund. Consequently, if the life assurance company should find itself in financial trouble, the bondholder could suffer loss on his investment despite the protection offered by the Policyholders' Protection Act 1975 (this Act provides that a policyholder would generally receive 90% of the benefits under his policy). It is mainly for this reason that great care should be taken before business is placed with new and small life companies. (In the case of unit trusts, there is not the same risk in dealing with newly established or small trusts due to the security provided by the trust deed.)

With most life companies, the investments are in a separate bond fund which operates similarly to a unit trust. The performance is measured by the investments in the fund, irrespective of the performance of the life company's other investments. Many bond funds themselves invest in unit trusts as well as directly in equities and other assets.

Underlying investments

Unit trusts
Unit trusts are authorised by the SIB to invest only in quoted securities (subject to 10% of the fund being allowed in unquoted securities).

The main types of unit trusts may be classified under the following broad headings:

(a) UK general;
(b) UK growth;
(c) UK equity income;
(d) UK mixed income;
(e) gilt and fixed interest;
(f) international growth;
(g) international income;
(h) North America growth;
(i) Europe growth;
(j) Japan growth;
(k) Far Eastern growth;
(l) others, e.g. Australia growth, commodities & energy, financial, funds of funds, index tracker funds, etc.

In recent months, the following major changes have taken place.

(a) The range of permitted investments has been widened in order to compete with other financial institutions. These investments include money market funds and property funds. Money market funds are able to invest in cash or deposits with, or loans to, banks and building societies; gilts; bank bills of exchange; bank and building society certificates; and other debt instruments.

(b) Managers of funds are permitted to invest up to 10% of the underlying investments in unquoted securities.

(c) A wider range of investments, including traded options, futures and forward currency transactions are available to hedge the fund against market risk, currency exchange or interest rate movements.

(d) The use of feeder funds is permitted whereby one fund invests exclusively in another (feeder funds are also allowed for personal pensions).

(e) Managers are allowed to borrow up to 10% of a fund's value, provided that equivalent amounts are due to accrue to the fund within one month.

(f) Funds are limited to holding a maximum of 10% of assets in each of four securities with each of the remaining holdings being limited to a maximum of 5% of assets.

(g) Funds of funds are able to invest in any unit trust, rather than only trusts managed by the same management group (see below).

(h) Greater disclosure of information is compulsory, with the aim of providing improved investor protection.

Investment bonds
Investment bonds are permitted to invest in an even wider range of assets than unit trusts, including investing in unit trusts themselves. The following are the main types of investment funds available:

(a) UK equity funds;
(b) international funds;
(c) North American funds;
(d) European funds;
(e) Far Eastern funds;
(f) money funds;
(g) fixed interest funds;
(h) index-linked gilt funds;
(i) property funds (including commercial property, residential property and agricultural land);
(j) commodity & energy funds.

A switching facility which is available with most bonds, enables the bond-holder to switch from one fund to another within the same policy at very low cost (typically one free switch in a policy year, with subsequent switches being charged at a rate of ½% of the capital involved, subject to a minimum charge of £10 and a maximum charge of £25). Since the switch is not considered to be a disposal by the bondholder, no tax is payable on the exercise of this facility.

However, despite the apparent attraction of the switching facility, timing and choice of funds are all-important. Therefore, unless this proves to have been mainly accurate, the value of the bond is likely to be lower than if the facility had not been exercised at all.

In the case of unit trusts, switching within the same management group often provides preferential terms, although the switch would normally be treated as a disposal by the investor for capital gains tax. The exception to this is the fund of funds which invests in other unit trusts within the same management group. In these circumstances, a switch between the underlying unit trusts by the fund manager would not be treated as a disposal for capital gains tax purposes.

Undertakings for Collective Investment in Transferable Securities (UCITS)

From October 1989, unit trust groups throughout the European Economic Community (EEC) will be able to market their schemes in any other EEC country. A European agreement on collective investments, UCITS, removes the barriers between individual countries by requiring minimum standards, with the effect that all the schemes will be comparable. (Under the Financial Services Act (FSA), other countries can become 'designated territories' if their financial regulations are at least as stringent as those in the UK. Consequently, from 1st March 1989, collective investment schemes in these territories could be marketed in the UK similar to unit trusts, provided they received permission from the SIB.)

UK unit trusts can therefore be sold elsewhere in the EEC and European funds can be marketed in the UK. However, each unit trust will operate under the regulations of its own country although it must abide by the marketing regulations of the country in which it is sold. A UK fund bought in Germany, while protected by the FSA, will be marketed under German regulations. A French unit trust bought in Britain does not offer investors the same protection as a UK fund under the FSA.

It was announced in the 1989 Finance Bill that, with effect from 1st January 1990, for all unit trusts which are UCITS there will be a reduction in the corporation tax rate from 35% to the basic rate of income tax, currently 25%. This will remove any UK tax charge on a trust which cannot be credited to unitholders. Tax relief will also be given for management expenses and interest paid on borrowings permitted under the SIB regulations.

Life assurance cover

Unit trusts
Since a unit trust is not a life policy, there is no life cover attached. Consequently, the realisation value on the death of the unitholder would be the bid value of the units. However, units do not necessarily have to be encashed by the executors, but can instead be passed to beneficiaries or held on trust created by a will.

Investment bonds
As mentioned above, a bond is a non-qualifying single premium life assurance policy and consequently on death (or death of the last survivor if applicable), the contract terminates and a lump sum is provided. This sum is normally determined by reference to the age of the individual at the time of his death, and the total amount payable will usually range from approximately 2.5 times the bid value of the units for younger ages to 1.01 times for older ages. An investor who does not provide evidence of health when submitting a proposal form would receive the minimum multiple, regardless of his age at death.

However, a small number of companies base the life cover on the age of the individual at the time he invests in the bond and on the amount of the original investment. On death, the amount receivable will be the greater of the life cover or the bid value of the units in the bond fund.

Personal requirements and investment objectives

Before a person invests in a unit trust or investment bond, he should first consider his personal requirements and investment objectives. These would include the following.

(a) Whether he requires capital growth, income, or a combination of the two, from his investment. Having decided on this, it is important to ensure that the purpose of the fund selected meets this objective.
(b) The degree of risk which he is prepared to undertake, remembering there is often a close correlation between risk and reward.
(c) The period of time for which it is intended to hold the investment. If the investment is being made on a long term basis, a general or managed fund providing the investment managers with the greatest flexibility is often the most suitable.
(d) If he wishes to invest in a specialised fund or geographical area, e.g. a fund investing in energy shares, or Hong Kong, it should be remembered that investment fashions can change and therefore it is important to be alert to dispose of the investment at short notice at an opportune time.
(e) Whether he would require the fund to be fully or substantially invested at all times, or whether it is required for the investment managers to take a view by going partially liquid if they think appropriate.
(f) Whether he requires to be exposed to a particular currency when making overseas investments.
(g) The particular purpose for which the investment is being made, e.g. an income unit trust can be very useful in a life tenant/remainderman type trust situation where the requirement is to provide a balance of income and capital growth between the two parties.

An investment bond is often ideal for a trust where income is to be accumulated until, for example, infant beneficiaries reach majority. However, it is unsuitable where income is required for a life tenant, as any withdrawals are regarded as capital repayments from which generally he is not permitted to benefit. However, it is essential that the trust contains a power to purchase investment bonds as they are not otherwise trustee investments.

Past performance

In measuring the past performance record of a unit trust or investment bond, it is most important that the results should not be considered in isolation if a realistic investment picture is to be obtained. Instead, the following matters should also be borne in mind.

(a) The results should be considered over a reasonable period, say a minimum period of two years, although it is often worthwhile to take a longer period.

(b) The trend of the past results. This could indicate changes which have taken place within the fund.

(c) The results of the fund under consideration should be compared with similar funds and also, where possible, with appropriate indices.

(d) It is normally preferable for the fund to have produced good results consistently, rather than outstanding results followed by mediocre performance.

(e) Whether there have been any changes in the management group or individual fund managers during the period under review. It should be borne in mind that where a change in management has taken place, the new investment manager may not have the same expertise as the person who was responsible for the past results.

It should also be remembered that a new manager may wish to change the structure of the investment portfolio in accordance with his own ideas and this could initially have an adverse effect on the investment performance. However, this could be less of a disadvantage than it initially appears, since the new manager will normally follow the overall investment policy of the group concerned and accordingly any changes are likely to be limited.

Assessing management expertise

Although it is not possible to *know* which investment fund managers will produce the best results in the future, a considered opinion can be formed as to which managers offer above average expertise. However, to do this, a certain amount of research must take place.

The following are indicators of management expertise which should help in the selection of a particular fund:

(a) the fund having a good past performance record, as already discussed;

(b) the management group and individual manager having a proven record in the specific sector or geographical area in which the fund will invest;

(c) the management group generally having a good all-round performance record.

Additionally, the investor should where possible attempt to form an independent opinion of the capabilities of the prospective group or fund manager by, e.g., reading any group literature (particularly that relating to the fund(s) he has in mind) and by reading the financial press. The investor could also ask the opinion of a professional financial adviser. The following information would be especially helpful:

(a) the general philosophy of the group as to the selection of investments and the degree of authority allowed to the individual fund managers;

(b) the general philosophy of the group as far as currencies are concerned when making overseas investments (this applies particularly to the extent to which the various funds are exposed or otherwise to any movements in the relevant currencies relative to the pound sterling);

(c) the practical way the group operates and how fund managers obtain their information, e.g. through stockbrokers, company visits, etc.;

(d) the length of time the individual fund managers have managed a particular fund together with their other responsibilities, previous experience, etc.;

(e) whether the fund manager has sufficient time to give proper attention to the fund and is not over-burdened with other responsibilities. In addition, whether the stated fund manager is only nominally responsible for the fund, with the day-to-day management delegated to another person.

In practice, it is unlikely that an investor would have sufficient time to be able to obtain the whole of the above information. Nevertheless, with the judicious use of publications such as *Money Management* or *Planned Savings*, he can still gain sufficient knowledge to make a reasonable assessment of a particular investment.

Unit trusts – general guidelines

The following general guidelines often apply in the selection of a unit trust.

General trusts v specialised trusts
The principal advantage of a general trust is that the fund manager has more scope in his choice of investments with fewer restrictions applying as to the type of investments which can be made. Due to the wider investment spread, general trusts are usually less volatile.

The main advantage of a specialised trust is that it enables an investor to back his own views if he favours a particular sector. In addition, a fund manager can concentrate his expertise on the sector concerned which should lead to improved results. However, if that sector should become unfashionable, it is difficult for the fund manager to avoid a loss. Consequently, an investor must be prepared to actively buy and sell unit holdings as his views of the investment prospects of different sectors change, although his capital gains tax position should be borne in mind.

Large funds v small funds
As a general rule, large funds are more likely to perform nearer to the average of the particular sector concerned, while in the case of small funds, an excellent or very poor performance is more likely.

However, although there is no clear evidence to show that the overall performance of small funds is superior to large funds, small funds would often have an advantage due to their greater flexibility. This would apply especially to particular types of trusts where the marketability of the underlying investments is restricted, e.g. unit trusts investing in small companies.

A steadily expanding fund would have a definite advantage, regardless of the size of the trust, due to the fund manager being able to build up liquidity if required without the need to sell the underlying investments. He could also change the 'slant' of the fund by applying new money differently from the existing investments and thereby avoid selling expenses in order to achieve this.

New trusts

The main advantage for an investor of purchasing units in a completely new trust is that the fund manager is often especially keen for the trust to perform well. In addition, the only investments in the trust would be those selected by the fund manager himself rather than having been inherited from a previous manager.

The principal disadvantage of subscribing to a new trust is that it is frequently launched after the particular sector in which the trust will invest has had a substantial rise. Consequently, the sector concerned may be over-valued and due for a fall.

Taxation of income

The tax borne by unit trusts and investment bonds on their income for the year ended 31st March 1990 is as follows:

	Rate
Franked investment income	25%
Unfranked investment income	35%

Note: Where investments made by unit trusts are confined to those the income from which is chargeable to tax under Schedule C as profits arising from UK public revenue dividends or under Case III of Schedule D, the rate of 25% would be chargeable. As a result, the income of fixed interest and gilt-edged unit trusts would normally be charged at 25%.

As mentioned earlier in this chapter, with effect from 1st January 1990, there will be a reduction in the corporation tax rate from 35% to 25% for all unit trusts which are UCITS. A similar reduction in corporation tax will apply to investment bonds from 1st January 1990.

Examples 3 and 4 below show the net return to an investor from a dividend (franked investment income) and bank interest (unfranked investment income) which is received by a unit trust and investment bond respectively and then distributed. From 1st January 1990, the position with regard to unfranked investment income will be similar to that for franked investment income in the cases of both investment bonds and unit trusts which are UCITS. While the income cannot be paid directly to a bondholder, the examples illustrate the net return on final encashment.

Example 3

A dividend of £75 is received by a unit trust and an investment bond and then distributed.

	Highest rate of income tax paid by individual	
	40% £	25% £
Unit trust		
Net dividend received by unit trust and distributed to unitholder	75.0	75.0
Tax credit	25.0	25.0
Gross distribution for tax purposes	100.0	100.0
Less: Personal income tax	40.0	25.0
Net return	60.0	75.0
Investment bond		
Net dividend received by insurance company	75.0	75.0
Tax credit	25.0	25.0
Gross income	100.0	100.0
Less: Corporation tax	25.0	25.0
Net income received and withdrawn by bondholder	75.0	75.0
Less: Tax payable by bondholder on encashment (higher rate less basic rate)	11.3	–
Net return on final encashment	63.7	75.0

Example 4

Bank interest of £100 is received by a unit trust and an investment bond and then distributed.

	Highest rate of income tax paid by individual	
	40% £	25% £
Unit trust		
Gross income	100.0	100.0
Less: Corporation tax	35.0	35.0
Net distribution payable to unitholder	65.0	65.0
Add: Tax credit — 25/75×£65	21.7	21.7
Gross distribution for tax purposes	86.7	86.7
Less: Personal income tax	34.7	21.7
Net return	52.0	65.0

	Highest rate of income tax paid by individual	
	40% £	25% £
Investment bond		
Gross income	100.0	100.0
Less: Corporation tax	35.0	35.0
Net income received and withdrawn by bondholder	65.0	65.0
Less: Tax payable by bondholder on encashment (higher rate less basic rate)	9.8	–
Net return on final encashment	55.2	65.0

Taxation of capital gains

0The following is the tax payable by unit trusts and investment bonds on their capital gains.

	Rate
Unit trusts	Nil
Investment bonds	
Realised gains (after making adjustment for the capital gains tax indexation allowance)	30% (25% from 1.1.90)
Deduction made in calculating the price of the investment bond in respect of the contingent liability of the life fund for capital gains tax on unrealised gains	usually between 10% and 30%

The example below shows the net return to an investor from a realised gain made by a unit trust and an investment bond investing directly.

Example 5

A realised gain of £100 is made before 1st January 1990 by a unit trust, an investment bond investing in a unit trust and an investment bond investing directly.

	Highest rate of income tax paid by individual	
	40% £	25% £
Unit trust		
Realised gain made by unit trust	100.0	100.0
Less: Effective capital gains tax payable by unit trust	–	–
Increase in value of unit trust	100.0	100.0
Less: Capital gains tax payable by individual on sale of units (assuming gain made within annual capital gains tax exemption)	–	–
Net return	100.0	100.0
Investment bond investing in a unit trust		
Realised gain made by unit trust	100.0	100.0
Less: Effective capital gains tax payable by unit trust	–	–
Increase in value of unit trust	100.0	100.0
Less: Deduction by bond in respect of contingent liability of life fund for tax on unrealised capital gains (say 20%)	20.0	20.0
Net increase in value of bond	80.0	80.0
Less: Tax payable by individual on encashment (higher rate less basic rate)	12.0	–
Net return	68.0	80.0
Investment bond investing directly		
Realised gain made by bond	100.0	100.0
Less: Effective capital gains tax payable by bond	30.0	30.0
	70.0	70.0
Add: Release of reserve for unrealised gain at say 20% of gain	20.0	20.0
Net increase in value of bond	90.0	90.0
Less: Tax payable by individual on encashment (higher rate less basic rate)	13.5	–
Net return	76.5	90.0

Note: The purpose of this example is not to compare a unit trust with an investment bond but solely to illustrate the operation of each. Therefore, no conclusions should be drawn from the figures shown.

Investment bonds — partial withdrawals

The taxation position of partial withdrawals from an investment bond is as follows.

(a) Any tax liability is based on the realisation proceeds and not the actual profit thereon. This can produce very harsh results where withdrawals are substantial (see planning hint (a) on page 42).

(b) Annual withdrawals of 5% pa of the original investment can be made with no immediate liability to tax but will be taken into account on final encashment.

(c) The 5% allowances operate on a cumulative basis so, for example, if withdrawals are not taken in the first four years, a tax deferred withdrawal of 25% of the original investment can be taken in the fifth year.

(d) Tax deferred withdrawals are limited to 100% of the original investment (e.g. 20 years at 5%).

(e) When a withdrawal is made in excess of the above allowances, a chargeable event is deemed to occur. The excess may then be liable to income tax at the difference between the bondholder's highest rate(s) and the basic rate.

(f) The tax payable is calculated with reference to top-slicing relief which is explained on page 42. However, the period over which the gain is top-sliced for partial encashments is limited to the number of years which have expired since the most recent chargeable event, or the start of the contract if there has not been a previous chargeable event.

This is illustrated in the following example.

Example 6

An investment bond is purchased for £10,000 with partial withdrawals having been made as follows:

during year 1	—	£ 500
during year 4	—	£1,400
during year 5	—	£2,500
during year 7	—	£2,000

Complete years held	Cumulative allowance (5% pa)	Withdrawals in year	total	Chargeable excess
	£	£	£	£
1	500	500	500	Nil
2	1,000	Nil	500	Nil
3	1,500	Nil	500	Nil
4	2,000	1,400	1,900	Nil
5	2,500	2,500	4,400	1,900
6	500	Nil	Nil	Nil
7	1,000	2,000	2,000	1,000

Note: For the purposes of top-slicing relief, the chargeable excess of £1,900 in year 5 is divided by 5 and the chargeable excess of £1,000 in year 7 is divided by 2.

(g) Chargeable excesses are assessed on a policy year basis, e.g.:
Bond purchased for £10,000 on 1.1.88;

Partial withdrawal of £4,000 on 10.1.89;

Tax based on policy year ending 31.12.89, i.e. in fiscal year 1989/90;

Cumulative allowances to 31.12.89 £1,000, resulting in chargeable excess of £3,000;

Tax due on chargeable excess payable in December 1990.

Planning hints
(a) Take out a series of smaller bonds in lieu of one larger bond to provide greater flexibility (this is often achieved by dividing a bond into a number of identical cluster policies or segments). In this way, the bondholder can totally encash a smaller bond if required, rather than resort to a partial encashment of a larger bond with the possible penal tax consequences.
(b) Postpone taking withdrawals when markets are low to avoid the encashment of an undue number of units in the bond fund. This also applies to any automatic withdrawal facility where the bondholder does not need to rely on the withdrawals for living expenses etc.

Investment bonds — final encashment

The taxation position on final encashment of an investment bond is as follows.

(a) Final encashment is considered to arise on complete surrender, death (or death of last survivor if applicable), or assignment for money or money's worth.
(b) The gain on the bond is calculated by taking the proceeds on final encashment plus any previous withdrawals and deducting the original cost of the bond and any chargeable amounts already established (known as chargeable excesses – see page 41).
(c) This gain will be subject to the higher rate of income tax, but not to basic rate tax, in the tax year in which encashment arises (not the policy year).
(d) The tax payable is calculated with reference to the top-slicing provisions. For final encashment, the gain on the bond is divided by the number of complete years that the bond has been held to arrive at the top-slice of the gain. This top-slice is added to the other taxable income arising in the year of encashment and the tax payable with and without the top-slice is then calculated. The difference less basic rate tax on the top-slice is multiplied by the complete number of years that the bond has been held to arrive at the tax liability.
(e) If a loss should arise on final encashment, this will only be allowed to the extent of the amount of the chargeable excesses which have already arisen on partial surrenders in policy years commencing after 13th March 1975. This loss will then be permitted as a deduction in calculating the bondholder's higher rate tax in the year of final encashment. (It should be noted that each policy is considered in isolation. Therefore, it is not permitted to use the loss on one policy to offset the gain on another.)

The following example illustrates the tax resulting from top-slicing.

Example 7
A married man aged 50 bought a single premium bond for £10,000 and in the eleventh year encashed it in 1989/90 for £13,000 having exercised a 5% pa withdrawal facility throughout. During the year of encashment his income was £25,000.

Under the top-slicing method, the gain of £8,000 (£3,000 on encashment plus previous withdrawals of £5,000) is divided by ten (the number of complete years the bond has been in force) to arrive at the top-slice of the gain, i.e. £800.

	Tax position without top-slice of the gain Income		*Tax position including top-slice of the gain* Income
	£		£
Income	25,000		25,000
Top-slice of gain	—		800
	25,000		25,800
Less: Personal allowance	4,375		4,375
	£20,625		£21,425
Tax payable thereon	£20,625 at 25% 5,156	£20,700 at 25%	5,175
		725 at 40%	290
	£5,156		£5,465

Total tax payable including tax on top-slice	5,465
Total tax payable without tax on top-slice	5,156
Tax payable including basic rate tax on top-slice	309
Less: Basic rate tax on top-slice — £800 at 25%	200
Higher rate tax on top-slice	£ 109
Total tax on gain — £109 × 10	£1,090

Planning hints
Although the maximum tax liability on a gain made on an investment bond is currently restricted to 15%, it is still worthwhile to keep any liability to a practical minimum. The following are some planning hints to enable an investor to do this.

(a) Encash bond in a tax year when the bondholder's marginal tax rate is low. This could be due to retirement, a period of employment overseas or unemployment.
(b) Rearrange the bondholder's affairs to make income low in the tax year of encashment, e.g. by reinvestment of assets in low or nil income producing securities.
(c) Hold the bond until death as the bondholder's income in that year is likely to be less than normal since it would be based on that received from the preceding 6th April to the date of death.

(d) Take out a series of smaller bonds as already mentioned. The bondholder will then be in a position to completely encash separate bonds over a number of years and thereby reduce the amount of the top-slice to be added to the other income each year. This is likely to have the effect of the gain being taxed at lower rates, if at all.

(e) Take out bonds on a joint life and last survivor basis. Where a bond is taken out by a husband and wife on a joint life and last survivor basis and the bond is not encashed until the second death, the tax charge will be postponed until that time.

If the husband was the first to die, it is likely that the widow's income would be lower following his death. This would then present a suitable opportunity for her to encash the bond if she required the capital sum.

A bond can also be effected by a single (rather than a joint) grantee but written on a joint or multiple life basis. This can offer the individual a greater opportunity for tax planning, e.g. if the bond is used as part of a legacy on the earlier death, and is the subject of a correctly drafted will trust, or passes absolutely to a person who pays basic rate tax only.

(f) Arrange for a bond to be taken out by the spouse paying tax at the lower rate. With the introduction of independent taxation in 1990/91 (see Chapter 10), a smaller tax charge may result on encashment of the bond after 5th April 1990.

(g) An additional investment into an existing bond is treated for top-slicing purposes as if made at the date of the original investment.

A considerable number of insurance companies include the facility whereby an additional investment can be added to an existing bond and treated for top-slicing purposes as if it was made at the date of the original investment. Consequently, any gain arising on final encashment on both the original and subsequent investments would be top-sliced over the whole period of the original investment with the result that the tax liability could be considerably reduced. This would not, however, reduce the tax liability on the original investment.

Particular care should be taken by a person who would normally qualify for age allowance, since chargeable excesses or gains on a bond are counted as income for the purpose of determining whether the age allowance should be reduced. Top-slicing relief has no effect in these circumstances. However, the 5% pa withdrawals can be taken without affecting the age allowance.

Position on death

Unit trusts
At the present time, there is no capital gains tax payable on gains at death. Consequently, if a unit trust is held until death, capital gains tax will be avoided.

Investment bonds
As already mentioned, death is one of the reasons for final encashment, when the bid value of the units of the bond fund is used in calculating the amount of the gain made on the bond. If the life cover exceeds the bid value of the units, the excess will not be taken into account in calculating the tax charge.

This charge will be an allowable deduction from the estate in calculating the inheritance tax liability.

Trusts and settlements

A bond can in certain cases be advantageous for some trusts and settlements in that it is a non-income producing asset and there is no tax liability on the settlor, trustee or beneficiary until it is encashed. However, before an investment is made in a bond, it is necessary to ensure that the trustees have the power to invest in non-income producing assets and also the power to invest in life assurance policies. A bond can be particularly suitable in the following circumstances:

(a) in accumulation and maintenance settlements for the benefit of children, especially where the settlor is not alive or is likely to die before the bond is encashed by the trustees;
(b) as gifts to children either absolutely or contingent upon their attainment of a certain age.

As previously mentioned, an income unit trust can be very useful in a life tenant/ remainderman type trust situation where the requirement is to provide a balance of income and capital growth between the two parties. Bonds are not suitable for this purpose.

Personalised bond funds

Some insurance companies permit an individual with large investments to have his own private bond fund for these investments. By this means, the individual would be able to retain control of the management of his investments while receiving tax treatment the same as that applying to investment bonds.

However, the transfer of existing investments into a bond fund is treated as a chargeable disposal and consequently capital gains tax may be payable.

Share exchange schemes

If an individual already owns stocks and shares, it will often be possible for him to exchange these investments for unit trusts or investment bonds on favourable terms such as the following:

(a) where the individual has stocks and shares with a minimum value of, typically, £5,000 and these investments are accepted into the portfolios of the unit trust group or insurance company, the offer or middle prices are normally allowed on the stocks and shares exchanged, with no deduction being made for selling expenses;
(b) where the stocks and shares have a ready market but the unit trust group or insurance company does not wish to take them into its portfolios, they will usually be sold on the individual's behalf, often with a refund of the selling expenses being made. Accordingly, where a refund is allowed, the gross

proceeds would be applied to the purchase of the unit trust holding or investment bond.

In all other cases, the individual would be required to dispose of his own investments.

Where a person exchanges his investments, this will be treated as a disposal for capital gains tax purposes.

Although the terms offered by some share exchange schemes are more advantageous than others, it should be remembered that it is the future performance of the unit trust or investment bond selected that will generally be of far greater importance.

Unit trusts or investment bonds?

Before a decision is taken as to which of these is the more suitable investment medium, it will be necessary to consider the following.

(a) Whether the particular fund being considered is available in the form of both a unit trust and an investment bond. In many cases, it is only in the form of one or the other.
(b) The current and future tax position of the individual. This is of particular importance in the case of investment bonds where the marginal rate of tax payable by the individual in the year of final encashment will be a major factor in determining the amount of any tax liability. Although the maximum personal tax liability is restricted to 15% in 1989/90, this is likely to change if there is an alteration in income tax rates in subsequent years.
(c) The age of the individual. A bond is not normally as suitable for a younger person (say under age 50) since it is more difficult for him to postpone final encashment until the time when his income is low such as following retirement. A bond may also not be suitable for a very elderly person since death may cause tax to become payable.
(d) The investment objective of the fund under consideration. If capital growth is the principal aim, a unit trust will usually be more suitable if the total gains made by an investor are within his annual capital gains tax exemption. Realised gains made within an investment bond are currently subject to capital gains tax at 30% (25% from 1.1.90) and this cannot be recovered by the bondholder.
(e) Whether a regular 'income' is required. Investment bonds normally provide greater flexibility in this respect.
(f) Whether the investment is to be used for a particular purpose, e.g. in an accumulation and maintenance settlement or as a gift to children.
(g) Whether the individual is likely to make use of the fund switching facility available on most investment bonds.

Investment trusts and unit trusts compared

Investment trusts, although quoted on the stock market, have many features similar to unit trusts including full-time professional management, a wide investment spread and the same tax treatment for investors. However, investment trusts have several characteristics which distinguish them from unit trusts.

(a) An investment trust is a public company with its shares bought and sold through a stockbroker. Consequently, for very small investors, the proportion of the investment taken in charges will be high (this also applies to other stock exchange investments). In the case of a unit trust, the units are bought and sold from the management company where charges are calculated as a percentage of the value of the purchase, irrespective of the size of the transaction. The unit trust management company does, however, set a minimum sum to be invested.

(b) The share capital of an investment trust is fixed. Consequently, an investment trust cannot experience redemptions. This is an important advantage in plummeting markets. With a unit trust, the number of units in issue can be increased or reduced. (A fund which is gradually expanding is normally easier to manage from an investment viewpoint than a fund which is static or contracting.)

(c) The share price of an investment trust fluctuates in accordance with the supply and demand for its shares, which can usually be purchased at a discount to the value of its underlying assets. However, although this is an advantage as far as income is concerned, it may not necessarily be one from a capital viewpoint if the shares are sold at a larger discount than that at which they were purchased. The price at which a unit trust is bought and sold is based directly on the value of its underlying assets (subject to the provisions regarding the calculation of the bid/offer spread).

(d) Being valued normally at a discount to assets, an investment trust could be subject to unitisation (when the investment trust is converted into a unit trust), with the result that the discount would be eliminated. Alternatively, an investment trust could be subject to a takeover (the buyer's object being to acquire an investment portfolio cheaply). In either case, the investment trust shareholder is likely to make a windfall profit.

(e) The mood of the UK stock market normally has a greater effect on the share price of an investment trust than on the price of a unit trust (the price of an investment trust can even be affected when its underlying assets are wholly invested outside the UK). Accordingly, investment trust prices will often show greater movements than their underlying assets, even before taking into account the effect of any gearing (see (g) below). This could therefore have an adverse result for shareholders wishing to dispose of their shares in a falling market when the discount on assets often widens, with the reverse applying in a rising market when the discount frequently narrows.

(f) An investment trust has the freedom to invest entirely in unquoted securities, while a unit trust is restricted to 10% of the portfolio being in unquoted investments.

(g) Although an investment trust is able to produce gearing by issuing prior capital in the form of preference shares, debentures, loan stocks, etc., this has not been a major factor in recent years as interest rates have generally been too high to make this attractive. (The effect of gearing on an investment trust is that an increase or decrease in the value of its total assets will have an exaggerated result on the value of the net assets per ordinary share. This arises because the holders of prior capital are entitled to a fixed return of capital if the investment trust is wound up, with the value of the remaining assets being divided between the ordinary shareholders. Gearing also has a similar effect on income.) A unit trust is only permitted to borrow within very strict limits (see page 32) and therefore gearing can only be introduced to a minor extent.

(h) A particular type of investment trust which could be suitable for investors seeking specifically either income or capital growth is a split capital trust. These trusts, which were first introduced in the mid-1960s, can have several different classes of share capital, including income shares and capital shares.

Holders of the income shares are entitled to all or most of the income arising from the trust's portfolio throughout its life, after paying all charges and dividends on other classes of prior capital, plus a predetermined capital value on liquidation.

Holders of capital shares, while receiving little or no income throughout the trust's lifetime, are entitled to all the surplus assets on liquidation after all other classes of capital have been paid out. This will usually take place during a specified future period.

The main advantages of capital shares over conventional investment trust shares for investors with an objective of capital growth are the provision of a final liquidation date when the discount on assets must disappear and the high level of gearing (although this is a disadvantage in a falling market).

For the holders of income shares, the main advantage is the high level of income gearing produced by the capital shares.

Other classes of capital can include zero dividend preference shares, stepped preference shares, warrants, etc., the terms and rights of which vary from company to company. Expert advice should always be sought when considering this type of investment.

A unit trust is not able to offer a similar type of structure to a split capital investment trust since it is only able to issue income units and accumulation units (holders of income units receive the appropriate amount of income to which they are entitled or have it applied to secure additional units, whereas the holders of accumulation units have the income accumulated to enhance the value of their existing units).

(i) An investment trust is effectively prohibited from advertising its shares in the way a unit trust can advertise its units.

(j) With effect from 1st January 1990, investment trusts investing in overseas markets will be at a minor disadvantage compared to unit trusts which are UCITS, since their income from overseas dividends, bonds and deposits will continue to be subject to corporation tax at 35%. As previously discussed, the rate applicable to unit trusts which are UCITS will be 25%.

Other considerations

(a) Except for very small investors, an investment trust usually has lower charges than those of a unit trust. One of the main reasons for this is that, unlike most unit trusts, an investment trust does not pay commission to the agent who, as a result, will have to rely on his own charges for his income.

(b) The average performance of investment trusts has been generally superior to the average performance of unit trusts over most periods. However, individual unit trusts have often produced the best (as well as the worst) results compared to individual investment trusts.

(c) Greater information is usually more readily available in the case of a particular unit trust than for an investment trust. Consequently, a potential investor can normally make a more informed decision regarding a unit trust than an investment trust.

Conclusion

Although the choice between an investment trust and a unit trust will depend on individual circumstances, the following factors are likely to be of particular importance in determining which will prove to be a better investment.

(a) The expertise of the particular investment managers. (This is discussed earlier in this chapter. Although dealing with the management of unit trusts and investment bonds, the criteria for investment trust managers are largely the same.)

(b) The size of the discount on assets at which an investment trust is bought and sold. However, this is likely to have a relatively less important effect on the result of the investment if the shares are held on a long term basis.

Unit trust and investment trust regular savings plans

Unit trust and investment trust regular savings plans are investment schemes whereby a fixed amount is invested on a regular basis (usually monthly) in a unit trust or an investment trust. These plans are particularly useful to an individual who wishes to spread his investment over a period, rather than commit a lump sum at a particular time. However, although a decision on timing is largely removed, it should be remembered that the investor will only benefit from rising values to the extent that he has already invested in a savings plan.

One of the benefits of regular savings plans is that of 'pound cost averaging', whereby more units are automatically acquired from the regular investment when prices are low than when they are high. Consequently, the average cost per unit purchased over a period is less than the average of the market prices during that period. Although pound cost averaging is likely to produce greater benefits with a volatile fund than with a more stable fund, it is even more important if a volatile fund is selected that the investor should have the flexibility to be able to postpone encashment until the market is considered high.

The same care should be taken in choosing a regular savings plan as with a lump sum investment. If large regular investments are to be made, it is normally worthwhile to divide the contributions into a number of different plans.

One particular problem which can arise with regular savings plans is capital gains tax. Since each contribution to a plan counts as a separate investment, a large number of capital gains tax calculations may be necessary when the plans are encashed. However, for disposals made after 5th April 1988, it is possible for an investor to apply for a simplified method to operate, whereby fixed monthly savings are aggregated each year and treated as a single sum invested, with the date of the deemed investment being on the seventh month of the anniversary of the savings plan. Additional payments can also be included, provided they do not exceed twice the regular monthly contribution. Otherwise, lump sums will be treated separately.

4. Investments under the Business Expansion Scheme

The main purposes of the Business Expansion Scheme (BES) are to increase outside investment in unquoted companies and thereby assist in providing additional employment and to revitalise the private rented residential sector on assured tenancy terms. In order to achieve this, the scheme gives investors relief at their highest income tax rates on the amount invested up to a maximum of £40,000 pa. (From 1990/91, a husband and wife will each be able to make investments of £40,000 pa which will qualify for relief.) In addition, no capital gains tax is payable on the first disposal of shares issued after 18th March 1986 unless the BES relief has been withdrawn from shareholders.

A BES investor is able to claim relief of up to one-half of the amount subscribed against his income of the previous tax year, subject to (a) the shares being issued in the first half of the tax year (between 6th April and 5th October inclusive) and (b) the carry-back being limited to £5,000. However, the overall maximum amount on which tax relief can be claimed in any one tax year remains at £40,000. The minimum investment permitted under the Scheme is £500 per company, but this does not apply to investments made through approved investment funds.

An individual can invest either directly in individual companies or indirectly via a fund which itself will make investments in a number of 'target' companies. In the latter case, shares in the target companies will often be transferred to the investor at the end of five years or sold en bloc with the relevant proportion of the sales proceeds being passed to the investor.

As a result of the changes in the 1988 Finance Act, whereby the total investment by a company which would qualify for BES relief is restricted to £500,000 (other than ship chartering companies and companies providing private rented accommodation where the limit is £5 million) and the top rate of both income tax and capital gains tax is 40%, the current situation is generally as follows.

(a) BES investments are often less attractive from an income tax viewpoint, although tax free capital gains may be more attractive.
(b) Conventional BES investments, as opposed to assured tenancies, are likely to be even more risky since:
  (i)   they will often be smaller issues;
  (ii) they will often be unsponsored as it may not be financially viable to have a sponsor.
(c) Prospectus issues are still usually more popular compared to funds despite the costs of providing a prospectus. (If the cost of a prospectus relating to a fully subscribed issue is £100,000, this would normally be 20% of the amount to be raised, except in the cases of ship chartering companies and companies providing private rented accommodation on assured tenancy terms.)

(d) In the case of an investment in an approved fund, tax relief is obtained in the year by reference to the closing date for investment in the fund rather than the date the fund invests in target companies.

(e) A large number of issues has been made by companies providing private rented accommodation. This is on the basis of assured tenancies which are discussed later in this chapter.

Main investment considerations

The following are some of the main considerations which should be borne in mind before an investment is made under the BES.

(a) Despite the tax reliefs provided, any investments made should be considered to be of a higher risk nature, especially in the case of direct investments in individual companies.

(b) Unless the investor has the necessary expertise himself, proper advice should be obtained as to the investment potential of the company under consideration. Although an investment fund will undertake such a review before the investment is made, it is still necessary for the expertise and experience of the fund managers themselves to be assessed. This varies considerably, with some fund managers having specialist knowledge of particular industries, etc.

(c) The prospect of being able to realise the investment at the end of the five-year qualifying period. For example, if it was considered likely that at the end of the five-year period the company would be able to buy back its own shares or arrangements would be made for the shares to have a full listing on the Stock Exchange, a quotation on the Unlisted Securities Market or be dealt in on the third market, this would be a major advantage.

(d) Whether the investment is to be made directly in a qualifying company or via an investment fund. The main advantage of a direct investment is that the individual is able to know beforehand in which company his investment is being made. With an investment in a fund, the individual does not know in what companies his monies will be invested until after the event.

The main advantages of an investment in a fund are as follows.

   (i) Specialist fund managers will select the investments to be made and then monitor them on a regular basis. This is likely to produce superior results than if this work is carried out by the investor himself unless he has access to the necessary information and expertise.

   (ii) By investing in a fund, the risk of the investment being a total loss is reduced due to the spread available. However, the likelihood of very large gains is also reduced. (It should be remembered that investment in a fund specialising in venture capital will normally be of a higher risk/higher reward nature than in a fund investing in companies mainly requiring development capital.)

(e) In the case of a private issue involving a direct investment in a qualifying company, consideration should be given to safeguarding against withdrawal of the tax relief allowed. Accordingly, it may be worthwhile for the investor to seek appropriate warranties and indemnities from the other shareholders, the company and its directors in the event of their non-compliance with all the conditions.

(f) If an investment in a fund is being considered, the level of charges should be carefully examined, bearing in mind that they can be levied by a number of different methods. Particular attention should be paid to option agreements, especially where they relate to a proportion of the target company's equity. These options, while providing incentives to the fund management company, can involve the equity available to investors being substantially diluted.

(g) Where a direct investment is being considered, it is important to find out:
  (i)   the experience and qualifications of the management;
  (ii)   the composition of the management and whether it makes a balanced team;
  (iii) whether the directors are investing their own money on the same terms as other investors, and if not, whether their incentives, including any options available, are realistic (where 'A' shares are involved, close examination should be made of the potential rewards provided);
  (iv)   whether the executive directors (often with outside interests) will devote sufficient time to managing the company's affairs;
  (v)   whether there is a reputable sponsor with an established record;
  (vi)   whether the overall costs of the issue are reasonable;
  (vii) the past results of the company (if any);
  (viii) whether the business concept of the company is sound;
  (ix)   the extent to which the investment is asset backed;
  (x)   the likelihood or otherwise of there being a satisfactory exit route at the end of the five-year qualifying period.

(h) In the case of an investment in a fund, it should be remembered that the fund is often only open to accept applications for a comparatively short period and therefore a quick decision on whether to invest is usually necessary.

(i) Funds can be either approved or non-approved (by the Inland Revenue). The main differences are as follows.

Approved funds
  (i)   All the investments are initially registered in the name of a nominee company which holds the shares on behalf of the individual participants. At the end of five years, the intention of the funds with regard to unquoted shares varies. However, in the case of shares in quoted companies, it is likely that they will be transferred into the names of the participants.
  (ii)   The offer can only remain open for a maximum period of forty days, although this may be extended.
  (iii) Every investor has an identical portfolio proportionate to the amount invested.
  (iv)   An individual must invest a minimum of £2,000 and the fund must make at least four investments. No single investment may exceed 25% of the fund.
  (v)   Tax certificates are normally issued in batches of £500 or half-yearly.
  (vi)   As previously mentioned, tax relief is obtained in the year by reference to the closing date for investment in the fund rather than the date the fund invests in target companies. However, at least 90% of the amount subscribed by the individual to the fund must be invested in eligible shares within six months of the closing date.

Non-approved funds
(i)   The investor is registered by the company as the beneficial owner with regard to each investment made. Consequently, he will receive the annual report and accounts plus other shareholder information in respect of all companies in which he holds shares.
(ii)   The offer can be open-ended both as to closing date and the maximum amount to be raised.
(iii)   An instalment plan is permitted.
(iv)   The manager selects investments for each investor, most of whom will have different portfolios. Comparing investment performance is therefore more difficult.
(v)   An individual must invest a minimum of £500 in each company.
(vi)   Tax relief is granted on each investment on a company by company basis.
(vii)   Tax relief is obtained by reference to the date the fund invests in target companies rather than the closing date for investment in the fund itself.

(j)   Under the changes in the 1989 Budget, it is now no longer possible for an individual to claim tax relief for the interest on money borrowed to buy shares in a close company where the shares also qualify for relief under the BES. Consequently, unless the shares had been allocated to the individual by 13th March 1989, the scheme was put to an end whereby approximately £100 million had been invested with the benefit of the double tax relief.

Due to tax relief being allowed against the investor's highest rates of tax, an investment made under the BES is more likely to be advantageous for higher rate taxpayers. This is illustrated below.

Example 8

An investment of £5,000 in a fund is realised after five years at 150% of cost.

Average rate of income tax relieved	40% £	25% £
Original cost of investment	5,000.00	5,000.00
Management fee — say 7% plus VAT	402.50	402.50
Total cost	5,402.50	5,402.50
Less: Tax relief	2,000.00	1,250.00
Net cost	£3,402.50	£4,152.50
Net proceeds of investment	£7,500.00	£7,500.00
Return on original net cost	120%	81%
Annual net compound return	17%	12½%

Note: If the investment was in a prospectus issue instead of a fund, tax relief would generally be obtained on the issue costs. Accordingly, both the returns shown in the example would be greater with the return available to a higher rate taxpayer still considerably more attractive.

Assured tenancies

In order to revitalise the private rented residential sector so as to alleviate the housing shortage, BES status was made available in the 1988 Finance Act to issues from companies providing private rented accommodation. These are made on the basis of assured tenancies which under the Housing Act 1988 allows full market rents to be charged to residential tenants. (To qualify for the tax treatment of investments made under the BES, the market value of each property to be let must not exceed £125,000 if it is in Greater London and £85,000 if it is elsewhere.)

However, before an individual decides to make an investment in an assured tenancy, the following matters should be taken into account.

(a) Large rises have already taken place in most properties, particularly in London and South-East England. The location of the assured tenancy is therefore very important.
(b) The quality of the management company may not always be high. In addition, since the Housing Act 1988 only came into force in January 1989, nobody has yet had more than very limited experience of assured tenancies.
(c) The likelihood of the company obtaining vacant possession at the end of the five-year qualifying period. If this does not happen, a reduced amount may be received on sale.
(d) The level of charges is often high and frequently complex.
(e) The position if there was a change of Government.
(f) The three main types of assured tenancy are as follows:
  (i)   a single company which is issued by means of a prospectus;
  (ii) a fund which invests in a range of BES companies at the manager's discretion;
  (iii) a scheme which offers investors a choice of companies and geographical regions.

5. Personal equity plans

In order to promote individual share ownership and to give investors a personal interest and direct stake in UK companies, personal equity plans (PEPs) were introduced with effect from 1st January 1987. Substantial improvements to PEPs were made in the 1989 Budget and these became effective on 6th April 1989. However, as a transitional measure, plan managers are given the option to operate both the old and new-style plans until 31st December 1989, thereby enabling an individual to make an investment in each.

Main details

The main details of the 1989/90 new-style PEPs can be summarised as follows.

(a) Any UK resident aged 18 or over is able to invest up to £4,800 pa in a PEP (plans may not be opened in joint names, but in the case of married couples both husband and wife may have independent plans). In order for the full £4,800 per person to be invested, some plan managers allow an additional payment to be made to cover their initial charges. New share issues, including privatisation issues, can be brought into a PEP within 30 days of allocation of the shares.

(b) The maximum permitted investment is calculated on the basis of a tax year (prior to 6th April 1989, the basis was on a calendar year). Investment within a PEP can continue indefinitely. However, after death the plan comes to an end.

(c) The PEP payment must be made to an authorised PEP manager. This includes members of the Stock Exchange, licenced security dealers, banks, building societies, insurance companies, unit trusts and other financial institutions who have registered with the Inland Revenue and been approved as a plan manager.

(d) Investments must be in ordinary shares in UK incorporated companies quoted on a UK stock exchange or dealt with on the Unlisted Securities Market. However, an individual is allowed to invest up to £2,400 of his PEP into unit trusts and investment trusts.

   The trusts themselves must invest a minimum of 75% of their underlying assets in UK equities by no later than 6th April 1990, subject to the following relaxations.

   (i) Investors have the option of investing up to £750 pa in a unit trust or investment trust which does not satisfy the above requirement. However, this is an alternative to investing up to £2,400 in trusts which do meet the 75% requirement.

   (ii) Third market and unquoted shares of companies held in a portfolio of a unit trust or an investment trust count towards the 75% rule.

    (iii)   Unit trust funds of funds qualify for inclusion in a PEP, providing they only invest in funds that are authorised schemes, complying with the 75% requirement.

    (iv)   Capital shares and income shares in split capital investment trusts count towards the 75% rule, but as with the funds of funds, the underlying investments must meet the 75% requirement.

    After the initial investment has been made, shares can be switched into unit trusts or investment trusts to a limited extent (the value of the holding in unit trusts and investment trusts immediately after the switch must not exceed half the value of the whole PEP portfolio). Investments in unit trusts or investment trusts can be switched without restriction to other unit trusts or investment trusts.

(e)   A recognised plan may be either non-discretionary, in which the plan manager simply executes the buy and sell orders of the investor, usually from a restricted list, or discretionary. A discretionary 'common management arrangement' is where the investment decisions are made by the plan manager.

(f)   No tax is payable either on capital gains or on dividend income, whether it is passed on to investors or reinvested in the plan, in respect of investments held within a PEP. However, interest arising from cash holdings is subject to composite rate tax in the same way as bank or building society deposits. The requirement prior to 6th April 1989 that plans must be held for a full calendar year in order to qualify for the advantageous tax treatment has been abolished. Accordingly, a PEP can be sold at any time without adverse tax consequences.

(g)   No tax relief is allowed on investments made.

(h)   There is no need for an investor to contact the Inland Revenue as the plan manager is responsible for reclaiming the tax on dividends and for all the paperwork.

(i)   An individual is allowed to take out only one PEP in a tax year and therefore it is not possible to split an investment and choose more than one PEP manager in the year. However, he is permitted by the legislation to 'top-up' his plan to the £4,800 maximum.

(j)   A PEP can be combined with earlier plans to form a unified portfolio. A PEP can also be transferred from one plan manager to another at any stage.

(k)   If requested by planholders, the PEP manager must arrange for them to receive the annual report and accounts of all companies in which they hold shares. Similarly, planholders can request to attend shareholders' meetings, exercise voting rights and obtain other shareholder information. A charge can be made by the PEP manager for these facilities.

(l)   Planholders must be sent regular statements, at least annually, showing details of all plan investments and cash held, the value of the investments, the prices at which purchases and sales have been made and details of all dividends, interest, etc.

(m) There is no limit to the amount of charges that can be made, but they must be clearly shown. Charges can include an initial fee, annual charges for both first and subsequent years, dealing costs, charges on the number of assets held, withdrawal from the plan (including switching to another plan manager), receiving the annual report and accounts and attendance at annual general meetings of companies where shares are held, and other sundry expenses mainly covering portfolio valuations additional to the first in a year.

Principal advantages and disadvantages

The following are the principal advantages and disadvantages of PEPs compared to other main savings media.

Advantages
(a) No tax is payable, either on capital gains or on dividend income, in respect of investments held within a PEP (this can be particularly advantageous where the main purpose of the investments is to produce a high income).
(b) An individual is able to invest up to £2,400 pa into unit trust and investment trust plans with the above tax advantages.
(c) PEPs can be discontinued at any time without loss of the tax benefits.
(d) All returns to the Inland Revenue are dealt with by the plan manager. An individual need not mention the investments on his own tax return.

Disadvantages
(a) A proper investment spread may not be obtained, with the result that risk would be increased.
(b) The costs of administration could be high in relation to the amount of the investments involved.
(c) The maximum investment is restricted to £4,800 pa per person, although a married couple can pay a total of £9,600 pa.

Other considerations

Other considerations which should be borne in mind are as follows.

(a) The quality of investment management in a discretionary plan is of paramount importance. This is likely to have a greater bearing on the final investment return than the level of charges.
(b) PEPs should normally be regarded as medium to long term investments due mainly to having relatively high initial charges but lower annual charges. By holding the PEP over a reasonable time, the initial charges would be diluted over the period. In addition, the tax benefits would be greater over a long term.

Conclusion

The tax reliefs provided are relatively small and in any event the majority of investors do not pay capital gains tax, as their gains are normally within the annual exemption. Accordingly, PEPs would seem to be most advantageous for higher rate taxpayers who already make use of their annual capital gains tax exemption. However, for those investors who wish to effect a unit trust or investment trust regular savings plan with contributions of up to £200 per month, an arrangement within a PEP would usually be more advantageous.

6. Pension arrangements for directors and executives

This chapter has been written primarily from the viewpoint of individual arrangements for directors and executives effected on a money purchase basis (the final benefits being based on the amount in the pension fund at retirement) and not on a final salary basis (where the pension benefits are funded as a proportion of final remuneration). It is not intended to cover medium or large group schemes (although much of the chapter may still be relevant to them), nor the state pension scheme, including the Social Security Act 1986. Personal Pensions are discussed in Chapter 7.

Maximum benefits

The maximum benefits, which may be provided under exempt approved pension schemes within the Inland Revenue limits, in respect of individuals who were members of schemes in existence before 17th March 1987, are as follows.

(a) Member's retirement pension of ⅔rds of final remuneration provided ten years' pensionable service has been completed by the normal retirement date.

(b) Lump sum on retirement of 1½ times final remuneration provided 20 years' pensionable service has been completed by the normal retirement date. However, if a lump sum is taken, the member's retirement pension would be reduced. Based on the maximum lump sum of 1½ times final remuneration being provided, the pension receivable would be approximately as follows:

	% of final remuneration
for a man aged 60	52
for a man aged 65	50
for a woman aged 60	53

(c) Widow's/widower's post-retirement pension of ⅔rds of the maximum pension that could have been approved for the member before any reduction for lump sum benefits.

(d) Widow's/widower's death-in-service pension of ⅔rds of the maximum pension that could have been approved for the member had he retired on incapacity grounds at the date of his death. This pension can take into account the whole of the potential service up to normal retirement age.

(e) Dependants' post-retirement and death-in-service pensions. These together with the widow's/widower's pension must not exceed the amount of the member's maximum approvable pension.

(f) Lump sum death-in-service benefit of £5,000 or four times' final remuneration, whichever is the greater (in this case, final remuneration may be defined more widely than for the calculation of other benefits). In addition, there can be a return of the member's contributions, with or without interest.

(g) Escalation of post-retirement and death-in-service pensions with the maximum increase being the maximum pension increased by the greater of the rise in the cost of living as measured by the RPI or 3% pa.

The above benefits are illustrated by the following bar chart.

Example 9

A man aged 65 has final remuneration of £18,000 and 20 years' pensionable service.

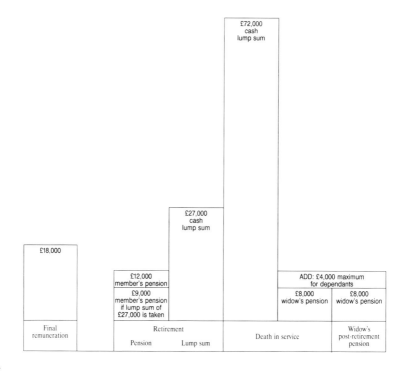

Notes:

(a) The amount of £12,000 for the member's pension assumes that a cash lump sum is not taken in commutation. However, if a lump sum of £27,000 is taken, the member's pension would be reduced to £9,000.

(b) The widow's/widower's pension plus dependants' pensions must not exceed the maximum pension that could have been approved for the member.

(c) In addition to the benefits shown in the chart, the post-retirement and death-in-service pensions can be increased in proportion to the increase in the cost of living or 3% pa, if greater.

From 17th March 1987, the following changes in general applied to all new schemes and arrangements set up prior to 14th March 1989 and to new members of existing schemes joining before 1st June 1989.

(a) The 'accelerated accrual' rate for pension benefits is replaced by a new scale permitting a pension of ⅔rds of final remuneration after 20 years' service (previously it was possible to qualify for a maximum of ⅔rds of final remuneration after ten years' service). For shorter periods, a 'straight line' maximum accrual rate of 2/60ths of final remuneration for each year of service will be allowed.
(b) The accelerated accrual rate for the tax free lump sum, with a maximum of 1½ times final remuneration after 20 years' service, can be used only if pension benefits accrue on the new accelerated scale. Otherwise, 3/80ths of final remuneration for each year of service (with a maximum of 40) will broadly apply, subject to certain relaxation.
(c) Due to final remuneration being generally restricted to £100,000 for the purpose of calculating the tax free lump sum on retirement, the maximum amount payable is £150,000.

Where a member joins his company late and so is unable to have 20 years' pensionable service, his maximum approvable retirement pension, expressed as a fraction of final remuneration, is as shown below.

Years of service to normal retirement age	Fraction of final remuneration Before 17th March 1987	On or after 17th March 1987 (see note (a) below)
1	1/60th	2/60ths
2	2/60ths	4/60ths
3	3/60ths	6/60ths
4	4/60ths	8/60ths
5	5/60ths	10/60ths
6	8/60ths	12/60ths
7	16/60ths	14/60ths
8	24/60ths	16/60ths
9	32/60ths	18/60ths
10	40/60ths	20/60ths
11	40/60ths	22/60ths
12	40/60ths	24/60ths
13	40/60ths	26/60ths
14	40/60ths	28/60ths
15	40/60ths	30/60ths
16	40/60ths	32/60ths
17	40/60ths	34/60ths
18	40/60ths	36/60ths
19	40/60ths	38/60ths
20	40/60ths	40/60ths

Notes:
(a) From 17th March 1987, the fractions of final remuneration shown in this column have in general applied to all schemes and arrangements set up since that date and to new members of existing schemes. The fractions in the previous column are applicable in other cases.
(b) Fractions of a year may be interpolated into the scale.
(c) Where the accelerated accrual rate is applied, benefits provided from previous occupations (retained benefits) must generally be taken into account to ensure that the total pension does not exceed ⅔rds of final remuneration.

For late entrants who are unable to achieve 20 years' pensionable service, the maximum approvable lump sum on retirement, expressed as a fraction of final remuneration, is as shown below.

Years of service to normal retirement age	Fraction of final remuneration
1-8	3/80ths for each year
9	30/80ths
10	36/80ths
11	42/80ths
12	48/80ths
13	54/80ths
14	63/80ths
15	72/80ths
16	81/80ths
17	90/80ths
18	99/80ths
19	108/80ths
20 or more	120/80ths

Notes:
(a) For all schemes and arrangements set up between 17th March 1987 and 13th March 1989 (and members who joined existing schemes between 17th March 1987 and 31st May 1989), lump sums based on the accelerated accrual rate (years 9 to 20 or more on the above scale) will be available only to those individuals whose pension is also based on the accelerated accrual rate. In any event, the maximum amount which can be taken as a tax free lump sum with regard to these schemes is £150,000.
(b) Fractions of a year may be interpolated into the scale.
(c) Where the accelerated accrual rate is applied, benefits provided from previous occupations must generally be taken into account to ensure that the total lump sum does not exceed 1½ times final remuneration.

Further changes have been proposed in the 1989 Budget which will affect all new schemes set up on or after 14th March 1989 and employees joining existing schemes from 1st June 1989.

(a) The benefits to be provided, both pensions and cash sums, will be based on remuneration of up to £60,000 only. This figure will be revalued each year in line with the RPI.
(b) Employees with at least 20 years' service may retire on a pension of ⅔rds final remuneration at any time from age 50 onwards. For shorter periods, $\frac{2}{60}$ths of final remuneration for each year of service will be allowed. Any shortfall in funding must be provided by augmentation.
(c) The tax free lump sum payable on retirement will be calculated as either $\frac{3}{80}$ths of final remuneration for each year of service (subject to a maximum of 40) or 2¼ times the annual pension, whichever is the greater. The maximum amount permissible will be £90,000 (1½ times remuneration of £60,000).

(d) Employers will be able to provide more generous benefits than the tax rules allow by establishing an unapproved top-up scheme, but the usual tax advantages will not apply. This second scheme can be on a funded or unfunded basis, although contributions to a funded scheme would be taxed as income of the employee. Benefits from an unfunded scheme would be taxed only when they are paid.

Employees who joined schemes before 1st June 1989 may elect that their benefits be subject to the new maxima shown above but this would include accepting the remuneration restriction in (a) above.

As a consequence of the changes which have occurred since 17th March 1987, many older and highly paid employees could be reluctant to change jobs since their pension and/or lump sum expectation may be reduced.

Final remuneration

The most usual definition of final remuneration is the remuneration for any one of the five years preceding the normal retirement date. However, where fluctuating emoluments arise such as commission or bonuses, they would usually be taken as the average of three or more years ending on the last day of the basic pay year. Directors' fees may rank either as basic pay or as fluctuating emoluments according to the basis on which they are voted.

In the case of a 20% director (a director, who either on his own, or with associates, is able to control 20% or more of the ordinary share capital of the company), benefits cannot be based on one year's earnings. Instead, final remuneration would normally be defined as the average of the total emoluments for any three or more consecutive years ending not earlier than ten years before the normal retirement date.

For either definition, remuneration may be dynamised in proportion to the increase in the cost of living for the period from the end of the year on which the remuneration is based up to normal retirement date. However, dynamised final remuneration may not be used to permit a greater lump sum retirement benefit in isolation.

Benefits in kind may be taken into account when they are assessed to income tax as emoluments under Schedule E, and will normally be regarded as fluctuating emoluments. If benefits are not assessable, they may not be included as part of final remuneration except with the agreement of the Inland Revenue Superannuation Funds Office (SFO).

With effect from 17th March 1987, the following changes have in general applied to all new schemes and arrangements and to new members of existing schemes:

(a) the definition of final remuneration excludes income and gains from share option schemes;
(b) employees earning more than £100,000 and any employee who has at any time within ten years prior to retirement been a 20% director have final remuneration defined as if they were 20% directors (see above).

Normal retirement date

The normal retirement age is usually within the range 60–70 for men and 55–70 for women. However, in the case where a woman is a 20% director, the earliest normal retirement age is 60.

It is also possible to obtain approval for a scheme where a retirement age is greater than 70, and in the case of certain occupations the SFO will approve earlier retirement ages than is the norm, e.g. footballers at 35. However, each case would have to be considered according to its own individual circumstances.

An individual may continue to work after the normal retirement date. In this case, he may elect to receive at that date or before he actually retires, the pension and/or lump sum benefit which would have been due if he had retired, rather than defer all benefits until actual retirement. Where benefits are taken after the normal retirement date, the 1989 Budget proposals will remove the basis for late retirement increases if the pension scheme provides uplifted benefits for early leavers and/or retirements.

Retirement earlier than the normal retirement date is allowed on grounds of incapacity, whatever the age, or if the individual is at least age 50 (a woman may retire before age 50, but not before age 45, if her normal retirement age is lower than 60 and she is already within 10 years of it).

If it is required to change the normal retirement date, this may be possible with specific approval from the SFO. However, where the change is to bring forward the retirement date, there must usually be a period of approximately five years from the date of request to the new retirement date.

Early leavers

The problem of individuals who leave their employment before normal retirement date in order to move to a new job and the advantages and disadvantages of portable pensions have in recent years been the subject of considerable debate. Mainly as a result of this, personal pensions were introduced in 1988 so that an employee can be given the opportunity to make his own arrangement.

The following are the main options which may be available to early leavers at the present time:

(a) contributions cease and the plan is made paid-up. It would then continue to participate in the investment performance of the fund;
(b) the transfer value of the plan is applied towards a new company's scheme if permitted by the scheme rules of both companies, provided that the individual leaves his employment at least one year before his normal retirement date. The new company would then take over the provision of retirement benefits;
(c) the transfer value of the plan is used to purchase a 'buy-out' bond from an insurance company (the value of which would depend on the growth of the underlying fund);
(d) the transfer value is paid to a personal pension;
(e) a paid up policy is issued in the member's own name.

Where the individual has less than two years' service with a company, he is not automatically entitled to benefits purchased by the company, unless this is specifically stated in the scheme rules. He may, however, receive a refund of up to the level of his own contributions, with or without interest, less a deduction for tax of currently 20%.

Commutation

It is usually advantageous to commute into cash the maximum amount of pension permitted by the Inland Revenue (up to 1½ times final remuneration), and if appropriate to use the cash to purchase an annuity. The reason for this is that the whole of the pension is taxable, whereas the capital element of the annuity is tax free with only the income element being subject to taxation.

Example 10

A single man aged 65 commutes £4,000 of his pension and applies the resultant cash lump sum to purchase a life annuity.

	Without commutation £	*With commutation* £
Pension	16,000	12,000
Other income	9,000	9,000
Income element of annuity	—	1,976
	25,000	22,976
Tax	5,781	5,048
Net	19,219	17,928
Capital element of annuity	—	1,976
	£19,219	£19,904

Notes:
(a) One quarter of the amount in the pension fund has been applied to purchase the annuity.
(b) The annuity is payable monthly in arrear, guaranteed five years.
(c) Although the £4,000 of gross pension forgone is replaced by a gross annuity of £3,952, the tax treatment results in an improved net income situation.

In practice, the purchase of the annuity should often be delayed until at least age 70 with the object of obtaining the benefit of improved annuity rates available at older ages (although the value obtained of purchasing an annuity at an earlier age would be equivalent). However, besides personal circumstances, this decision would also be influenced by the general level of interest rates prevailing at the time together with their future outlook (prevailing high interest rates which are expected to fall in the near future would often indicate that the annuity should be purchased immediately).

Simplified schemes

Simplified occupational pension schemes providing 'no frills' benefits designed to suit the small employer first became available in 1987. The Inland Revenue will provide on request standard documentation enabling approval for these schemes to be automatically forthcoming. There are two types of scheme to allow a choice so that benefits can be related to final salary (a 'defined benefit' scheme) or contributions (a 'defined contribution' scheme). In order to achieve the simplified procedure, special restrictions are imposed on both types of scheme.

Immediate tax free cash for elderly company directors

Arrangements can be created for directors and employees, who are over normal retirement age but are not members of a company pension scheme, whereby they can receive an immediate tax free cash sum from their companies, whether or not they retire. The amount would be based on 3/80ths of final remuneration for each year of service, with a maximum of $1\frac{1}{2}$ times final remuneration after 40 years and an overriding limit of £90,000. However, in calculating this amount, it is necessary to take into account any tax free lump sum receivable from a personal pension or retirement annuity policy if it arose from current employment.

The arrangement is not made with an insurance company, but is on an unfunded basis which allows the payment to be made directly from the company to the director. Where the company does not have sufficient cash resources to do this, it may still be possible for the payment to be made to the director if he makes a loan of a similar amount back to the company. He can then draw on his loan account in lieu of his normal remuneration and thereby avoid income tax and national insurance contributions.

A pension can also be provided under this arrangement and if this is received instead of remuneration, national insurance contributions would again be avoided.

If required, approval can be obtained from the Inland Revenue for the arrangement before it is effected.

Taxation position

The provision of private pensions is favourably regarded by the Government and, in order to encourage their development, the following advantageous taxation treatment currently applies.

(a) Investment income and capital gains accumulate within the pension fund free of all UK tax.
(b) The resulting pension is treated as earned income.
(c) Lump sum benefits arising on death and at retirement are normally received tax free. The main exception to this is where the trustees of the pension scheme do not have discretion to nominate who should receive the lump sum death-in-service benefit, with the result that the payment is made into the estate of the deceased member.

(d) Annual contributions payable by a company are allowable as an expense for corporation tax purposes. However, the contribution should be paid and cleared through the bank account before the end of the company's accounting year in order to obtain tax relief in that year. The contributions are not taxable as a benefit of the member.

In order for a scheme to be approved, the company's contributions must not be insignificant (generally, a minimum of 10% of the total contributions payable).

(e) Special contributions (contributions which are not ordinary annual contributions) made by the company to purchase additional benefits for a member in respect of past service may have to be spread for corporation tax purposes. The amount allowed in a single year is the greater of: (i) £20,000; or (ii) the amount of the annual contribution. For this purpose, the annual contribution is the total amount paid by the company in respect of all members to all schemes and not that relating to just the member or scheme concerned.

Where the special contribution exceeds the amount stated above, the general rule for determining the period over which the contribution is to be spread is calculated by dividing the contribution by the greater of £20,000 or the amount of the annual contribution, subject to a maximum of five years.

(f) Contributions by a member of up to 15% of his annual remuneration are treated as allowable deductions for income tax purposes. Remuneration for this purpose must not exceed £60,000 in 1989/90 (increasing in subsequent years in line with the increase in the RPI).

(g) Where a refund of contributions is taken, a deduction for tax is made, currently of 20%.

(h) Although not strictly a taxation advantage, no national insurance contributions are payable either on pension contributions made by a company or on the resulting pensions.

Main uses of pension arrangements

Some of the main uses of pension arrangements are outlined below.

(a) Retirement planning for directors and executives. Additional benefits over those of the main scheme can be provided as appropriate for the individual.

(b) Mitigation of corporation tax liabilities. Payment of pension contributions is an allowable expense in whole or in part (if a special contribution, it may be necessary for it to be spread) against corporation tax in the accounting year of payment.

(c) Reduction of the value of the shares in a company for both capital gains tax and inheritance tax purposes. By paying pension contributions, the value of a company is generally reduced.

(d) In inheritance tax planning, viz:

    (i)   a good pension arrangement provides a continuing income for the member and his wife, and it is therefore more likely they would be willing to dispose of assets during their lifetimes and thereby benefit from the annual exemptions or even avoid inheritance tax entirely (lifetime transfers which are potentially exempt become completely exempt after seven years, but will be chargeable if death occurs within that time);

   (ii)   a lump sum death-in-service benefit may be provided free of tax for the benefit of children, dependants, etc. by way of an 'expression of wish letter' to the trustees of the pension scheme. This letter should be regularly reviewed in case it becomes appropriate to change the individuals nominated.

(e) Funding for cash. A member's retirement pension may be commuted into cash up to the Inland Revenue limit, i.e. up to 1½ times final remuneration. In order to receive the maximum cash (which must not exceed £90,000 in the cases of all new schemes set up on or after 14th March 1989 and employees joining existing schemes from 1st June 1989 onwards), individuals who were members of schemes in existence before 17th March 1987 will need to complete 20 years' pensionable service by retirement. In other cases, 40 years' service will often be necessary.

Maximising benefits

Due to the considerable advantages offered by company pension schemes, it is a major benefit to directors and executives if their pension arrangements can be maximised. In order to achieve this, the amount treated as final remuneration should be the highest permitted and the pension contributions paid should be as large as possible without over-funding. The following are some of the ways in which these requirements can be met.

(a) Dynamising past salaries. As previously mentioned, remuneration may be dynamised in proportion to the increase in the cost of living for the period from the end of the year on which the remuneration is based up to normal retirement date. Therefore, when the rate of inflation has exceeded the actual increases in remuneration, notional final remuneration should be calculated by taking the actual remuneration for an earlier period and applying the increase in the RPI or other suitable index up to normal retirement date. This would then produce a larger amount on which pension benefits can be based that the final remuneration actually paid.

(b) Arranging for the normal retirement age to be the earliest allowed by the Inland Revenue. As a result of this, larger contributions would be required for the pension fund to build up to produce the required benefits, due to the shorter period available and fewer contributions payable. In addition, a larger fund would be required to provide the pension benefits as they would normally be payable for a longer period.

(c) Assuming that remuneration will increase by 8½% pa (the maximum permitted) until normal retirement date in order to determine in advance final remuneration for the purpose of funding pension benefits.

(d) Funding for post-retirement pensions to escalate by the maximum permitted (the increase in the cost of living, as measured by the RPI).

(e) Maximising all death-in-service benefits.

(f) Employing wives and making them directors where appropriate. In this way they can be paid salaries and be provided with pensions in their own right.

(g) Paying additional voluntary contributions (AVCs) to provide benefits within the permitted maximum. However, it is no longer allowed to commute any of the benefits from AVCs into a tax free lump sum, except in the circumstances mentioned below.

Additional voluntary contributions

As mentioned above, a further method which may be available to directors and executives to increase their pension benefits is for them to make additional voluntary contributions (AVCs), with the maximum permitted being 15% of their annual remuneration up to £60,000 in 1989/90 (this would include any contributions which they already pay).

Scheme members are able to pay 'free-standing' AVCs to a pension plan of their own choice. The individual will be able to deduct basic rate tax before paying the AVC to the pension provider who will then reclaim this amount from the Inland Revenue and apply it on the employee's behalf to the contract. A higher rate taxpayer should claim relief at the higher rate through his tax coding or assessment. The overall limit on personal contributions will remain at 15%, but with a maximum of £9,000 pa, revalued each year in line with the RPI, in the cases of all new schemes set up on or after 14th March 1989 and employees joining existing schemes from 1st June 1989 onwards. Since benefits provided by free-standing AVCs will have to be taken in the form of pension, it will not be possible to commute any of the benefits into a tax free lump sum. This also generally applies to employees joining new or established AVC schemes on or after 8th April 1987, although employees who were already in such schemes on 7th April 1987 may commute pension benefits within the Inland Revenue limits.

Free-standing AVCs have not been as successful as had been anticipated because of the possible reduction in the main scheme benefits if Inland Revenue limits were exceeded at retirement. In addition, there was a requirement for the pension provider to obtain certain information from the employer which had also caused administrative problems. Proposals in the 1989 Budget aim to make it easier and more attractive for employees to pay free-standing AVCs by simplifying the procedures. For payments up to £2,400 a year, the pension provider would carry out a small number of simple checks which would not involve the employer. Further checks before retirement would not normally be necessary. Should the benefits at retirement exceed the Inland Revenue limits, the amount in respect of the excess benefits would be returned to the employee subject to a tax charge which would broadly correspond to the tax relief received on contributions and on the build-up of funds.

The payment of AVCs may be worthwhile in the following cases:

(a) where the benefits offered by the pension scheme are low. Moreover, although commutation from the AVC scheme may no longer be allowed, it might still be possible to increase the overall pension benefits by the payment of AVCs and then take the maximum tax free lump sum at retirement from the main scheme. However, this would cause a reduction in the pension provided from the main scheme and consequently post-retirement increases may be lost, although the AVC fund can be used for this purpose (see (f) below);

(b) although the company may have introduced improved benefits for directors, they may not have been made retrospective due to the cost involved;

(c) the pension scheme may have been introduced late in the individual's working life with the result that he may receive only low pension benefits at retirement;

(d) a change of job may not allow an individual sufficient time in his new pension scheme to build up the maximum pension;

(e) earnings for the purposes of the pension scheme may not accurately reflect an individual's total earnings, e.g. commissions or bonuses may not have been taken into account;

(f) no provision may have been made in the pension scheme for escalation of post-retirement pensions.

However, before an individual decides to pay AVCs, the following matters should be borne in mind:

(a) the likelihood or otherwise of the company improving pension benefits before the individual retires, making the payment of AVCs unnecessary;

(b) the fund built up from the AVCs will be locked in until retirement when the pension benefits become available;

(c) the position with regard to the monies in the pension fund accumulated from AVCs made should the individual change his job before retirement.

Whether it is preferable for pension contributions to be made by the individual in the form of AVCs or in the form of salary sacrifice, whereby the individual's salary is reduced but the company pays an additional pension contribution for his benefit, will depend on the exact circumstances.

With the removal of the upper earnings limit on employers' national insurance contributions from 6th October 1985, salary sacrifice can be an ideal method for a company of reducing the salaries paid to directors and executives and thereby mitigating the additional national insurance costs.

However, from the individual's viewpoint, the advantage of AVCs is that the limits on pension and death-in-service benefits are based on the gross remuneration and not on the remuneration after the deduction of the contributions. (As previously mentioned, remuneration for this purpose must not exceed £60,000 in 1989/90, increasing in subsequent years in line with the RPI.) Moreover, in the event of the individual's death-in-service, the normal lump sum death benefits may be increased by the return (with or without interest) of his own contributions.

It can therefore be seen that there are now conflicting factors operating on the choice between AVCs and salary sacrifice.

The following example shows AVCs as an investment.

Example 11

A married man is aged 45 next birthday with a normal retirement age of 65 and current remuneration of £26,000 pa. AVCs of £1,000 pa are to be paid:

	Contributions paid £	Contributions not paid £
Gross remuneration	26,000	26,000
Less: Additional voluntary contributions	1,000	—
	25,000	26,000
Less: Allowances	4,375	4,375
	£20,625	£21,625
Income tax payable	£ 5,156	£ 5,545
Net income	£19,844	£20,455
Difference in net income	£611 pa	

Illustrative benefits provided by pension scheme at age 65 in respect of £1,000 pa payable for 20 years

Illustrated fund   £71,700

Net return is approximately 15% pa compound based on £611 pa

Notes:
(a) The illustrated fund shown at £71,700 is based on the rules laid down by the Life Assurance and Unit Trust Regulatory Organisation (LAUTRO) and assumes that contributions, after allowing for a deduction for expenses, will be invested to earn 13% pa.
(b) In the event of death before age 65, the full amount of the accumulated fund would be returned.
(c) Since employees joining new or established AVC schemes on or after 8th April 1987 cannot commute any of the benefits into a tax free lump sum, the benefits will have to be taken in the form of pension.

Insured schemes

The main types of insured schemes are as follows.

(a) With profits. Under this method, the pension fund is increased each year by the declaration of bonuses which, once declared, cannot be taken away. In addition, most insurance companies also pay terminal bonuses, the amount of which will be mainly based on the investment surplus at retirement. Many insurance companies now write these contracts on a unitised basis whereby bonuses increase the rate of growth in unit prices.
(b) Non-profit. This type of scheme can be suitable when it is required that the amount in the pension fund or the pension itself at pension age should be guaranteed. It is not normally recommended except in cases when there is a comparatively short period to retirement.
(c) Unit-linked. The value of the pension fund under this method will fluctuate with the value of the underlying assets on which the price of the units is

based. Unit-linked schemes, although capable of producing very good results, usually involve a greater risk.

(d) Deposit administration. This method is often operated in a similar way to a bank deposit account where interest is added periodically to the amount in the pension fund. Therefore, the value of the fund is guaranteed to show annual growth and cannot depreciate.

It is now normal practice in the case of all types of insured schemes for an open market option to be available without penalty. (An open market option is where the full value of the member's benefit is made available to purchase a pension from an insurance company other than that with which the pension scheme was effected. The amount normally transferred would be the fund after payment of any retirement lump sum.) Therefore, it is usually worthwhile for several quotations to be obtained at retirement from leading life assurance companies in the annuity market and then for the pension benefits to be taken with an appropriate company.

Small self-administered schemes

Small self-administered schemes have taken longer to gain popularity than was generally predicted. The maximum benefits that can be provided, the normal retirement ages permitted and the definition of final remuneration are identical to insured pension arrangements. The main difference is that the administration and the management of the investments are undertaken by the trustees, who can be nominated by the company, so that control of the assets of the scheme is not passed to an insurance company.

Although small self-administered schemes have been in existence for a number of years, it was not until February 1979 that proper guidance was given when Memorandum No. 58 was issued by the Inland Revenue Superannuation Funds Office (SFO).

Since then, many insurance companies have brought out their own hybrid schemes (part insured, part self-administered) and loanback schemes, mainly to compete with the pure self-administered schemes.

A 'small' scheme is one with less than 12 members, and in this interpretation the Inland Revenue will ignore relatively low-paid employees with derisory benefits whose inclusion brings the total membership to 12 or slightly more.

It is necessary for every small self-administered scheme to have a pensioneer trustee (an individual or body, widely involved with occupational pension schemes and having dealings with the SFO, who is prepared to give an undertaking to the SFO that he will not consent to any improper termination of a scheme of which he is a trustee). A pensioneer trustee is not a watchdog for the Inland Revenue in any other area.

In order to obtain Inland Revenue approval for a small self-administered scheme, its purpose must be pension provision and not tax avoidance. The SFO will permit a company to have only one small self-administered scheme.

Suitability
Small self-administered schemes, which are mainly appropriate where the beneficiaries under the scheme also own the shares in the company, are more likely to be suitable in the following circumstances:

(a) where the minimum annual contribution is say £10,000;
(b) where all the beneficiaries are not due to retire in the near future, i.e. until at least five years from the inception of the scheme;
(c) where the fund will be used to make specific investments such as a loan to the company or an investment in property when the company may be the lessee. However, in these cases, the transactions must be arranged at arm's length and on full commercial terms.

Advantages and disadvantages
The main advantages of small self-administered pension schemes compared to insured schemes are as follows:

(a) greater investment freedom, since:
   (i)   direct control of the investments of the pension scheme is with the trustees who often include the directors of the company;
   (ii) the choice of investment is very wide;
   (iii) it is usually possible to change investment managers at low cost;
(b) greater flexibility as to the amount and timing of contributions. Consequently, there is less risk to future cash flow;
(c) generally lower costs for larger contributions. However, charges which are based on a percentage of the size of the pension fund can be extremely high;
(d) if the fund purchases a property, either owned by the company or which can be leased to the company, the rent is paid to the fund with no liability to tax. When the property is sold, any capital gain is tax free;
(e) if assets are built up in a fund rather than in a company, it is often possible to transfer substantial sums from one generation to another, free of inheritance tax.

The principal disadvantage is that there is often more administration. As a result, additional costs may be incurred. Also, responsibility must be assumed for investment. It should be remembered that the size of the pension to be received will mainly depend on the success or otherwise of the scheme's investments.

Possible future changes
A discussion document was issued by the Inland Revenue in September 1987 which proposed changes to the conditions set out in Memorandum No. 58. The main proposals were as follows:

(a) all loans to the company must be properly secured and, if made during the first two years of a scheme, should not exceed 25% of the scheme's assets. For this purpose, no account is taken of the value of any payments transferred from a previous pension scheme (including any pension policies which have been assigned to the scheme).
(b) regulations will be issued to provide that no investment in residential property will be approved unless it is occupied by an 'arm's length' employee (such as a caretaker) who is required to live close to the company's premises.
(c) approval will not be given to investments in works of art, valuable chattels or similar investments.
(d) if a scheme currently holds assets that will be prohibited by the proposed changes, those assets may still be retained (provided that they were consistent with existing practice). Once such assets are disposed of, they should not be replaced by assets of a similar nature.

(e) certain scheme investments will require automatic notification to the SFO together with an undertaking that the investment does not infringe current requirements.
(f) the pensioneer trustee must notify the SFO of any transaction which, in his opinion, is likely to infringe the requirements for approval. Failure to do so is likely to lead to withdrawal of 'pensioneer trustee' status.

The conditions necessary in order to be recognised by the SFO as a pensioneer trustee are being relaxed. Any reputable professional person with pensions experience will be regarded as competent to act as a pensioneer trustee.

7. Personal pensions

Introduction

Personal pensions (PPs) were introduced in the Finance (No. 2) Act 1987 and came into effect on 1st July 1988, replacing the Section 226 self-employed retirement annuity. They can be effected by either self-employed persons (including partners) or persons not in an occupational pension scheme. An employee, covered for death-in-service benefits only under an occupational scheme, is allowed to arrange a PP. PPs can be provided by life assurance companies (including friendly societies), building societies, banks and unit trust management groups.

Unlike pension arrangements made through a company where the limits are determined by final salary and length of service, the benefits under PPs are restricted by the maximum contributions which it is permissible to pay. These contributions are based on a percentage of net relevant earnings and the maximum varies according to the age of the person concerned at the beginning of the tax year to which the relevant assessment relates. Net relevant earnings may be broadly defined as any income which is chargeable to tax and to which no approved occupational scheme relates, or earnings from a business etc. less certain deductions such as expenses, trading losses, capital allowances, etc. Personal charges such as mortgage interest are not deducted.

Main benefits

The following are the main benefits available under PPs.

(a) Retirement pension. This could normally commence at a minimum age of 50 with the maximum age at which the pension must be taken being 75. However, for certain professions and occupations, the Inland Revenue have agreed earlier retirement ages (see Appendix 2).

As an alternative to a full pension, a lump sum on retirement may be taken together with a reduced pension. It is proposed in the 1989 Budget that the maximum cash sum allowed is 25% of the overall fund, including the value of any benefits for dependants, but excluding the value of the 'protected rights fund' (see 'Contracting out' on page 75). For contracts made on or after 17th March 1987 but before the date on which the Finance Act 1989 is enacted, there is an upper limit of £150,000 for each contract. The inability to take the total benefits in the form of a lump sum is one of the very few disadvantages of PPs compared to other forms of savings.

In practice, it is generally worthwhile to take the lump sum together with the reduced pension since the lump sum could then be used to purchase an annuity. If this was done, a higher net income would normally be obtained

than from the full pension, as part of the annuity is tax free (see example 10 in Chapter 6).
(b) Dependant's retirement pension (this must not exceed the amount of the individual's pension) payable to a spouse or other person financially dependent on the retired person.
(c) Annual increases in the individual's and dependant's retirement pensions.
(d) Lump sum death-in-service benefit with the maximum allowed being the value of the pension fund at the time of death.
(e) Supplementary death-in-service benefits to provide a cash lump sum or pension for any named individual. These benefits can be provided only by an insurance company or friendly society.

Contracting out

Employed persons can use a PP as the vehicle to contract out of the State Earnings Related Pension Scheme (SERPS). It is then described as an 'appropriate personal pension scheme'. Such a scheme can be divided into two parts. The first part is the compulsory minimum contribution which is equal to the national insurance contracting out rebate (see below) and is paid by the Department of Social Security (DSS) direct to the pension provider chosen by the individual. The fund built up by these contributions is called the 'protected rights fund', the benefits from which may be taken only from state pension age or later. The second part is an additional contribution which may be made by either an employer and/or the employee (see 'Contributions' below).

The national insurance rebate at the present time is 5.8% of 'band earnings', i.e. earnings between the lower and upper earnings limits (between £43 and £325 per week in 1989/90) for the five-year period which ceases on 5th April 1993. A 2% incentive payable by the DSS applies to PPs effected in the same period. This is also based on band earnings. However, not all employees qualify for the incentive; those who leave a contracted out occupational scheme voluntarily without leaving service on or after 6th April 1988, having been members for more than two years, are not eligible.

Contributions

Contribution limits based on age rather than date of birth were introduced with effect from 6th April 1987 and these limits applied to PPs when they were introduced on 1st July 1988. Under the changes in the 1989 Finance Bill, the allowable contributions from 6th April 1989 will be substantially increased as follows.

Age at 6th April	Maximum contributions (% of earnings)
35 or less	17.5
36-45	20
46-50	25
51-55	30
56-60	35
61-75	40

Since 6th April 1980, there has been no salary ceiling for the calculation of maximum pension contributions payable by the self-employed and those in non-pensionable employment, but the new limits for PPs apply only to earnings up to £60,000 for 1989/90. It is proposed that this figure will be increased each year in line with the RPI.

Where a contract is effected by an employee, it will also be possible for a contribution to be paid by his employer, although the overall limits shown above must not be exceeded. Minimum contributions and incentives paid by the DSS for an arrangement which is used to contract out of SERPS are not included when determining the maximum contributions payable.

The maximum contributions qualifying for tax relief in respect of the provision of death-in-service benefits are limited to 5% of net relevant earnings. The contributions paid would reduce the maximum contributions available to provide the benefits (a) to (d) under 'Main benefits'.

Taxation position

As with company pensions, the provision of PPs is regarded very favourably by the Inland Revenue with the taxation position being broadly as follows.

(a) Contributions up to the maximum permitted are effectively allowed against the highest income tax rates payable in the tax year in which the contribution is paid. For the self-employed, contributions are paid gross and the tax relief claimed from the Inland Revenue at the end of the tax year in which they are paid. For those in employment, contributions are paid net of basic rate tax. Any claim for higher rate tax relief can be made in the same manner as for the self-employed.
(b) By election, a contribution paid in one tax year may be treated for tax purposes as having been paid in the previous tax year. Where there are no relevant earnings in the previous tax year, an election may be made to go back to the last but one tax year.
(c) Where contributions paid in a fiscal year are less than the maximum contributions permitted, the difference (known as unused relief) may be carried forward for up to six years. Relief will be given in the year in which the excess contribution is paid, or deemed to have been paid, at the tax rates applicable for that year.
   Before unused relief can be utilised, the maximum contribution permitted must first be paid in respect of the current tax year against which it is to be set for tax relief. Thereafter, any excess contributions paid will be applied as unused relief, starting with the earliest years on a first in, first out basis.

(d) Investment income and capital gains accumulate within the pension fund free of all UK tax.
(e) The resulting pension is treated as earned income.
(f) The lump sum benefit on retirement is tax free.
(g) The lump sum death-in-service benefits are free of income tax. These benefits, apart from any payable in respect of the protected rights fund, are usually paid at the scheme administrators' discretion and are therefore free of inheritance tax liability. It is also possible to make all lump sum death-in-service benefits the subject of an individual trust and this will again remove any inheritance tax liability.

Options available

PPs are very flexible contracts, with the following options often being available.

(a) Regular contribution contracts can be increased, decreased, temporarily stopped and restarted, or entirely omitted. Contracts may also be set up on payment of a 'one-off' single contribution.
(b) Switching facilities are now available within the same pension plan whereby both the existing fund and/or future contributions can be switched from a with profits basis to a unit-linked basis and vice versa (under these plans, with profits funds are themselves on a unitised basis).
(c) Waiver of contributions under regular contribution contracts can be arranged by the payment of small additional contributions. These would qualify for tax relief in the same way as the normal pension contributions. Consequently, if the person concerned was unable to work due to a prolonged period of disability, the contributions falling due would be waived, thus enabling benefits to be maintained (without the waiver of contribution option, benefits could not be maintained due to the lack of net relevant earnings, even if the individual had the necessary money to pay the contributions). This option is particularly important when the tax free lump sum on retirement is to be used to repay a loan.
(d) In the event of death before retirement, the amount of the contributions paid can be returned, either with or without interest. Alternatively, the amount of the pension fund itself can be returned.
(e) An open market option is generally available whereby the pension fund can be built up with one pension provider but the actual pension taken with a different company if this offers higher annuity rates at retirement. However, financial penalties are imposed by some companies if this option is exercised.

   Although the open market option can be very important, it is the general level of interest rates prevailing at the time the pension is taken that is likely to have an even greater influence on the actual amount to be received.
(f) At retirement, it is usually possible for a person to elect for his pension benefits to be guaranteed for a period of up to ten years or taken on a joint life, second death basis. This can be particularly useful if he is not in the best of health at that time. If the individual has only a short life expectancy, it may be worthwhile for him to delay taking his benefits. In these circumstances, the amount payable on death before retirement will often exceed the guaranteed retirement benefits.

(g) An option is often available for the pension benefits to be taken in stages rather than the entire benefits commencing at the same time (however, unlike company arrangements, if a cash lump sum is taken, the corresponding pension must also commence at the same date). This phased retirement is normally arranged by the pension plan being divided into multiple policies which can then be dealt with independently.

(h) Instead of taking level pension benefits, it is possible to arrange for them to increase in accordance with one of the following methods:
    (i)   by a fixed percentage annually;
    (ii) on a with profits basis (a guaranteed annual increase plus bonus);
    (iii) in line with the RPI;
    (iv) in line with the value of the underlying fund in the case of a unit-linked policy (under this method, the amount of the pension can also decrease).

    Where an increasing pension is taken, it will generally commence at a significantly lower amount than the corresponding level pension, and consequently it will usually take several years before the amount of the level pension is reached. Therefore, unless the person concerned believes he has an above average life expectancy or expects the increasing pension to rise rapidly, a level pension is normally more attractive.

(i) Term assurance can be taken out with tax relief effectively allowed at the individual's highest rates of income tax payable. The benefits can be written under trust to pass free of inheritance tax to any dependant.

    If net relevant earnings should cease, an option may be available to convert the policy into a standard term assurance policy with no medical evidence required. However, the contributions payable under the new policy would normally relate to the age of the person at the date of conversion.

(j) Loan facilities are often available prior to the proposed retirement date (the main advantages of loan facilities are discussed later in this chapter).

(k) The benefits under a PP may be transferred to most other types of pension arrangement but special conditions apply to the benefits, if any, in the protected rights fund. Transfer payments from any pension arrangement may be made to a PP, although in certain cases it may be necessary for additional restrictions to be imposed and guarantees may be lost.

With profits policies

The main types of insured schemes available for PPs are similar to those for company pension arrangements for directors and executives and have already been considered in Chapter 6.

The following are the principal types of with profits policies together with their characteristics.

(a) Funding for cash. Under this type of contract, a cash fund is built up by the addition of reversionary bonuses to the guaranteed basic sum. A terminal bonus, representing mainly the investment surplus earned over the lifetime of the policy, will also often be added to the pension fund when the policy proceeds are taken. At retirement, if beneficial, the open market option can be applied to the amount in the pension fund.

(b) Deferred annuities with guaranteed cash conversion rates. Unlike the funding for cash contract, this type of arrangement provides a guaranteed basic pension to which pension additions are made in the form of reversionary bonuses and a terminal bonus, if applicable. At retirement, guaranteed conversion factors from pension to cash are applied based on the age and sex of the person concerned. The open market option can then be applied to the converted cash sum. The level of benefits under this contract generally tends to be less volatile than in the case of the funding for cash contract.

(c) True deferred annuities. This type of arrangement operates in a similar way to (b) above except that there are no guaranteed conversion rates with the pension being unaffected by the rates of interest at the time of retirement. The pensions receivable under this contract are likely to be more predictable than for the more common with profits contracts shown under (a) and (b) above.

Unit-linked policies

The main considerations relating to unit-linked policies are as follows.

(a) The amount of the pension benefits receivable under a unit-linked policy (and also largely under a with profits policy) will mainly depend on the cash fund at retirement, which has had regard to:
   (i) the amounts and dates of the contributions paid;
   (ii) the performance of the investment fund;
   (iii) the charges levied by the life office;
   and the translation of this fund into pension, which depends on:
   (i) the sex of the individual and the age at retirement;
   (ii) the level of annuity rates at the time the pension commences;
   (iii) the form in which the benefits are taken — cash/pension and such factors as guaranteed period, escalation rate, dependant's pension, etc.

(b) Although unit-linked policies are normally of a higher risk/higher reward nature than with profits policies, this need not necessarily be the case. For example, by switching into a deposit fund whereby the pension fund is credited with a rate of interest, the value of the fund cannot fall but must increase with interest additions.

(c) Investment market conditions are reflected more immediately in the value of unit-linked policies, whereas there is an averaging effect in the case of with profits policies.

(d) It is normally possible to switch at low cost both the amount already accumulated and future contributions between the available underlying investment funds.

(e) Equity linked funds are often suitable when it is possible to have flexibility in choosing a retirement date in order for it to coincide with a time when stock market values are considered high. However, if this flexibility is not available, consideration should be given to switching into a deposit fund shortly before retirement at a time when stock market values are considered high.

(f) Charges on unit-linked policies can be incurred in the following ways:
   (i) policy fees;

(ii) bid/offer spread, or other initial charge;
(iii) unit allocations;
(iv) capital levy, usually on units allocated during the first one or two years;
(v) periodic fund management charge;
(vi) early retirement penalties which represent the outstanding balance of the capital levy.

General principles

Before any firm recommendations can be made, it is necessary to consider the exact circumstances of the person concerned. These would include:

(a) the age of the person;
(b) the number of years until the pension is to be taken and whether the pension date is flexible;
(c) the degree of risk the person is prepared to take;
(d) the likelihood of the person remaining self-employed or not joining an occupational pension scheme;
(e) the extent to which earnings are likely to fluctuate;
(f) the state of health of the person.

Subject to the particular requirements and circumstances of the person concerned, the following general principles will normally apply.

(a) Since contributions paid cannot be carried forward for tax purposes, the ability to vary the amount of the payments can be extremely important.
(b) The more volatile funds available under unit-linked policies are usually more appropriate for younger persons, unless the retirement date is flexible.
(c) Non-profit policies are often more suitable for persons within, say, three years of retirement.
(d) In many cases, it is appropriate to spread the contribution payable over two or more types of policy, e.g. to pay an annual contribution based on the minimum anticipated earnings to a with profits policy and top up with single contributions to a unit-linked policy. It is also normally recommended that the total contributions to be paid over the period to retirement should be spread over several different life companies.
(e) Due to the higher charges made by some companies in respect of longer term annual contribution contracts, policies should often be written to age 50 as the retirement age. Late retirement rarely incurs a penalty.
It is generally advantageous to start the payment of contributions to a PP at the earliest possible age. By so doing, the amount of the pension to be received is usually considerably enhanced.
This is illustrated in the following examples.

Example 12

Two men aged 39 next birthday and 40 next birthday with a retirement age of 60 pay pension contributions of £1,000 pa for 21 and 20 years respectively.

	Man aged 39 next birthday paying 21 contributions £	Man aged 40 next birthday paying 20 contributions £
Illustration of benefits at age 60:		
Cash value of		
pension fund	86,300	75,800
Tax free lump sum	21,500	18,900
Annual pension	7,680	6,740
Increase in illustrated pension fund by payment of additional contribution	13.8%	

Example 13

Two men aged 39 next birthday and 40 next birthday with a retirement age of 60 each pay a single contribution of £1,000.

	Man aged 39 next birthday £	Man aged 40 next birthday £
Illustration of benefits at age 60:		
Cash value of		
pension fund	11,100	9,910
Tax free lump sum	2,790	2,470
Annual pension	994	882
Increase in illustrated pension fund by earlier payment of contribution	12.0%	

Notes:
(a)   The figures shown in examples 12 and 13 are based on the rules laid down by the Life Assurance and Unit Trust Regulatory Organisation (LAUTRO) and assume that contributions, after allowing for a deduction for expenses, will be invested to earn 13% pa. Immediate annuity rates are based on an interest rate of 10% pa.

(b)　In the event of death before retirement, the full value of the pension fund would be paid.
(c)　The pension is payable monthly in advance for a guaranteed period of five years.

Where other resources are available at retirement, it is often preferable to take the pension benefits as late as possible due to the favourable taxation treatment of the pension fund and improved annuity rates at older ages.

However, it may be that an individual could afford to pay a contribution only if the pension benefits were received immediately. Such an arrangement (known as an immediate vesting PP) can be advantageous, particularly for higher rate taxpayers, but is subject to the following requirements:

(a)　The individual should normally be aged between 50 (or within a few weeks thereof) and 75.
(b)　The contribution must be eligible for tax relief by reference to current net relevant earnings, or those of the previous tax year where an election is made, together with unused relief from earlier years, if appropriate.
(c)　The amount to be paid must not exceed taxable earned income, even if this was permitted.
(d)　Preferably, the individual should be in good health so that he is likely to live for a longer period than that for which the pension is guaranteed.

The following example illustrates an immediate vesting PP for a man paying tax at the higher rate.

Example 14

A man aged 49 years 11 months subject to tax at 40% on the top part of his income pays a single contribution of £10,000 and chooses to take the pension benefits at age 50.

	£	Net cost £
Gross contribution		10,000
Tax relief at 40%		4,000
		£6,000

Benefits provided

Tax-free lump sum payable at age 50		£2,425
Gross annual pension	825	
Less: tax payable at 40%	330	
		£495

Notes:
(a)　The pension is payable monthly in arrear for life, but in any event guaranteed for five years. Therefore, the man or his estate would receive in the first five years after retirement, based on present tax rates, a total amount after tax of £4,900 (lump sum of £2,425 plus annual pension of £495 payable for five years).
(b)　The net cost of the single contribution of £10,000 would be recovered in full within seven years four months (one month after payment, a lump sum of £2,425 is receivable, followed by a net monthly pension of £41.25 for seven years three months, assuming the man survives for that

period). If his top rate of tax payable should fall below 40% after retirement, the net cost of the single contribution would be recouped more quickly.
(c)   For individuals with a higher retirement age than 50 who carry out a similar exercise a month before retirement, both the tax free lump sum and annual pension would be greater. Therefore, the cost of the net contribution would be recovered even earlier.

As mentioned in the previous chapter, it is often worthwhile for a self-employed man to employ his wife in his business and pay her a salary. As a result, she could then be provided with pension benefits in the same way as an employed person under a company arrangement. Moreover, if her salary was not greater than either the amount of the wife's earned income allowance (£2,785 in 1989/90) or the amount at which social security contributions commence (currently £2,236 pa), no liability for income tax or social security contributions would arise. In addition, the resulting pension would be free of income tax up to the amount of the wife's earned income allowance.

As an alternative to the wife being an employee, it may be advantageous for her to be taken into partnership with mainly similar results to the above except that higher remuneration can often be justified.

With the abolition of life assurance premium relief for policies effected after 13th March 1984, the provision of term assurance under a personal pension contract has become even more advantageous compared to conventional life assurance contracts.

However, it should be remembered that the contributions payable to provide term assurance under a personal pension contract would have to be included within the overall contribution limits permitted. Therefore, if a person wishes to pay the maximum possible contributions for pension benefits, it is generally expedient for any term assurance to be obtained through a life assurance contract.

Main advantages of loan facilities

There are now many different types of loan facility in association with PPs available on the market, all with varying terms and requirements. (Pension mortgages are discussed in Chapter 11.) However, it should be remembered that although the loan facility can be important, in the majority of cases the provision of the maximum pension at retirement is of even greater importance.

By careful selection of the appropriate loan facility, a number of advantages can be obtained compared with alternative sources of capital.

(a)   There need not be any restrictions regarding the purpose of the loan and borrowing can be arranged as and when required. It is not always necessary for evidence of financial status to be provided and there need be no limits on borrowing directly related to income. Liquid funds may be made available regardless of the economic situation.
(b)   Interest may be rolled-up and both the capital and interest repaid on retirement. However, in order to obtain tax relief on interest relating to a qualifying loan, the interest must normally be paid. Tax relief would then be allowed in the year of payment.
(c)   For qualified persons in professional practice, it is possible to obtain loans on an unsecured basis.

(d) Larger loans may be obtained, usually by means of a multiple of the annual contribution or a percentage of either the projected or accumulated pension fund.

Regular or single contribution policies?

Where a person is eligible to pay PP contributions, it will be necessary for him to decide whether regular contribution or single contribution policies should be effected. The main advantages of regular contribution policies are as follows.

(a) Higher minimum guaranteed pensions are usually provided.
(b) Due to the ongoing nature of the contract, there may be a greater personal commitment to maintain the regular payment of contributions, thereby providing larger pension benefits.
(c) The need to shop around each year for a particular policy is avoided with the consequent saving in time.
(d) The accumulation of a large number of policies is avoided.
(e) The following facilities are available under regular contribution policies (but not generally under single contribution policies):
   (i)   waiver of contribution option;
   (ii)   larger loans can be arranged by way of a multiple of the annual contribution;
   (iii) pension mortgages.
(f) Existing regular contribution policies are less likely to be affected by any adverse future legislation unless this is made retrospective.

The principal advantages of single contribution policies are as follows.

(a) Greater flexibility is provided. This is particularly important in the following cases.
   (i)   Since contributions cannot be carried forward for tax purposes, the risk of overpayment is reduced.
   (ii)   Single contribution policies are very suitable for mopping up unused relief from earlier years.
   (iii) If a person suffers a reduction in his earnings or ceases to be eligible to pay contributions, he can reduce or stop the payment of contributions without penalties being incurred. This is often not the case with a regular contribution policy if it is varied or made paid up within the first three to five years of the contract.
   (iv)   Similarly, if adverse future legislation should be introduced, contributions can again cease without penalty.
(b) A series of single contribution policies effected with one insurance company will usually produce superior results to a regular contribution policy arranged with the same company. This is mainly due to the higher initial charges of the latter contract, principally caused by the payment of larger introductory commissions and the longer investment term.
(c) The individual has the ability to assess the market each year in order to arrange the policy of his choice at that time.

Before a decision is reached whether regular contribution policies are more suitable than single contribution policies, or vice versa, all the circumstances should be considered. However, in many cases it will be appropriate for a regular contribution policy to be effected based on the minimum amount of net relevant earnings which is likely to be maintained and topped up each year with single contribution policies for the balance of the contributions permitted.

Friendly societies

Friendly societies have been in existence since the Middle Ages although it was only in the last century that they started to thrive as mutual insurance societies. The advent of the National Health Service removed the need for some of the benefits which friendly societies had previously provided. Registration is with the Registrar of Friendly Societies in accordance with the Friendly Societies Act 1974. Several societies provide savings plans (see Chapter 8).

Small self-administered pension schemes can be attractive to company directors especially where flexibility and control of the investments are important. The problem for partners and the self-employed is that such schemes are not available to them. However, friendly societies can issue PPs (they also used to be able to issue Section 226 retirement annuity contracts) and tax exempt status still applies if benefits are provided for members who are employees of the same employer. Partners in the same firm are classed as being in this category so that if there is a group of at least seven partners, a friendly society can be set up.

Each partner can contribute any amount up to the usual maxima and there is no commitment for all contributions to be paid to the society. Contributions can be paid into a pooled fund or each partner can have his own separately managed fund. If the partnership wishes to buy a property, some or all of the partners can pool their assets to form a property fund with the participating partners sharing the assets in the fund. There could, of course, be more than one property fund.

When a partner wishes to take his retirement benefits, his investments would be realised with the normal options being available to him (see page 74).

Neither the friendly society nor the accompanying legislation was designed for the provision of pensions for partners. However, there are now in excess of one hundred partnership friendly societies operating successfully, providing what are in effect self-administered pension schemes for partners.

Personal pensions or company pension arrangements?

If a company director or executive is in non-pensionable employment, it may be that he has the option to effect his own PP or alternatively to be provided with pension benefits through his company. There are advantages to both options.

Advantages of personal pensions
(a) PPs are more simple to set up. There is less documentation and no delay in obtaining Inland Revenue approval.
(b) Greater flexibility is provided, e.g. the amount of the contributions paid can be varied more easily. In addition, it is unnecessary for contributions to be paid before the end of the current tax year due to the relating back and also possibly the unused relief provisions.

(c) If an individual changes his employment near retirement, PPs will often allow higher benefits. Unlike an arrangement made through a company where a minimum of 20 years' service by retirement is necessary in order to obtain maximum pension benefits, the benefits received under a PP are not affected by length of service.
(d) Loans to an individual can often be more conveniently arranged. It is also usually possible for larger loans to be obtained based on a multiple of the annual contribution or a percentage of the projected or accurulated pension fund.

Advantages of company arrangements
(a) It is normally possible for greater pension benefits to be obtained with the actual amounts receivable based on final remuneration.
(b) The whole or a substantial part of the amount in the pension fund can in some cases be taken in the form of a tax free cash sum.

Where an option is available between the two types of arrangement, all the circumstances need to be considered before a decision can be reached. However, in general, if large or maximum benefits are required, a company arrangement is likely to be more appropriate.

Consideration also needs to be given as to whether it is worthwhile for an employee to opt out of a company pension scheme on a final salary basis and effect a PP in lieu. The main points are as follows.

Advantages of PPs for employees
(a) There is greater personal control and freedom of choice.
(b) Where an appropriate PP scheme is effected, normal national insurance contributions will apply. However, the rebate payable by the DSS will qualify for basic rate tax relief.
(c) It is easier for employees to take their pensions with them if they change jobs.
(d) The 2% incentive will be available until 5th April 1993.

Disadvantages of PPs for employees
(a) There may be no contributions from the employer.
(b) Any life assurance provided by the employer may cease.
(c) The final benefits are dependent on investment returns and are not related to final salary (this can also be an advantage).
(d) The contribution from the DSS is not usually expected to be paid until up to six months after the end of the tax year.
(e) Economies of scale are not available as in a group pension scheme.

As a general rule, subject to the particular circumstances, PPs will normally be more suitable for younger employees (say under 40 for men and under 35 for women), while older persons will benefit by remaining in a final salary pension scheme. However, much will depend on:

(a) whether the person concerned is likely to change jobs, and if so, the period remaining to retirement after the change;
(b) future salary increases;
(c) future investment returns;
(d) the level of employee contributions to the pension scheme;
(e) the level of pension scheme benefits provided.

Section 226 contracts

Prior to 1st July 1988, pension arrangements for the self-employed and those in non-pensionable employment were made under Section 226 of the Income & Corporation Taxes Act 1970 (which was consolidated as Section 620 of the Income & Corporation Taxes Act 1988). Contracts in force before that date remain governed by the Section 226 legislation and most allow for contributions to continue even where only single contribution contracts have been arranged.

Most of the PP details in this chapter apply equally to Section 226 contracts with the following exceptions.

(a) The £60,000 earnings limit does not apply to Section 226 contracts but the contribution limits have not been increased. The limits applying to Section 226 contracts are as follows:

Age at 6th April	*Maximum contributions* (% of earnings)
Up to and including 50	17.5
51-55	20
56-60	22.5
61 or more	27.5

(b) The retirement pension cannot normally commence before age 60. As an alternative to a full pension, a lump sum on retirement may be taken together with a reduced pension. The maximum lump sum allowed is three times the amount of the remaining pension (it is permissible for the calculation to be on the basis that the pension is payable yearly in arrear with no guaranteed period, thus increasing the lump sum available).

(c) For each contract made on or after 17th March 1987, the maximum lump sum allowed is £150,000 (at the present time, for a man aged 65, the maximum lump sum is approximately 32% of the amount in the pension fund with the proportion in other cases mainly depending on the level of interest rates and the age of the person at the time the benefits are taken).

(d) A transfer payment can be received only from another Section 226 contract.

(e) Complex calculations as to maximum contributions can arise where a person has a Section 226 contract and a PP, especially where net relevant earnings are in excess of £60,000.

(f) A Section 226 arrangement cannot be used to contract out of SERPS.

8. Life assurance policies as investments

The principal purpose of this chapter is to discuss the two main types of regular premium investment policies which can be particularly useful in personal financial planning. These are (a) endowment with profits contracts; and (b) maximum investment plans. Also discussed are friendly society plans and some of the more usual methods of funding a life policy from capital.

Endowment with profits policies

Under this type of policy, a basic sum assured is provided to which reversionary bonuses are added, normally on an annual basis, with terminal bonuses also being paid by most insurance companies on maturity of the policy (or on the death of the life assured, if earlier). A with profits endowment policy is therefore likely to offer an individual a low risk investment medium with capital appreciation and guarantees. However, the choice of the right life assurance company will be of the utmost importance in determining the amount of the benefits ultimately to be received (for policies maturing on 1st February 1989, contracts with the best results over 10 years and 25 years paid out 63% and 141% more respectively than the contracts with the worst results).

Before consideration can be given to the selection of a particular contract, certain basic information, such as the person's age and state of health and the date when the policy is required to mature, will need to be ascertained. It will then be possible to consider the particular company with which the contract should be taken out with careful attention being paid to:

(a) past performance;
(b) surrender values;
(c) underwriting;
(d) other considerations.

Past performance
The following matters should be borne in mind when considering past performance.

(a) It is normally worthwhile to select a life company which has produced consistently good results over a reasonable period. However, it should be remembered that good past results are no guarantee of good future results.
(b) The trend of past performance is very important, but it should be remembered that with a long term policy, the results could be largely based on earlier conditions which no longer apply. This could be due to changes in investment managers, policy, etc.

(c) The mutual offices have tended (with exceptions) to produce better results than the proprietary companies (all profits of a mutual office are retained for the benefit of policyholders, whereas in the case of proprietary companies, up to 10% of distributable profits are allocated to shareholders). However, if additional capital is required for future development, etc., proprietary companies are likely to have greater flexibility.

(d) Large companies have usually produced results superior to those of small companies.

(e) Terminal bonuses are much more volatile than reversionary bonuses (which are largely based on a company's investment income, and once declared, cannot be taken away) and mainly reflect a company's investment surplus at the time the policy benefits are paid. However, sometimes a proportion of terminal bonus is also paid when a policy is surrendered. (Despite the above, it should be remembered that bonuses reflect investment returns, with no absolute distinction between income and capital appreciation.)

Some companies have regularly paid large terminal bonuses, while other companies have not paid any, or only small terminal bonuses, or bonuses which have shown major fluctuations in accordance with market conditions at the time the policies have matured.

(f) A company may have declared a special reversionary bonus out of successful investment operations not expected to recur. Such a bonus, unlike the terminal bonus, cannot be withdrawn once declared and added to the policy. A special reversionary bonus is less of a burden to a life company than a reversionary bonus since there is no commitment to make the same ongoing payouts.

(g) The average results of a ten year endowment with profits policy maturing on 1st February 1989 for a male aged 30 next birthday at entry, paying £30 per month, would have achieved a net return of 12.3% pa compound ignoring the benefit of tax relief on the premiums (the best result over the same period would have produced a net return of 17.2% pa). This compares very favourably with the underlying rate of inflation (7.5% as measured by the increase in the RPI for the year to 1st February 1989), the average annual inflation rate over the previous ten years up to 1st February 1989 (7.9%), and also with other types of investment offering the same degree of security. In addition, life assurance cover is provided by the policy.

Surrender values
Although a life assurance policy would not normally be taken out as a short term savings contract, unforeseen circumstances can occur which require the policy to be surrendered before its maturity date. It is for this reason that surrender values are important and in order to provide some guide to the treatment by life companies of policies surrendered prematurely, the actual surrender values offered over different periods should be considered.

It should also be borne in mind that by surrendering a policy, a charge to higher rate tax could arise (the tax would be calculated in a similar way to the charge on investment bonds – see Chapter 3).

Due to the relatively low values normally offered on surrender, especially in the early years, a policy should usually be maintained if possible. This applies particularly to a policy effected before 14th March 1984, as any policy subsequently arranged to replace the policy surrendered will not attract life assurance premium relief. Accordingly, where it is necessary to raise capital, policy loans may be appropriate. Most companies will lend up to 90% of the surrender value, with interest rates normally in line with market rates.

Another possible alternative to surrendering a policy is to make it paid-up with the benefits being reduced. Consequently, no further premiums would be payable. However, if this course of action was taken, a charge to higher rate tax may arise when the paid-up benefits are subsequently received.

Where, however, a decision has been taken that a policy should be surrendered, it is useful to bear in mind that there are at least three organisations which specialise in arranging the sale of second-hand life policies. In these cases, the price fetched will often exceed the surrender value offered by the life company, with the taxation position being the same as if the policy was actually surrendered.

Underwriting
The degree or level of underwriting required by life assurance companies varies considerably. This can have an important bearing in the selection of a particular contract, as generally the more demanding companies have tended to produce the better results due to their more favourable mortality experience.

Therefore, before a particular policy is selected, details of the person's occupation, recreational pursuits and state of health, including smoking habits, should first be obtained and the information considered before proceeding further. If there are health problems, a joint medical examination can often be arranged for the use of more than one company.

In recent years, the medical information requested by life companies has generally been considerably reduced other than for larger proposals, mainly due to the expense and time involved. (The main exception is in respect of individuals whose health or lifestyle might bring them under suspicion of being possible victims or carriers of AIDS. In these cases, blood tests or full medical examinations are usually required.) An example of this is that many companies allow an endowment policy to be arranged within defined limits for the purpose of repaying a mortgage and seek only the minimum medical evidence (for a short period, a number of companies allowed policies to be effected without any underwriting whatsoever, but due to adverse experience, this practice was discontinued).

Other considerations
In choosing a particular company, the following points are important.

(a) The financial strength of the life company. It should be remembered that bonuses will be paid from the surplus of a life company and this will largely depend on the investment performance, together with the amount of the company's expenses.
(b) The service provided by the life company.
(c) In order to maintain bonuses at present levels in respect of a ten year endowment with profits policy, returns of approximately 17% are generally required. Consequently, if a long term fall in interest rates was to occur, it can be expected that many life companies would reduce their reversionary bonuses, although this may be offset by increases in terminal bonuses.

Low cost endowment policies
Low cost endowment policies are a variation of the with profits endowment policy and are usually a combination of a normal with profits endowment and a

decreasing term assurance (see Chapter 11). (These policies are normally designed as endowment assurances which contain a guaranteed minimum death benefit at a level higher than that used for bonus purposes.)

Maximum investment plans

Maximum investment plans are unit-linked qualifying life assurance policies and thus incorporate the usual tax advantages. Therefore, income accruing within the life fund is taxed at a maximum rate of 35% (25% from 1st January 1990) and the policy proceeds are normally completely free of any personal tax liability to income tax and capital gains tax, provided that premiums have been paid for a minimum period of ten years (or three-quarters of the term, if less, in the case of an endowment-type policy).

The main characteristic of these plans is that they are essentially investment vehicles and consequently will normally combine the minimum life cover permitted to retain qualifying status, with the maximum percentage of each premium being invested in units. There is normally a higher allocation invested in units for larger premiums.

Although policy charges are important, it is the actual investment performance of the underlying fund that will normally determine whether a particular policy will prove to be of good value.

Options available
As already mentioned, it is the performance of the underlying investments which will usually be the most important factor in the success or otherwise of a policy. Accordingly, the policyholder is normally given the option to switch both the existing fund and/or future premiums between the funds available. In order to provide the policyholder with maximum flexibility, virtually all the life companies writing maximum investment plans permit a plan to be divided into a number of identical cluster policies.

At the end of ten years, the following options are available to policyholders on plans from a number of life companies:

(a) to take the accumulated cash as a tax free lump sum;
(b) to stop paying premiums and leave the capital to accumulate with the life office;
(c) to continue paying the premiums in full for a further ten years (a higher investment allocation than that provided at the outset of the policy is generally given);
(d) to take a tax free income (this will normally be on the basis of the plan being written as a number of different policies which can then be encashed separately to provide a stream of proceeds without affecting the tax status of the remaining policies).

The option to take a tax free income after ten years can be particularly advantageous and is especially suitable in the following cases:

(a) to increase the net spendable income of a higher rate taxpayer;
(b) to supplement a pension;
(c) to provide for school fees.

However, in the cases of supplementing a pension and providing for school fees, it is normally expedient that the policy should be linked to a stable rather than to a volatile fund.

As far as the higher rate taxpayer is concerned, by taking a tax free income instead of a tax free lump sum and then reinvesting the capital, the tax that would have been payable on the resulting income is avoided, although the income arising within the life fund would still be taxed at life assurance company rates (currently, franked investment income is taxed at 25% and unfranked investment income at 35% with a rate of 25% being applicable to both types of income from 1st January 1990).

In the case of a husband and wife, a policy written on a joint life and last survivor basis should be considered. This would have two advantages over a policy written on a single life basis:

(a) the policy would continue until the second death — as a result, the tax free income facility could continue after the first death;
(b) a higher investment allocation into units would usually be obtained as any death benefit payment by the life company would normally be postponed.

It should be noted that, for many individuals who wish to invest on a regular basis in equities, a savings plan directly into a unit trust is likely to produce superior results to a unit-linked life policy (this is mainly due to the generally advantageous capital gains tax treatment of unit trusts). The main exception to the above could be in the case of higher rate taxpayers or where the annual capital gains tax exemption is fully utilised each year in respect of other investments. However, if the savings plan is within a PEP, this is likely to be even more advantageous since no tax at all is payable either on capital gains or on dividend income.

Friendly society plans

Due to their advantageous tax treatment, these plans should generally produce satisfactory results, although the maximum premiums which can be paid are very low. Their main characteristics are as follows.

(a) They are written as ten-year savings plans.
(b) Policyholders must be between the ages of 18 and 70.
(c) Investment income and capital gains accumulate within the friendly society investment fund free of all UK tax (this can be particularly advantageous where the main purpose of the fund is to produce a high income).
(d) For contracts arranged on or after 1st September 1987, the maximum annual premiums payable are £100 (£110 if premiums are payable more frequently than annually). However, some societies permit a lump sum to be paid to fund the premiums which at the current time generally varies between £800 and £1,000. (It is also possible to combine a friendly society plan with a conventional policy, which may provide a saving in expenses compared with two completely separate policies.)
(e) The charges made on friendly society plans are frequently very high when expressed as a percentage of the premiums paid.

(f) Although it is no longer necessary that a minimum of 50% of the underlying investments of the fund should be in narrower-range investments, most friendly societies have not changed their practice. This restriction can be an inhibiting factor as far as investment performance is concerned.

(g) At the end of ten years, the policyholder is usually provided with certain options (these are often similar to those under maximum investment plans) but this will depend on the particular plan.

(h) If the plan is surrendered within seven and a half years when written as an endowment policy, or within ten years when written as a whole life policy, the penalties can be severe (the maximum surrender value allowed is a return of the gross premiums).

(i) Supervision of a friendly society rests with the Registrar of Friendly Societies and with the Life Assurance and Unit Trust Regulatory Organisation (LAUTRO) if the society is engaged in long term investment business. Although friendly societies are not covered by the Policyholders' Protection Act 1975, they are covered under the Friendly Societies Protection Scheme which provides policyholders with similar protection. It would therefore seem advisable for an individual to choose a plan with a society which is covered by the above Scheme.

Funding a life policy from capital

In addition to paying premiums from income, a life policy can be funded from investment of a capital sum by one or more of the following methods (these packages are generally known in the market as capital conversion plans).

(a) Temporary annuities. These have the main advantages of having returns guaranteed, and of simplicity and convenience. The disadvantages are that capital is locked in, the investment return is often not competitive, and the annuity ceases on early death.

(b) A series of guaranteed growth bonds. Again, these have the advantages of having returns guaranteed, and of convenience, but the disadvantage of the investment return not being competitive in early years.

(c) Investment bonds. The principal advantage of this method is that the return could be very competitive, as underlying investments are not restricted to fixed interest investments. In addition, some insurance packages are administratively easy to operate. The main disadvantage is the risk of the need to provide funds from other resources to pay the premiums if the value of the investment bond fails to show sufficient growth.

(d) A series of low-coupon government securities or corporation stocks. On the plus side is that returns are guaranteed, and usually competitive. The main disadvantage is that the method is cumbersome and often inconvenient.

Note: A further method would be to realise capital from existing investments on a regular basis to meet the premiums as they fall due.

The actual method selected would depend upon all the circumstances of the case, including the return on the various investments at the particular time and the financial and tax position and age of the person concerned.

Capital conversion plans can also be used to generate an income for ten years with the subsequent return of capital at the end of that period. In this case, only part of the total amount arising each year from the capital sum is used to fund the life assurance premiums, with the balance being available as income.

9. Protection through life assurance

In the previous chapter, life assurance policies were considered as investments. However, their original purpose was to provide protection in the form of life cover and it is this application that is now discussed.

For most individuals, subject to their state of health, appropriate protection policies should be arranged in order to provide the required level of life cover before investment is considered. These policies can normally be effected very cheaply, with UK insurance companies offering amongst the most competitive rates in the world.

Although it is not always possible to distinguish completely between protection and investment policies (this can be seen later in this chapter when flexible unit-linked whole life policies are discussed), better results can often be achieved if the protection and investment needs are dealt with separately.

The amount of life cover required will vary depending on the individual circumstances. For example, a man approaching retirement would normally need less cover to protect his family than a younger person with dependent children, although it is more likely that he would wish to effect a policy for inheritance tax purposes. In any event, before a particular type of policy can be selected, the following matters should be considered:

(a) the exact needs of the individual;
(b) the ages of the individual and his dependants;
(c) the health of the individual, including his smoking habits;
(d) the resources to pay for the cover;
(e) the existing level of cover, if any, and to whom payable;
(f) the existing estate after inheritance tax which would be available to the dependants in the event of the life assured's death.

The two main broad categories of protection policies are term assurance policies and whole life policies, each of which can be further sub-divided into its own appropriate type. These policies can usually be effected in the following ways:

(a) on a single life basis;
(b) on a joint life basis payable on the first death;
(c) on a joint life and last survivor basis payable on the second death.

Where a policy is arranged in order to provide protection for the family of the life assured, it will often be advisable for it to be written in trust for the wife or children or, alternatively, on a life of another basis. The particular method will depend on the precise circumstances.

Term assurance policies

Although there are several classes of term assurance, they all have the same principal purpose of providing a tax free lump sum if death should occur within a preselected period. If the individual concerned should survive until the end of that period, the policy would automatically expire without value.

There are no surrender values or paid-up values on term assurance policies. If premiums should cease, the policy would automatically lapse with the insurance company having no further liability.

In each of the types of term assurance mentioned below, there would be no personal liability to income tax or capital gains tax on the benefit payable under the policy. However, unless the policy was written under a suitably worded trust (see Chapter 14), the proceeds could form part of the deceased's estate for inheritance tax purposes. Therefore, it is advisable, whenever appropriate, to write this type of policy under a suitable trust, in order to avoid the proceeds enhancing the deceased's estate, with the resultant adverse inheritance tax consequences.

The following are the most common types of term assurance policies which can be effected through life assurance contracts (death-in-service benefits under company pension arrangements and personal pensions have already been considered in Chapters 6 and 7 respectively):

(a) level term;
(b) decreasing term;
(c) mortgage protection;
(d) convertible term;
(e) convertible, renewable term;
(f) family income benefit.

Level term
This is generally a very straightforward type of term assurance enabling a tax free lump sum to be provided in the event of the death of the life assured within the preselected period. Apart from making provision for the death of the bread-winner, one of its more usual practical applications is in connection with a bank or other loan arranged on an interest-only basis, whereby the life of the borrower would be insured for the full amount of the loan.

Decreasing term
Under this assurance, the amount of the life cover reduces each year or lesser period by predetermined amounts throughout the duration of the policy. Like level term assurance, decreasing term assurance is often effected in conjunction with a loan but on the basis of the capital being repaid by equal instalments. The life cover provided would then decrease in line with the amount outstanding under the loan.

Mortgage protection
This is another form of decreasing term assurance with the amount of life cover being sufficient to repay the outstanding mortgage at death. Since the cover reduces more slowly in the early years than under a decreasing term assurance, the cost of a mortgage protection policy is normally greater.

Mortgage protection policies usually match the outstanding capital when a loan is being repaid by regular instalments of capital and interest. Any deviation from the original terms of the loan may upset the relationship between the capital outstanding and the cover provided.

Before a mortgage protection policy is arranged, it is worthwhile to investigate the options available, and particularly the position should mortgage interest rates rise substantially. If this was to happen and the policy lacked flexibility, the individual could find himself under-insured.

Where the mortgage repayments depend upon the joint incomes of the husband and wife, it is often advantageous for two single life policies to be effected rather than one policy written on a joint life payable on the first death basis, especially if the couple have dependent children. This would then provide two sets of benefit if both parents should die within the term, usually at little extra cost. In addition, in the event of the break-up of the marriage, matters would normally be considerably simplified.

Convertible term

This type of policy is similar to level term assurance except that the policyholder usually has the option to convert to another life policy throughout the term, subject to conversion taking place before a maximum age of normally 60 or 65, regardless of his state of health at the time the option is exercised. The premium rate applicable to the new policy would be based on the individual's age at the time of conversion.

Before a person decides on a specific policy, it is important for him to consider whether he is likely to exercise the conversion option and, if so, into what type of policy. Policyholders will normally be allowed to convert into a whole life or endowment contract while other options often include conversion into unit-linked or level term policies. Consequently, the competitiveness of the policy after conversion can be of greater significance than the initial cost of the term assurance itself.

Convertible term assurance can be a particularly useful contract for a younger person who requires immediate life cover but cannot afford the cost of a more permanent policy at the time the convertible term assurance is effected. By subsequently being allowed to switch into, say, a whole life or endowment contract, irrespective of his state of health at that time, a very valuable option is offered at a relatively low cost.

Convertible, renewable term

These are usually short term policies, typically five or six years, offering maximum flexibility but with minimum commitment. Two basic options are provided: to convert the policy into another contract; and to renew the policy at the end of the original term.

The conversion option under this contract operates in a way similar to the option provided under a normal convertible term assurance policy. The conversion option can be taken up at any time during the term of the contract with many insurance companies also allowing partial conversion.

The renewal option allows the policyholder to renew his policy at the end of each term without further medical evidence until normally age 60 or 65. The premium will usually increase at renewal in line with the rates for his age at the time.

This policy therefore enables an individual to obtain guaranteed life cover in most cases until retirement age but with only minimum commitment. In addition, he is provided with the opportunity to convert the policy into a different contract more appropriate to his needs.

In the 1970s, an increase option was often built in to these contracts in response to high rates of inflation. This option allowed the sum assured to be raised at regular intervals, e.g. by an amount of 10% pa or by an amount in line with the increase in the RPI, without recourse to medical evidence. This option has now generally been withdrawn by insurance companies, or modified to exclude the AIDS risk (see 'Underwriting' on page 108).

Due to the number of variations in the terms offered, it is important to compare like with like, as far as this is possible, when selecting a particular contract. The options which are likely to be exercised in the future should also be considered, bearing in mind that some contracts may offer very competitive rates at younger ages but uncompetitive rates at older ages. Therefore, if the original intention is to renew the policy throughout, the cheapest contract at the outset may not necessarily be the most suitable.

Family income benefit
This policy is another form of term assurance contract whereby a tax free income is provided from the date of death of the life assured to the expiry of the preselected term (an option is also often available to commute the future income payments into a cash lump sum). Therefore, a family income benefit contract is effectively a decreasing term assurance. (Although termed 'income', the payments are actually instalments of the sum assured under the policy, and therefore do not create any personal liability to income tax or capital gains tax.) Policies requiring higher premiums are also available which provide increasing payments to combat the effects of inflation.

Although a family income benefit policy may be effected on the joint lives of a husband and wife with the benefits payable on the first death, it is often preferable to take out two single life policies instead, especially where the couple have young children. If the husband should die before the children can become financially independent, there could be considerable financial hardship for the rest of the family. Consequently, it is usually advisable that a policy should be effected at the time of the birth of a child for the period of likely dependence.

The husband should also consider arranging a family income benefit policy on the life of his wife where she looks after the children or where he is dependent on her earnings. If the wife should die prematurely, the husband may need additional income, either to pay for home help and the supervision of the children while he is at work or to replace her lost earnings.

Due to the reducing nature of the life cover and to any death benefit only being paid in instalments (unless a cash lump sum is taken in commutation), this contract provides higher initial life cover for the same premium than other types of term assurance policy. Consequently, because of this and the important need it serves, a family income benefit policy is an essential requirement for many families.

The following example illustrates some of the more competitive rates for effecting the principal types of term assurance policies.

Example 15

Two men aged 30 next birthday and 40 next birthday respectively, both in good health and non-smokers, arrange £100,000 initial life cover over a period of 20 years through the main types of term assurance policies. Premiums are to be paid annually.

	Man aged 30 next birthday	Man aged 40 next birthday
	Annual premium £	Annual premium £
Level term	256.00	466.00
Decreasing term	144.34	220.00
Mortgage protection (see note (a))	186.24	331.74
Convertible term	279.36	511.00
Convertible, renewable term (see note (b))	172.96	277.21
Family income benefit (see note (c))	56.50	141.00

Notes:
(a) Although in practice a mortgage protection policy for £100,000 cover would be unusual, it has been included above for comparison purposes. The premium rates shown are based on rates of interest not exceeding 16% pa.
(b) The convertible, renewable term assurance is for a period of six years only. However, at the end of that time and each succeeding six year period up to age 65, there is an option to renew the policy without further medical evidence. The premiums for the new level of cover will be based on the age when the option is exercised.
(c) The family income benefit assurance provides a tax free income of £1,250 per quarter from the date of death to the end of the 20-year period.

Whole life policies

Unlike term assurance policies where the sum assured only becomes payable if death should occur within a predetermined period, the death benefit under a whole life policy will become payable whenever death occurs. In addition, a whole life policy acquires both a surrender value and a paid-up value, except generally in the first two years of the contract. Due to the certainty of eventual death, a whole life policy is usually considerably more expensive to arrange than a term assurance policy.

The following are the more usual types of whole life policies:

(a) whole life non-profit;
(b) whole life with profits;
(c) low cost whole life;
(d) flexible unit-linked whole life.

Whole life non-profit
Under this policy, a fixed amount becomes due on the death of the life assured. Although this may appear to be sufficient to meet requirements at the time the policy is effected, allowance should also be made as far as possible for the effects of inflation.

Mainly due to the relative costs involved, a term assurance contract is often preferable to a whole life non-profit contract with the principal exception being where the latter is effected for a specific purpose such as providing for inheritance tax.

Whole life with profits
This type of policy provides a basic sum assured payable on death (similar to a non-profit policy). However, reversionary bonuses are also declared and added to the sum assured, normally on an annual basis. In addition, terminal bonuses are paid by most insurance companies at the time of the death claim and sometimes on surrender.

Low cost whole life
This policy is usually a combination of a whole life with profits policy and a decreasing term assurance policy. The principle behind a low cost whole life policy is that the life cover provided by the term assurance will decrease by the same amounts as reversionary bonuses are added to the whole life policy until the cover provided by the term assurance ceases (in calculating the life cover, reversionary bonus rates are generally taken to be at the same level throughout the duration of the policy. Terminal bonuses are disregarded for this purpose). Thereafter, the amount of cover under the low cost whole life policy will increase with the addition of further reversionary bonuses plus any terminal bonus which is added when a claim arises. (A low cost whole life policy can also be designed as a whole life with profits policy containing a guaranteed death benefit at a level higher than that used for bonus purposes.)

The main advantage of a low cost policy compared to a full with profits policy is that it is much cheaper to effect due to part of the initial cover being provided by term assurance. However, against this, the longer the life assured should survive, the greater will be the difference between the two policies in the amount of the death benefits.

The low cost whole life policy is also usually significantly cheaper to arrange than a whole life non-profit policy, except for older individuals. In addition, it has the further advantage that a higher level of cover may eventually be provided, although this would depend on the number of years the life assured should survive, the current level of bonuses being maintained and the period of the decreasing term assurance.

Flexible unit-linked whole life
This is a more modern type of whole life policy (often known as a flexible, universal life policy) which has been given considerable publicity by a number of insurance companies. It combines a mix of insurance and investment and is designed to cover an individual's life assurance needs throughout his life. A wide degree of flexibility is offered in the amount of cover which can be chosen and in the extent to which the emphasis can be varied between cover and investment during the term of the policy.

The general operation of a flexible unit-linked whole life policy is broadly as follows.

(a) Premiums are paid to an insurance company from which charges are deducted for setting up and administrative costs, etc. The balance of each premium is then invested in units in one or more of the insurance company's unit-linked funds, with the normal switching facility usually being available (this type of policy can also be effected on a single premium basis).

(b)   The appropriate number of units is encashed each month to pay for the life cover, with the actual number depending on the value of the units allocated to the policy at the time, the amount of cover chosen and the age and sex of the policyholder. The units remaining provide the investment element of the policy.

(c)   The insurance company sets the maximum amount of cover that can be chosen by assuming a growth rate for the value of the units, usually 7% or 7½% pa. Some insurance companies base this maximum on the level of cover that could be maintained throughout the policyholder's life. Other companies offer a considerably higher maximum on the basis that it is maintained only for the first ten years of the policy, after which time the cover or premium may need to be adjusted.

(d)   The premiums and life cover are reviewed at the end of the first ten years and at regular intervals thereafter (generally every five years, but usually more often for elderly policyholders). Between reviews, the insurance company agrees not to seek to change the amount of the premiums or life cover. However, the policyholder is still normally provided with the option to increase his cover each year without waiting for the next review date, although in some cases evidence of health may be required.

At each review, the insurance company would look at both the value of the remaining units and the current premium level in order to decide whether they were sufficient to maintain the chosen level of cover until the next review. If they were not sufficient, either the premiums would have to be increased or the level of cover reduced.

If the value of the units had increased at a growth rate higher than that assumed, many insurance companies would allow this to be used in order to obtain a greater level of cover, although medical evidence would generally be required. However, only a small minority of companies would permit a reduction in the amount of the premiums.

(e)   On the death of the life assured, the policy would pay out the greater of the chosen amount of life cover or the value of the units.

(f)   If the payment of premiums should continue for a minimum period of ten years, similar options to those applicable with maximum investment plans will be available (these options have already been considered in Chapter 8). Alternatively, life cover can continue to be provided, subject to the value of the units being sufficient to meet the costs involved.

(g)   Where premiums are paid for less than ten years, any value attaching to the policy could be used to take a lump sum, although a charge to higher rate tax may arise. As further options, the units could be left to accumulate or be utilised to pay for continued life cover, assuming they had sufficient value.

The main advantages of flexible unit-linked whole life policies are therefore as follows.

(a)   The convenience of having only one policy to serve both the protection and investment needs of an individual together with the flexibility to make changes without excessive administration.

(b) Competitive premium rates. By regularly reviewing the progress of a policy, together with the ability to make adjustments when considered appropriate, an insurance company need not use the same conservative actuarial basis as when a guaranteed sum assured is provided over a very long period. As a result, it is possible for a less cautious approach to be adopted, with the consequent beneficial effect on premiums.

(c) The choice of funds and a switching facility are generally provided.

If mortality trends improve, this can be taken into account when making reviews (however, if the trends are worse than anticipated, this is likely to be a disadvantage).

Despite the above advantages, improved investment results may often be obtained if separate insurance policies are effected to provide the required life cover, with the balance of the funds available being used exclusively for investment. Accordingly, suitable term assurance policies plus direct investment in unit trusts or in the stock market would be preferable in many cases.

Where an individual does decide to effect a flexible unit-linked whole life policy, its exact purpose should clearly be borne in mind before a specific contract is chosen, due to the varying terms and different options available. In addition, if the main purpose of the policy is to provide life cover, the investment link should be with a relatively stable fund, e.g. a managed fund, rather than with a volatile fund.

The following example illustrates some of the more competitive rates for effecting the principal types of whole life policies.

Example 16

Two men aged 30 next birthday and 40 next birthday respectively, both in good health and non-smokers, arrange £100,000 initial life cover through the main types of whole life policies. Premiums are to be paid annually throughout life.

	Man aged 30 next birthday *Annual premium* £	*Man aged 40 next birthday* *Annual premium* £
Whole life non-profit	691.96	1,082.38
Whole life with profits	1,746.36	2,456.40
Low cost whole life	393.56	755.45
Flexible unit-linked whole life	536.38	907.70

Notes:
(a) Premiums payable in respect of the low cost whole life policy will reduce as follows:
    for the man aged 30 next birthday — from year 47 to £195.80;
    for the man aged 40 next birthday — from year 38 to £415.33.
These reductions are due to the expiry of the term assurance element of the policy.

(b) Premiums for the flexible unit-linked whole life policy have been set to remain unaltered throughout life on the basis that the price of the underlying units grows by 7½% pa.

Back to back arrangements

A further use of whole life policies is in connection with back to back arrangements which combine purchased life annuities with regular premium whole life policies written under trust for named beneficiaries. The arrangements are mainly designed for elderly higher rate taxpayers in reasonable health with their main purposes being (a) to increase the net spendable income of the policyholder; and (b) to increase the net estate available to the beneficiaries.

In order to avoid the associated operations provisions, it is necessary that:

(a) the life policy is issued on full medical evidence of the health of the life to be assured (this must follow the normal requirements and limits set by the particular company);
(b) the terms on which the life policy is issued should have no regard to the purchase of the annuity. (It is therefore usually advisable to arrange for the two contracts to be effected with different life assurance companies.)

Generally, for the payment of annual premiums not to be subject to inheritance tax, they must fall within the annual exemptions. For this purpose, in order to qualify for the normal expenditure out of income exemption, the following conditions must be satisfied:

(a) the gifts must be part of normal expenditure, i.e. they must be habitual (in the case of a life assurance policy, it is accepted that this is covered by the nature of the contract to pay regular premiums);
(b) the gifts must be made out of after tax income (the capital element of an annuity does not count as income for this purpose);
(c) after allowing for all the gifts forming part of normal expenditure, there must be sufficient income to maintain the usual standard of living.

If the normal expenditure exemption is not appropriate, the other annual exemptions could be utilised (see Chapter 10).

The following example illustrates the benefits resulting from a back to back arrangement.

Example 17

A woman aged 81 next birthday, in reasonable health and a non-smoker, pays income tax at 40% with her estate subject to an inheritance tax marginal rate on death of 40%. She purchases a level annuity without guarantee for £27,750 and effects a whole life non-profit policy written under trust for named beneficiaries paying an annual premium of £2,250.

Increase in net spendable income	£	£
Annual income from annuity:		
Capital element		3,619
Income element	2,188	
Less: Tax at 40%	875	
		1,313
		4,932
Less: Annual premiums on whole life policy		2,250
Surplus to be used as income		2,682
Less: Loss of income on £30,000 at, say, 12% from capital		
used for purchase of annuity and payment of first		
annual premium	3,600	
Less: Tax at 40%	1,440	
		2,160
Increase		£522
Increase in net estate to beneficiaries		
Guaranteed sum from whole life policy		27,635
Less: Amount used to purchase annuity and pay first		
annual premium	30,000	
Less: Inheritance tax at 40%	12,000	
		18,000
Increase		£9,635

Note:
In this example, the net spendable income from the capital invested has increased by approximately 24% and the net estate passing to beneficiaries by approximately 53%. The balance between increased income and net estate depends upon the proportions of the capital invested in the annuity and the first premium on the whole life assurance.

Other insurance contracts

Although not strictly life assurance policies, other insurance contracts can be arranged for protection purposes. The most usual of these contracts are as follows:

(a) permanent health insurance;
(b) personal accident and sickness insurance;
(c) hospital insurance;
(d) private medical insurance;
(e) dread disease insurance.

Permanent health insurance
The purpose of permanent health insurance is to provide an income for an individual during prolonged disability following sickness or accident.

Although only a relatively small number of permanent health insurance policies have been arranged compared to many types of life assurance policies, they nevertheless serve a very important need. According to available statistics, there is a greater likelihood of a man aged 25 being disabled for three months or more before reaching retirement age than there is of him dying within the same period.

The following are some of the more important characteristics of individual permanent health insurance policies

(a) The contract cannot be cancelled by the insurance company after it has been effected (hence the word 'permanent'). Neither can the company refuse to renew the contract if the health of the policyholder should deteriorate.
(b) There are different definitions of disability. Some insurance companies are very harsh in their interpretation, while others take a more lenient approach. It is therefore very important to investigate a company's attitude to this before effecting one of its policies.
(c) Some occupations are not normally acceptable to insurance companies, while others may attract special terms or restrictions.
(d) Benefits are not usually payable immediately from the time of disablement but after a deferred period (normally after a minimum of 4 weeks and a maximum of 52 weeks). The longer the deferment period, the lower will be the premiums. Policies are usually written to age 60 or 65. Benefits generally cease at the age selected even if disability continues.
(e) The maximum amount of benefit which can be received is usually limited to $\frac{2}{3}$rds of earnings or 75% of earnings less the single person's basic national insurance invalidity pension. Stricter limits are generally applied where the individual has a very high income.
(f) The level of insured benefits may be arranged at the outset, either to remain constant or to increase on an annual basis by a fixed percentage or in line with the RPI. Where benefits increase, usually the premiums will also rise each year. Benefits following a claim can likewise be arranged to increase annually, usually by a fixed percentage of either 5% or $7\frac{1}{2}$%.
(g) Benefits are not taxed until they have been received for one full tax year, but become taxable thereafter. Consequently, they can be received for a period which can extend almost to two years before they become taxable, with the precise period depending upon the point in the tax year when the benefits commence.

Personal accident and sickness insurance
The purpose of this contract is to enable a person to insure against accident or sickness, the benefits being in the form of either a lump sum or an income. The lump sum could become payable on death, loss of sight or a limb or on permanent total disability.

The following are some of the more relevant features of personal accident and sickness insurance policies.

(a) The contract is of an annual nature and subject to state of health each year. It can therefore be cancelled or special provisions made at the option of the insurance company at each renewal date.
(b) The amount of the premiums depends mainly on the level of benefits to be insured and the occupation and sex of the person concerned.
(c) In the case of the sickness insurance, benefits are normally payable after one week. However, there is usually an option for the benefits to be deferred for a longer period with the consequent reduction in premiums.

(d) The amount of the benefit is usually restricted to a percentage of earnings, often 75% thereof.
(e) Benefits are normally paid for up to a maximum of two years if the person is unable to work as the result of an accident or illness.
(f) The lump sum benefits are generally not taxable. The income benefits are treated similarly to those from permanent health insurance policies, i.e. they are not taxed until received for one full tax year.

Mainly due to the ability of the insurance company to cancel the policy each year, this contract is not generally of prime importance for many individuals.

Hospital insurance
The purpose of hospital insurance plans is to provide the policyholder with funds to mitigate the loss of his earnings while he is in hospital and also to cover incidental expenses, e.g. the cost of relatives' travel to and from the hospital. In addition, the plans usually provide further benefits such as a lump sum for a loss of a limb or eyesight.
    Some of the more important aspects of hospital insurance plans are as follows.

(a) The premiums on these policies are written on a renewable annual basis. Depending on the amount of the premiums, which are normally limited, the policyholder obtains a predetermined sum for each day or night that he stays in hospital.
(b) No medical evidence is required before a plan is effected. However, there may be problems when a claim is made due to the exclusion clauses contained in the policy.
(c) The policy conditions require careful consideration due to their varying terms, e.g. most of the companies will not pay out the benefits during the first two years of the policy if the claim relates to a recurrence of an illness which the policyholder had before the policy was effected.
(d) The taxation treatment of the benefits received is similar to personal accident and sickness insurance, i.e. the lump sum benefits are normally not taxed, with the income benefits not being taxed until received for one full tax year.

Unless an individual thinks that he is likely to suffer ill-health, these policies are not normally a priority. The premiums paid could usually be better applied elsewhere to provide the additional funds which might be required to meet the costs of a stay in hospital.

Private medical insurance
The purpose of being a subscriber to a private health insurance scheme is to enable medical treatment to be arranged privately, rather than through the National Health Service, for an individual and his family. This will usually provide the following advantages:

(a) there are effectively no waiting lists;
(b) the patient can choose the time for his treatment;
(c) the patient can select a hospital for his own convenience and also often choose a particular surgeon;
(d) miscellaneous benefits are provided such as a private room with better amenities and more flexible visiting hours;

(e) some health insurance schemes provide a daily cash benefit to pay for incidental expenses while in hospital, such as telephone calls.

Despite the benefit of being a subscriber to a private health insurance scheme, approximately 30% of the people who use private medicine in the UK still finance the costs out of their own funds without medical insurance. The view taken by many of these people is that it is less expensive to meet the costs of private medicine directly, as and when necessary, than it is to pay the subscription to an insurance scheme each year. Whether this proves to be the right decision will very much depend on the extent that private medical treatment is required by the individual and his family.

The Government has announced that it intends to introduce tax relief on premiums for eligible private medical insurance for individuals aged 60 and over, to take effect from 6th April 1990. The main features will be:

(a) basic rate income tax relief will be given by deduction at source (similar to the MIRAS scheme for mortgages);
(b) the basic rate relief will be available both to non-taxpayers and taxpayers;
(c) any higher rate tax relief due will be given to the payer of the premiums by adjustment to his PAYE tax code or through the end of year assessment;
(d) the person paying the premiums will be entitled to the relief available, whether or not he is the insured person.

In recent years, due to the mutual benefits provided, it has become increasingly common for private medical insurance to be arranged by a business for its staff and their families (it should be noted that this is regarded as a 'benefit in kind' and therefore a personal tax liability may be incurred by the employees on the notional premium paid by the employer for their membership).

Dread disease insurance
The purpose of this insurance is to provide a lump sum payment in the event of the insured person suffering a critical illness. The range of illnesses covered varies between insurance companies, but includes one or more of the following: heart attack, cancer, stroke, coronary bypass surgery, endstage kidney failure, major organ transplant, multiple sclerosis, paralysis and paraplegia.

Dread disease cover was introduced in 1986 and is currently offered by approximately 16 insurance companies. In every case the cover is provided as an addition to a life assurance policy. In the event of a claim under the dread disease insurance, the main policy will either cease or the sum assured be reduced by the amount of the payment to the insured person.

Underwriting

Underwriting in connection with investment policies has already been discussed in Chapter 8. As far as protection policies are concerned, underwriting will generally be of greater relevance due to the extra risks involved, arising from the higher level and longer periods of life cover normally required. Consequently, life assurance companies are likely to take more stringent measures in obtaining medical information.

A particular example of the above is with regard to smoking habits. Many insurance companies now provide two different levels of premium rates for their protection policies with the particular level depending on whether the individual is a smoker or non-smoker (the definition of this can vary widely). The discount offered to non-smokers can be as much as 33⅓% off the smoker rates.

Consideration of the risks of contracting AIDS and associated medical problems has had a much greater effect on protection policies than on investment contracts. Many insurance companies have ceased to write convertible or increasable contracts, or have made such options subject to fresh enquiry into the AIDS risk at the time of the options being exercised. Generally, premiums have increased substantially, particularly for the younger age groups.

New policies for permanent health insurance, personal accident and sickness, hospital insurance and private medical insurance generally exclude the AIDS risk (the possible exception to this is for group permanent health schemes, where greatly increased premium rates would usually be applied).

Taxation position

Life assurance premium relief was abolished for all life policies effected after 13th March 1984. The position with regard to policies arranged on or before 13th March 1984, which provide for the benefits to be increased or the term extended after that date, is as follows.

(a) Where a policyholder exercises his *option* to increase or extend his cover, e.g. in a convertible, renewable term assurance, he would lose the tax relief on the whole of the subsequent premiums.
(b) Where a policy has an in-built *automatic* increase for which the policyholder contracted at the outset, the premiums would still qualify for tax relief.
(c) Where the mix of insurance and investment within one policy can be altered *without* a change in the amount of the premiums, e.g. in a flexible unit-linked whole life policy, the policyholder would continue to obtain life assurance premium relief, even if he chooses to increase the life cover.

With effect from 6th April 1989, life assurance premium relief has been reduced from 15% to 12½%. Consequently, the net premium payable in respect of these policies is now 87½% of the gross premium.

Some specific uses of protection policies

The following are some specific uses of life assurance protection policies:

(a) funding for inheritance tax;
(b) partnership and share purchase assurance;
(c) keyman assurance.

Funding for inheritance tax
Life assurance protection policies written under trust for the benefit of nominated persons are often required in funding for inheritance tax. The

circumstances in which they may be used together with the appropriate type of policy are shown below:

(a) to meet the inheritance tax payable on death — a whole life policy;
(b) to meet the inheritance tax payable on the death of a surviving spouse — a whole life policy written on a joint life and last survivor basis;
(c) to meet the inheritance tax payable if death should occur within seven years of a potentially exempt transfer (PET) — seven year irregularly decreasing term assurance, where the sum assured remains level for the first three years and reduces each year thereafter by 20% of the starting amount. This may need to be varied if more than one PET has been made and the intervals are less than seven years;
(d) to meet the extra inheritance tax liability on a donor's death, resulting from adding back to his estate any PET, as reduced by taper relief (see Chapter 10), made in the seven years preceding his death – seven-year level term assurance;
(e) to meet any extra inheritance tax payable on death, which arises on a transfer that was chargeable during lifetime but the tax is recalculated as death occurs within seven years – a specially tailored decreasing term assurance.

Partnership and share purchase assurance
The purpose of partnership and private limited company share purchase life assurance arrangements is to assist in providing the funds required by the surviving partners to buy the share of a deceased partner or by the remaining shareholders to buy a deceased's shareholding.

Partnership assurance enables the necessary funds to be received by the surviving partners with the following advantages:

(a) it removes the need for the surviving partners to borrow, liquidate assets or use existing funds already earmarked for other purposes in order to provide the money to buy the deceased's share;
(b) the less attractive solutions are avoided, such as finding a new partner with capital or the widow becoming involved in the business;
(c) the persons entitled to the deceased's estate, usually the widow and dependants, will be able to benefit from the readily available funds.

Since partnerships and companies can vary considerably in their constitution and organisation, each case should be considered on an individual basis. The following information should be ascertained before a life policy is effected:

(a) the number of partners or directors, together with their ages, sex, state of health and smoking habits;
(b) the likelihood of future changes in the composition of the partnership or the board of directors;
(c) the current resources available;
(d) the value of the partnership shares or shareholdings;
(e) whether there are any relevant provisions in the articles of association, partnership agreement, etc.;
(f) whether there are any existing life assurance arrangements.

The main policies which can be suitably used in partnership or share purchase assurance to provide life cover for the appropriate period, normally up to the anticipated dates of retirement, are shown below:

(a) level term assurance;
(b) convertible term assurance;
(c) convertible, renewable term assurance;
(d) term assurance provided under personal pension plans;
(e) flexible unit-linked whole life policies.

Due to the abolition of life assurance premium relief, life policies effected by a partner or shareholder on his own life in trust for other partners or shareholders no longer have a tax advantage over policies written on the life of another basis (these policies were not eligible for tax relief even if effected before 14th March 1984). Consequently, it may be more appropriate to adopt the life of another basis so that the individuals paying the premiums can obtain direct benefit from them. This can considerably simplify matters both with regard to inheritance tax and also by ensuring that the cost of the arrangement is on an equitable basis. However, life of another arrangements can be very rigid. Therefore, it may be preferable to use the own life route using a flexible trust wording, especially where frequent changes are a possibility.

Keyman assurance
The purpose of keyman assurance is to cover the loss of profits to an employer arising out of the death of a key employee. This assurance could therefore be required where:

(a) the owner has only provided the capital but the keyman has the detailed knowledge of the business, etc.;
(b) the keyman has important personal and business connections;
(c) any other situation where the loss of the keyman's services will be critical to the business, and will result in a financial loss to the business or an extra burden, e.g. costs of recruiting a replacement, etc.

The premiums payable will be allowed as a business expense providing the following conditions are met.

(a) The sole relationship of the life assured to the company is that of employee to employer. (For this purpose, the employee should not be a significant shareholder.)
(b) The assurance is intended to meet the loss of profits resulting from the loss of the keyman's services. (The Inland Revenue will accept a level of cover normally up to a maximum of ten times the keyman's salary, but this will particularly depend on his status within the company and can be any amount actually justifiable in the given circumstances.)
(c) The life policy is an annual or short term assurance. This can normally be defined as not exceeding five years, although in exceptional circumstances terms of up to ten years or more may be acceptable.

If the premiums are allowed against corporation tax, the proceeds when received would be taxed as income in the hands of the company. This should be taken into account in determining the sum assured. In addition, it may be worthwhile to arrange for the sum assured to be paid in annual instalments over a period of, say, three to five years in order to mitigate the potential tax liability in the year of the keyman's death.

If the premiums had not been allowed, e.g. where a whole life policy had been arranged, the benefits will normally not be taxed in full, if at all. Consequently, the company should attempt in these circumstances to clear such an arrangement with the Inland Revenue, preferably *before* the keyman assurance is effected. Where such an agreement can be obtained, it will often be worthwhile for the premiums paid to be disallowed in order that any benefits may be subsequently received without being taxed in full.

Under the changes in the 1989 Finance Bill, qualifying policies, which were taken out by companies on or after 14th March 1989, will be treated in the same way as non-qualifying policies with regard to taxation of benefits. Consequently, in the case of a whole life policy, if the surrender value at the time of payment of any benefit is greater than the premiums paid, the gain would be liable to corporation tax.

In addition to the benefits payable on the death of a keyman, it is also possible to arrange for them to be paid if he should become disabled. This will then provide the company with the resources to seek a replacement for the keyman or for any other required purpose.

One particular consequence of arranging this type of assurance is that where benefits are received on the keyman's death, the value of the business may be inflated by the cash received. Therefore, where the keyman is a shareholder, the value of his shares may be increased, with the result that his estate may be subject to a larger inheritance tax liability.

10. Tax planning

Tax plays an extremely important part in financial planning for an individual since the main financial objective of most people is to increase their capital and/or income *after tax*. However, saving tax will generally be of secondary importance to personal, practical and investment considerations.

Many of the tax saving and planning aspects with regard to individuals are discussed in this book in the chapters to which they relate. The purpose of this chapter is to mention some of the other more important matters which have not been covered elsewhere. These can be shown under three main headings:

(a) income tax;
(b) capital gains tax;
(c) inheritance tax.

Income tax

The following matters should be considered in relation to income tax.

(a) All personal allowances and reliefs to which an individual is entitled should be claimed. Elections, where appropriate, should be made within the relevant time limits.
(b) From 1990/91 onwards, a husband and wife will be independently taxed for both income tax and capital gains tax. For income tax, each of them will have a separate personal allowance. There will also be a married couple's allowance which, if not used by the husband, can be transferred in whole or in part to the wife. Accordingly, planning is required in many cases to enable the wife to utilise her personal allowance, and preferably also her basic rate tax band (£20,700 in 1989/90).

Consideration should therefore be given to transferring income producing assets to the wife where she does not have sufficient income to absorb her personal allowance and basic rate tax band. This can be done free of capital gains tax (and also usually inheritance tax), but to be effective there must be an outright unconditional gift of the asset.

Investment by the wife in bank deposit and building society accounts will not be tax effective to absorb her personal allowance as the tax suffered is not repayable. Therefore, investments where tax is repayable such as gilts, National Savings Income Bonds or in a National Savings Investment Account or offshore deposit account, should be considered where appropriate.

It may also be possible to defer the taxation of investment income into 1990/91 or later, when the income may be taxed at a lower rate, by investing in a sterling offshore roll-up fund.

The ownership of a business which is likely to give rise to a loss needs to be carefully considered, as from 1990/91 losses of one spouse will not be available for relief against income of the other spouse.

It is important to decide who should be assessed on interest received on joint deposit accounts or obtain relief for interest paid on joint mortgages, and again this will have to be determined according to the tax levels of each spouse.

(c) In any situation involving separation or divorce, there is only a small amount of relief (£1,590 in 1989/90) for maintenance payments under arrangements set up after 14th March 1988. Consequently, the most tax effective way of providing for a former spouse is now usually by way of a capital settlement as the income from it will be taxed at a lower rate. However, this may not always be possible and, in any event, the payer does not obtain any tax relief.

(d) New deeds of covenant are no longer an effective means of transferring income to a person with unused allowances. Instead, it is necessary to make an outright gift of a capital sum to generate sufficient income, or create a settlement with a similar sum in favour of the individual concerned. This will not be effective in the case of a settlement by a parent in favour of a minor unmarried child, unless it is a 'bare trust' under which the child becomes absolutely entitled to the capital at 18 and the income is accumulated in the meantime. The child's personal allowance can then be used against the income.

Before it is decided to set up a trust, it should be remembered that there may be both capital gains tax and inheritance tax consequences. Therefore, the total position must be considered.

(e) With effect from 28th February 1986, the accrued income scheme was introduced to combat 'bondwashing', whereby income accruing on certain fixed interest securities was converted into capital form so that it was chargeable as a capital gain rather than as income. Broadly, the intention of the accrued income scheme is to treat interest on securities, e.g. gilts, local authority bonds, and non-convertible company debentures and unsecured loan stocks, as accruing on a day-to-day basis between interest payment dates and separated from the capital value of the investment. Interest accrued at the date of sale will be taxable as income, and in the case of a purchase, accrued income bought will be offset for tax purposes against interest subsequently received. The accrued income scheme applies to all UK residents except for those holding securities with a nominal value of £5,000 or less.

(f) Favourable income tax treatment can be obtained by individuals on certain transactions and investments. Shown below are some of those which are especially advantageous:

(i) National Savings Certificates (see Chapter 2);
(ii) investments under the Business Expansion Scheme, which now embraces assured tenancy schemes (see Chapter 4);
(iii) personal equity plans (see Chapter 5);
(iv) additional voluntary contributions (see Chapter 6);
(v) personal pension contributions (see Chapter 7);
(vi) private medical insurance for individuals aged 60 and over in respect of premiums paid after 5th April 1990 (see Chapter 9);
(vii) mortgage interest payments which qualify for tax relief (see Chapter 11);

(viii) school fees composition schemes and educational trusts (see Chapter 12);

(ix) covenants to charities with full tax relief obtained;

(x)   Lloyds' Underwriters;

(xi) purchase of an interest in an industrial or commercial building in an enterprise zone, either directly or through one of the property trusts set up for this purpose. The cost of the building, insofar as it exceeds rental income of the year of assessment, can be set off against other income (but not capital gains). The net cost after tax relief can therefore be as low as 60% of the cost of the building;

(xii) in certain situations, income arising to an offshore trust where the settlor or his spouse is not a beneficiary can be free of UK income tax.

Capital gains tax

The main considerations with regard to the planning of capital gains tax are as follows.

(a) Timing of disposals is of the utmost importance. This is illustrated below:

(i)   if a disposal is postponed until just after 5th April, the payment of any capital gains tax would be delayed for one year;

(ii)   if disposals are spread over more than one tax year so that the realised gains in each year, after adjusting for indexation relief, do not exceed the annual exemption (£5,000 for 1989/90), no capital gains tax liability would arise (in the case of most trusts, the annual exemption for 1989/90 is £2,500);

(iii) if realised gains (as adjusted for indexation relief) in excess of the annual exemption have been made in a tax year, consideration should be given to disposing of assets showing a loss (again, after adjusting for indexation). This can be offset against the gains made, thereby reducing or eliminating the potential capital gains tax liability. (Losses brought forward from previous year(s) can also be used in a similar manner. In this instance, such losses will be used only to reduce realised gains to £5,000, the exemption limit, with any unused balance being again carried forward.)

However, despite the possible action above to mitigate capital gains tax, it should be borne in mind that the timing of disposals should first be considered from an investment viewpoint. As previously mentioned, a poor investment even with good tax planning is unlikely to produce a satisfactory result.

(b) Every person, including a minor, is entitled to his own exemption. Consideration should therefore be given to husbands and wives spreading the ownership of investments in a family so that each member is able to realise tax free gains. This can be particularly advantageous if use can be made of 'hold-over' relief (it is proposed in the 1989 Budget that this will be available only for business assets, shares in unquoted trading companies, heritage assets and chargeable transfers for inheritance tax purposes). Therefore, for ordinary investments showing a gain, there is no tax saving in transfers amongst the family prior to sale. Consequently, it will usually be necessary to plan ahead by spreading the ownership of shares etc. between various members of the family from the outset.

(c) From 1990/91, each spouse will have an annual capital gains tax exemption. In order to make maximum use of this, it may therefore be worthwhile for them to transfer shares to each other. For example, one spouse may have losses brought forward which would offset a gain to be made by the other spouse. No stamp duty would normally be payable on such gifts, but all the formalities of transfer of ownership should be carried out before any sale. Any such transfer should be unconditional.

(d) 'Bed and breakfast' transactions (the sale and subsequent repurchase of shares, generally on the following day, in the same stock exchange account; a similar procedure applies to unit trust holdings)became effective again as a consequence of the 1985 Finance Act. There are two principal reasons for these transactions. The first reason is to enable an individual to establish an allowable loss to be used against taxable gains made in the same year. Such transactions should only be used to reduce the net gain to the annual exemption level. (It should be remembered that this also reduces the base cost of the investment and may, therefore, add to the tax liability in future years.) The second objective is to realise a gain up to the exemption level while retaining the investment and increasing its base cost to reduce future tax liability.

Whether bed and breakfast transactions are worthwhile will depend mainly on the cost involved and the benefit obtained.

(e) With effect from 2nd July 1986, gains and losses arising on the disposal of gilts and other qualifying corporate bonds (this includes local authority bonds and non-convertible company debentures and unsecured loan stocks) became completely exempt from capital gains tax. Consequently, from that date, investors were able to pursue a policy entirely on investment criteria without being concerned with the tax consequences of any decision.

(f) Since capital gains tax is not payable on death, it is often advisable for a person with a very short life expectancy to avoid realising substantial gains during the remainder of his lifetime.

(g) As it is now possible to 'rebase' values to 31st March 1982 for all disposals made after 5th April 1988, consideration should be given, for the purpose of calculating capital gains, to making an irrevocable election for all assets acquired before 31st March 1982 to be treated as if acquired for the value on that date. If this election was made, the original cost of the assets would be ignored.

(h) Careful attention should also be paid to the effect of the indexation rules on the capital gains tax position. In choosing which investments to sell, particular note should be taken of the indexation relief available on the individual investments, related to their base cost (or 31st March 1982 values if purchased before that date) and the time they have been held.

(i) If an individual wishes to make a large gift to a charity, it is usually beneficial, where it can be arranged, for the gift to be in the form of a chargeable asset showing a sizeable capital gain, and not the equivalent cash value. Since gains arising on gifts to charities are completely exempt from capital gains tax, the potential tax liability would be avoided.

(j) Where an individual becomes the owner of two homes, he should within two years of acquiring the second home make an election as to which home is to be treated as his main private residence. Since only one residence is exempt from capital gains tax, he should usually select the home likely to show the greater increase in value.

(k) Where a person is the owner of shares in a family trading company and works full-time in it as a director, or is a sole trader, or a partner in a firm, he is entitled to capital gains tax retirement relief on all or part of a gain not exceeding £125,000 if the business is sold (or gifted), provided he is at least age 60 (or has to retire earlier due to ill-health). The exemption is reduced proportionately where the business has not been owned for the whole of the previous ten years before the date of sale, or in the case of a family company, where the director has not been a full-time working director for that period.

One half of the gain in excess of £125,000 (or the proportionately reduced figure, if applicable) up to a maximum of £500,000 is also eligible for relief. Effectively, the tax rate on this element of the gain is therefore reduced to a maximum of 20%. If the disposal is of shares in a family company, the gain qualifying for relief would be in the proportion of the company's chargeable business assets to the total chargeable assets (chargeable assets are all assets on which a chargeable gain or allowable loss would arise if the company disposed of them).

In order to maximise retirement relief, it is usually worthwhile for the following action to be taken by an individual, when practicable:

(i)   postpone the disposal of the business until age 60 and also, in the case of a family company, continue to work in it until that time;

(ii) postpone the disposal of the business until it has been owned for ten years;

(iii) arrange for the wife to work full-time in the business and to own part of it. She will then also obtain retirement relief against her own gains on disposal of the business.

In all cases, it is recommended that detailed professional advice is obtained as the conditions which have to be satisfied can be complex.

(l) With the reintroduction of gains on a person becoming absolutely entitled to trust assets, consideration should be given to prolonging the life of the settlement if the beneficiary is prepared to receive the income but not the capital. This can be achieved by conferring on the beneficiary an interest in possession at age 25 instead of absolute entitlement. By this means, liability for capital gains tax is deferred, sometimes indefinitely.

Inheritance tax

With effect from 18th March 1986, capital transfer tax (CTT) was renamed inheritance tax (IHT) and the structure of the tax was radically changed. IHT is now a tax on certain lifetime gifts and on an individual's estate on his death and is effectively a combination of CTT and estate duty. It operates on a cumulative basis and, subject to certain exemptions and reliefs, is chargeable on the cumulative total of:

(a) at death, on certain lifetime gifts made within the previous seven years;

(b) at death, on lifetime gifts with reservation (see below);

(c) gifts into discretionary trusts, whether in lifetime or on death;

(d) the value of the assets passing on death.

For transfers made on or after 6th April 1989, it is proposed that the first £118,000 of cumulative chargeable transfers (the nil rate band) is exempt from IHT and any excess is taxed on death at a rate of 40%.

To some extent, IHT can be described as a voluntary tax due to the many exemptions and reliefs available. With early planning, it is often possible to reduce or entirely eliminate potential IHT liabilities, and this is helped by a husband and wife each having their own exemptions and rate bands. However, all assets are potentially liable to IHT on death with only estates (including cumulative transfers) within the nil rate band not giving rise to a tax charge at all. Since an individual's house must be included in calculating the value of his assets, IHT will affect many individuals who otherwise have only relatively modest estates.

For the purpose of calculating the value of a transfer, it is the loss suffered by the donor on the transfer, rather than the benefit received by the donee, which is relevant for IHT.

Classes of transfer
Transfers can be broadly classified as follows:

(a) exempt (see below);
(b) potentially exempt;
(c) chargeable.

A potentially exempt transfer (PET) is a lifetime gift made on or after 18th March 1986 by an individual to one of the recipients shown in (a), (b) and (d) below — in the case of (c), the relevant date is on or after 17th March 1987:

(a) another individual;
(b) an accumulation and maintenance trust;
(c) an interest in possession trust;
(d) a disabled person's trust.

A PET is treated as an exempt transfer on which no IHT is payable at the time of the gift and if the donor survives for seven years after the gift is made, no tax will be payable. If the donor dies within those seven years, the PET is treated as a chargeable transfer from the time it was made and IHT may become due at the date of death. However, a PET will still provide the following benefits.

(a) Although the PET may have become chargeable, the amount on which the charge is based is the value at the time of the actual gift and not the value at the date of death when the charge arises. If the property gifted has increased in value, this 'freezing' of its value will often be advantageous. Where the value of the property has fallen since the gift, the lower value may be used in most circumstances.
(b) Payment of IHT is postponed until after the death of the donor, rather than becoming payable shortly after the gift is made.
(c) IHT is charged at the rates in force at the date of death where they may be lower than those applying at the time of the gift. If the gift is made more than three years before the date of death, the tax payable is subject to taper relief as shown below:

Time between gift and death	% of full rate payable
up to 3 years	100
3 to 4 years	80
4 to 5 years	60
5 to 6 years	40
6 to 7 years	20

A lifetime gift which does not qualify as an exempt transfer or a PET is regarded as a chargeable transfer at the time it is made, and, subject to the nil rate band, will be immediately liable to IHT at one-half of the death rates in force at that time. For this purpose, any chargeable transfers which have been made in the previous seven years would be taken into account. If the donor then survives seven years, there are no further IHT consequences. However, if he does not do so, the tax charge is recalculated using the full rates in force at the date of death but reduced by any taper relief. If this produces a higher charge than the tax already paid on the lifetime transfer, a further liability arises. Where the calculation shows a lower charge, the difference is not repayable.

When making a chargeable transfer, the following options are normally available:

(a) the donor pays the tax based on the value of the transfer *plus* the tax; or
(b) the donee pays the tax calculated on the transfer value only. In this case, the tax does not decrease the donor's estate and consequently both the amount of the transfer and the inheritance tax are lower.

Exemptions
The main IHT exemptions are as follows.

(a) Transfers between husband and wife, whether made during lifetime or on death. The exception to this is where a husband or wife, domiciled in the UK, makes a transfer to a foreign domiciled spouse. In these circumstances, only the first £55,000 is exempt.
(b) Lifetime transfers in each tax year up to £3,000. Any unused part of the exemption may be carried forward for one year only for use in the following tax year after the exemption for that following year has been utilised.
(c) Outright lifetime gifts to any one person not exceeding £250 in each tax year with no limit to the number of recipients. However, this exemption cannot be claimed in respect of gifts to a particular person where more than £250 is given to that person in a tax year.
(d) Normal expenditure out of income. This covers transfers of net income after tax, provided that they form part of normal (i.e. habitual) expenditure and leave sufficient income for the donor to maintain his usual standard of living. For this purpose, the capital element of a purchased life annuity is not treated as being part of the donor's income.
(e) Gifts in consideration of marriage. The following amounts are exempt:
    (i)   £5,000 from each parent;
    (ii) £2,500 from each grandparent;
    (iii) £2,500 from one party of the marriage to the other;
    (iv) £1,000 from any other person.

(f) Lifetime gifts for the support and maintenance of children and dependent relatives.

(g) Gifts to charities both during lifetime and on death. This exemption can be of particular relevance to individuals with no relatives who prefer their favourite charities to benefit rather than the Crown.

Gifts with reservation

With effect from 18th March 1986, anti-avoidance provisions relating to gifts with reservation were introduced with the aim of ending various 'have your cake and eat it' schemes such as inheritance trusts. The rules regarding gifts with reservation are essentially the same as the old estate duty provisions, with gifted property subject to a reservation if:

(a) the donee does not assume full possession and enjoyment of the property at the time it is gifted or at least seven years before the donor's death; or

(b) the donor retains a benefit or enjoyment from the property at any time in the last seven years of his life.

The consequences of a gift with reservation depend on whether or not the reservation ceases during the donor's lifetime, or whether it is still in existence at the time of his death. If the donor releases the reservation before death, he is treated as having made a PET of the gifted property at the time the reservation is released. Where the donor dies without releasing the reservation, the gifted property is treated as part of his estate at death. IHT is charged according to the value of the property at that time, and consequently the original gift has no effect for estate planning purposes.

The gift with reservation provisions particularly affect many individuals with medium sized estates who may now feel unable to pass on their property before death.

IHT planning

The following matters are of the utmost importance in IHT planning.

(a) Subject to the individual circumstances, it is often beneficial from an IHT viewpoint for the assets of a husband and wife to be divided between them so that they are both able to take advantage of the various exemptions and the nil rate band. However, care should be taken to ensure as far as possible that the 'associated operations' rules do not apply, in order to avoid the transfer between the husband and wife, and the subsequent transfer from the recipient, being treated as one transaction. (In practice, the Inland Revenue is unlikely to use the associated operations provisions where a husband shares capital with his wife who then chooses to make gifts out of the money she has received. The exception to this is where there is a blatant case of a husband's gift to his wife (or vice versa) being made on condition that she should at once use the money to make gifts to others.)

A further advantage to a married couple of dividing their estates could be if a wealth tax was introduced. Since it seems likely that this would be calculated on the separate estates of a husband and wife at progressive rates, less tax would be payable on two smaller estates than on one larger one.

(b) Maximum advantage should be taken to make gifts within the various exemptions available. In this way, a considerable amount can be transferred from an estate over a period of years without any IHT liability.

(c) In addition to exempt gifts, an individual with a large estate should consider making further outright gifts during his lifetime, rather than waiting until death, for the following reasons.

    (i)   Cumulative chargeable lifetime gifts may be made within the IHT nil rate band (£118,000 for transfers made on or after 6th April 1989). Gifts made more than seven years previously drop out and consequently further gifts can be made within the nil rate band without attracting IHT. The rate bands are increased each year by not less than the increase in the RPI, with the result that an individual will be able to make additional transfers.

    (ii)   If the gifts were treated as PETs, the benefits mentioned earlier in this chapter would apply. Accordingly, it will often be particularly advantageous to gift those assets which are likely to increase in value, e.g. shares in a family company for which a USM listing may be sought in the future. In particular, the stronger life should make PETs and this may involve transferring assets from one spouse to the other prior to making a PET.

(d) In order to avoid redrafting a will each time the nil rate band changes, the will can be drawn up on the basis that an amount equivalent to the current nil rate band, less any chargeable gifts made within the previous seven years, is left to a discretionary trust.

(e) As previously mentioned, it is the loss suffered by a donor on a transfer, rather than the benefit received by the donee, which is relevant for IHT purposes. Therefore, an individual should be aware of the circumstances where a gift providing only a small benefit for the donee can give rise to a large potential IHT liability, e.g. a gift of 2% out of a 51% family company shareholding. Although in this case the gift may be of little value to the recipient, the donor would lose control of the company with the result that a large reduction in the value of his estate would be likely.

(f) If appropriate, business property relief and/or agricultural property relief should be claimed. Where relief is available, the transfer will be assessed for IHT purposes at a reduced value. (In this connection, it is very important that ownership of a farmhouse should not be retained without some of the farmland, otherwise it will not enjoy agricultural property relief.)

(g) If a loan is obtained, it should be secured against non-business assets where possible. A loan secured against business property will reduce the amount of business property relief available.

(h) The setting up of a trust may be especially useful to pass capital to children, grandchildren or other dependants, but at the same time enabling some flexibility and control over the assets to be retained, e.g. a gift into a discretionary trust up to the amount of the nil rate band. The particular type of trust would depend on the exact circumstances.

(i) Funding for IHT through life assurance policies (see Chapter 9) is now likely to play an even greater role in IHT planning due to the treatment of gifts with reservation and the proposed changes to capital gains hold-over relief for gifts.

(j) Where a life or pension policy is arranged in order to provide protection for the family of the life assured, it is often advisable for it to be written in trust or under nomination to pass free of IHT to the dependant concerned.

(k) Even after death, a variation of a will or a disclaimer may be effected. These can produce considerable IHT savings (see Chapter 13).

(l) On certain assets, an option is provided to pay an IHT liability by interest free instalments over ten years. Where this is permitted, it is usually beneficial to exercise the option. In other cases, the IHT liability may also be paid by instalments but interest would be payable. In this connection, the order of gifts made in a lifetime can be critical. If a PET becomes chargeable, it is important that where it is a gift of an asset on which tax can be paid by instalments, it is not the part of the estate which is within the nil rate band.

Overriding considerations

Although this chapter has been written from a tax planning viewpoint, the following overriding considerations should be borne in mind.

(a) Personal and family happiness is of greater importance than saving tax (the possibility of the children being financially immature or having unsatisfactory marriages should be taken into account).

(b) Although tax considerations are often vital in making a financial decision, the investment aspects will normally be paramount.

(c) Advice which may be suitable for most people will need to be adapted to the practical circumstances of the particular case, e.g. in IHT planning, assets should generally only be passed to children or grandchildren provided the surviving spouse has been left with sufficient capital and/or income on which to live. It may also be unwise to pass assets of high value to relatively young children until they are more responsible. (It might also be unwise on the death of the first spouse to split the ownership of the family home, as this may severely affect the future well-being and lifestyle of the surviving spouse.)

(d) In the light of court cases and Inland Revenue statements in recent years, considerable caution should be exercised before proceeding with certain tax mitigation schemes.

(e) It is usually advisable to keep matters simple and for any scheme to be as flexible as possible. It should be remembered that not only will an individual's family and financial circumstances change, but so also will governments and tax legislation.

(f) Income and capital should not be considered separately for tax planning purposes. Frequently, a higher net return can be obtained by making capital gains than by creating income.

(g) A course of action should be considered from the viewpoint of all forms of tax and not just one tax in isolation, e.g. while a lifetime gift may be advantageous as far as IHT is concerned, the benefit could be outweighed by the capital gains tax payable.

(h) Tax planning can be very complicated. It is therefore generally worthwhile for an individual to obtain professional advice before entering into any arrangement where a large sum of money is involved.

11. Mortgages

Apart from the personal satisfaction and enjoyment of owning one's home, it is very often one of the best investments an individual can make. In order to arrange the purchase, it is quite usual for a mortgage to be obtained from a building society, bank or other lender.

Guidelines on amount which can be borrowed

The maximum loan which can be obtained will normally be limited by reference to the size of the borrower's income and the value of the property. This is discussed below.

The size of the borrower's income
(a) Lenders usually base their loans on a multiple of income. For a single person, the multiple normally varies from 2½ times income to 3½ times income.
(b) In the case of couples, both of whom are earning, the basis of the loan would often be the greater of:
    (i)   2½ to 3½ times the main income plus once the second income; or
    (ii)   2 to 3 times the joint income.
(c) Some lenders operate low start schemes (usually for first time buyers) whereby a higher multiple of income is accepted. However, such schemes usually result in larger repayments being made over the total term of the mortgage.
(d) The definition of 'income' varies between lenders. Some allow overtime, bonuses or commission while others automatically exclude them.
(e) For self-employed persons, the loan is usually based on the income of the previous year. The lender will also normally wish to examine audited accounts for the last three years.

Since the amount of the mortgage repayments depends on the level of mortgage interest rates as well as the size and term of the loan, a lender will often be more strict on the amount he will advance when mortgage interest rates are high than when they are low. However, in the latter case, if there was an increase in interest rates and an individual had taken out a mortgage which he could only just afford, there would be no leeway within his income to make the inevitable higher repayments.

The value of the property
(a) The normal maximum amount that a building society or bank will lend varies between 85% and 100% of the agreed purchase price or valuation, whichever is the lower. Since the property is used as security for the loan, the lender will wish to ensure that its value is adequate.

(b) If the loan required is very large or it is to be used to purchase an older or less common type of property, there may be a further restriction on the percentage offered.

(c) Where a mortgage greater than the typical 80% (the percentage is often less for larger loans) of the agreed purchase price or valuation of the property is required, it will generally be necessary for the borrower to pay a premium (this is on a once and for all basis) for an indemnity guarantee insurance policy to cover the risk of default in the repayment of the loan. The borrower himself cannot benefit from this policy as it is effected for the protection of the lender only.

(d) If a lender is unwilling to provide a larger mortgage, it may still be possible to obtain a top-up loan by way of a second mortgage from an insurance company. However, in this case, it will usually be a condition for obtaining this additional loan that the amount borrowed under the original mortgage, in addition to the amount of the top-up loan, be repaid by way of a life policy effected with the insurance company providing the top-up loan.

Taxation position

In order to encourage private home ownership, successive governments have provided assistance to individuals in the form of tax relief on mortgage interest and exemption from capital gains tax on the profit made from the sale of the main home.

The taxation position with regard to mortgages at the present time is as follows.

(a) Tax relief on interest paid in respect of loans up to £30,000, or the first £30,000 of larger loans, used to buy the only or main residence, is allowed against basic rate and higher rate taxes. Where more than one loan is arranged in respect of a property, the £30,000 limit relates to the property, not to each individual borrowing (different rules apply to multiple loans on the same property arranged by unmarried persons before 1st August 1988).

(b) Tax relief is also allowed in addition to the purchase of the main residence where a property was purchased before 6th April 1988 for a former or separated spouse or a dependent relative (this includes a widowed, divorced or separated mother). However, the £30,000 limit takes into account all properties.

(c) Where an individual is an employee and lives in accommodation provided by his employer, he may purchase a separate house which he might wish to occupy at a later date, e.g. at retirement. In this case, tax relief will be allowed on the first £30,000 of a loan used to purchase that property.

(d) In addition to the new mortgage, a bridging loan of up to £30,000 will qualify for tax relief for normally up to one year (or longer at the discretion of the Inland Revenue) on a change of residence.

(e) In April 1983, mortgage interest relief at source (MIRAS) was introduced. Under this system, tax relief at the basic rate is automatically deducted at source from the amounts charged to borrowers. The non-taxpayer gains considerable benefit from this since the tax deducted is not subsequently recovered by the Inland Revenue.

For loans larger than £30,000, tax relief is deducted at source only up to that figure (loans made before 6th April 1987 which were outside MIRAS at that date can continue on the same basis, although in practice they will usually have been subsequently brought into the MIRAS system).

Higher rate taxpayers also receive basic rate tax relief through the MIRAS system but obtain relief at the higher rates through their tax codings or assessments.

Main types of mortgage

The method selected to repay a mortgage will depend on the exact circumstances of the individual including his age, state of health, tax position, etc. The main types of mortgage are as follows:

(a) repayment mortgages;
(b) endowment mortgages;
(c) pension mortgages.

Repayment mortgages
Under this method, both part of the capital and interest on the outstanding loan are paid to the lender monthly under the MIRAS system. In addition to the monthly loan repayments, it is usually advisable for a mortgage protection policy or other term assurance to be effected in order to provide life cover for the outstanding mortgage.

With this type of mortgage, an increasing proportion of the regular payments is applied each year to reduce the capital outstanding. The two most common types of repayment mortgage, constant net repayment mortgages and gross profile mortgages, are discussed below.

Constant net repayment mortgage This is the most usual type of repayment mortgage, whereby if interest rates and the basic tax rate remain static, a constant amount is paid, net of basic rate tax, throughout the entire mortgage term. Constant net repayment mortgages are offered by the large majority of building societies, although not generally by banks.

Gross profile mortgage With this type of mortgage, the loan repayments are calculated on the basis that if interest rates remain static, constant gross payments are made each year, although in fact the payments are made net of basic rate tax. Consequently, as more interest is included in the payments in the early years than in the later years of the mortgage term, the net amount payable will gradually rise throughout. However, the initial payments will be considerably lower than with the constant net repayment mortgage, although greater over the entire mortgage term. As a result, a gross profile mortgage is usually more attractive to a first time buyer who has no surplus income, with a constant net repayment mortgage often being more suitable for a person already established in the property market.

The capital repayments will also start at a lower level under the gross profile mortgage, but rise more quickly than under the constant net repayment mortgage. Accordingly, if an individual moves house, a larger proportion of his mortgage will remain outstanding. Gross profile mortgages are generally offered by banks, but only by a minority of building societies.

The following example compares the two most common types of repayment mortgage.

Example 18

A person paying tax at the basic rate takes out a £30,000 mortgage repayable over 25 years, compared on constant net repayment and gross profile bases. Gross interest of 13½% is charged in both cases.

Year	Constant net repayment mortgage		Gross profile mortgage	
	Monthly payment £	Year end balance £	Monthly payment £	Year end balance £
1	278.07	29,700.64	267.99	29,821.65
5	278.07	28,167.84	270.44	28,832.72
10	278.07	25,200.33	275.89	26,634.07
11	278.07	24,415.00	277.45	26,001.32
12	278.07	23,550.17	279.23	25,283.14
15	278.07	20,393.90	286.15	22,492.78
20	278.07	12,609.02	305.48	14,692.43
25	278.07	repaid	341.88	repaid
Total repayments	£83,421.23		£86,781.57	

Note: As shown by the above example, the monthly payments under the gross profile mortgage start to exceed those under the constant net repayment mortgage in the 12th year.

Endowment mortgages
Payments made under an endowment mortgage consist of two separate parts, interest to the lender (in most cases, this will be at the same rate as for a repayment mortgage), and life assurance premiums to an insurance company.

The interest is payable throughout the term of the mortgage and will vary only with movements in interest rates and any change in the basic rate of taxation.

The proceeds from the life policy are used to repay the mortgage at the end of the term with any surplus arising being available to the borrower. Both unit-linked and with profits policies can be taken out to repay a mortgage, and although the former are offered by an increasing number of life companies, with profits policies are normally more appropriate due to the greater certainty provided. Endowment without profits policies are also available but are generally not competitive.

The main type of with profits policy which is used to repay a mortgage is a low cost endowment policy. Occasionally a full with profits endowment policy may also be suitable (these policies are considered in Chapter 8).

Most low cost endowment policies are effectively a combination of with profits endowment assurance and decreasing term assurance, but since future bonus rates are not known, the life cover under the term assurance is not defined. (In reality, these policies are endowment assurances with a guaranteed death benefit which is higher than the amount on which bonuses are declared.) A low cost endowment policy can also be a combination of a with profits endowment policy and a level term assurance.

Since the total death benefit under the low cost endowment policy would be guaranteed to equal the amount of the mortgage, the policy would provide sufficient cover to repay the loan in the event of the death of the borrower while the loan is still outstanding.

The more usual basis for a low cost endowment policy to be accepted by lenders is for the with profits endowment element to be calculated on the basis that if reversionary bonuses are maintained at their current rate, then the basic sum assured together with 80% of the resulting total of reversionary bonuses would repay the loan at the end of the borrowing term (this leaves a reasonable margin if the bonus rate is not maintained). However, there is no guarantee given at the outset that the maturity proceeds would repay the full amount of the loan.

The main advantage of a low cost endowment policy as compared to a full with profits policy is that it is much cheaper to effect due to part of the initial cover being provided by term assurance. Against this, the longer the policy runs, the greater will be the difference in the amount of the proceeds between the two policies.

However, even where an individual has sufficient resources to be able to afford to repay his mortgage by way of a full with profits endowment policy, it would not usually be advisable for him to do so. Instead, it would normally be advantageous for him to effect a low cost endowment to repay the mortgage and arrange an additional savings contract for the uncommitted funds. In this way, the additional contract will not be charged to the lender and could therefore be used for other purposes.

Pension mortgages

These mortgages, which are usually arranged by self-employed persons or employed persons not in an occupational pension scheme, have similarities to endowment mortgages. However, a personal pension policy is effected instead of a life assurance policy. Furthermore, while an endowment policy can be assigned to a lender, this is not possible with a personal pension policy providing retirement benefits. Consequently, the lender will normally require a separate term assurance policy to be assigned to him to cover the event of the borrower's death before the loan is repaid. (It is also possible for a pension mortgage to be taken out by a director, executive or other person through a company pension arrangement. In these cases, the criteria discussed in Chapter 6 will apply.)

The main advantage of a pension mortgage compared with the other methods is the very favourable tax position in respect of both the contributions paid and the pension fund itself. As mentioned in Chapter 7, contributions up to the maximum permitted are effectively allowed against the highest income tax rates payable by the individual, while investment income and capital gains accumulate within the pension fund free of all UK tax. As a result, pension mortgages are particularly advantageous for higher rate taxpayers.

However, against these advantages, only a proportion of the amount in the pension fund at retirement can be received in the form of cash, with the balance being taken by way of pension. The proposals in the 1989 Budget to introduce an earnings limit of £60,000 to the level of salary or relevant earnings which can be considered in relation to pension contracts, may further reduce the cash sum which can be withdrawn. From the cash sum, the mortgage would be repaid (provided the investment return under the pension policy was sufficient).

Despite the attractions of a pension mortgage, the following matters should be considered before a decision is taken to use this method to repay a loan:

(a) it will not normally be possible to repay the mortgage nor receive the pension and any surplus cash before age 50 in the case of a personal pension, or age 60 in other cases (although the proposals in the 1989 Budget include the possibility of an individual retiring at age 50 with no penalty);

(b) by using the tax-free cash to repay the mortgage, the cash benefit available for retirement purposes would be reduced (this is particularly important where maximum contributions are already being paid);

(c) if the earnings are volatile, there may be a restriction in poor years on the amount of the contributions which can be paid;

(d) if the person concerned should cease to be self-employed or become a member of an occupational pension scheme, he would be ineligible to pay contributions into the existing contract and consequently would have to make alternative arrangements.

It would therefore seem that pension mortgages are mainly suitable for those persons who are able to predict their future with a reasonable degree of certainty. These will be largely high-earning, self-employed professional people who are unlikely to work for an employer in the future, or directors and executives who are able to utilise their potential benefits under a company pension scheme or individual pension arrangement. In any event, before the pension method is decided upon, consideration should be given to the position which would arise if, at a future date, contributions cannot be maintained.

It is also important to remember that future legislation could be introduced reducing the tax advantages of a pension mortgage, e.g. the lump sum available when the benefits are taken could be further restricted or become taxable. Consequently, a person considering this method would be advised to have an alternative means of repayment available.

The following example illustrates the more usual ways of repaying a mortgage.

Example 19

A man aged 40 next birthday paying tax at the basic rate takes out a £30,000 mortgage repayable over 25 years. He is in good health and a non-smoker. The gross interest rate charged under each type of mortgage is 13½%.

	Constant net repayment mortgage £	*Low cost endowment mortgage* £	*Pension mortgage* £
Net monthly payments			
To lender	278.07	253.13	253.13
To insurance company:			
endowment premiums		42.70	
term assurance premiums	10.20		9.83
pension contributions			68.84
	£288.27	£295.83	£331.80
Illustrative benefits at end of mortgage term			
Illustrated value of life policy/pension fund	Nil	£40,800	£163,600
Surplus tax free cash after repayment of loan	Nil	£10,800	£10,900
Annual gross pension	Nil	Nil	£15,500

Notes:
(a) The illustrated values of the life policy and pension fund are based on the rules laid down by the Life Assurance and Unit Trust Regulatory Organisation (LAUTRO) and assume that contributions, after allowing for a deduction for expenses, and the cost of life cover (in the case of the life policy), will be invested to earn 10½% pa net of tax and 13% respectively. For the purpose of calculating the annual gross pension, immediate annuity rates are based on an interest rate of 10% pa;
(b) The term assurance premiums relate to a mortgage protection policy in respect of the repayment mortgage and a level term assurance effected under a personal pension policy in respect of the pension mortgage. The pension policy would also repay the accumulated value of the fund in the event of death before retirement;
(c) Comparisons between the different house purchase methods will vary with the age of the person concerned and the level of interest rates.

Early repayment of a mortgage

From a financial viewpoint, it is not normally advantageous to repay a mortgage early even if a lump sum should become available to do so. This is because it is often possible, at least for a higher rate taxpayer, to obtain a greater net return by investing the lump sum than the net saving which could be achieved by repaying the mortgage.

In addition, once a borrower has made an early repayment, the capital so used cannot be applied for other purposes with the result that flexibility is lost. To re-borrow, other than for the purposes of house purchase etc. would be capital raising and therefore not eligible for tax relief. It should also be borne in mind that interest rates on most other forms of finance are higher than those on house mortgages.

However, early or partial repayment of a mortgage is generally worthwhile in the following circumstances.

(a) Where a mortgage is in excess of the tax relief limit. In this case, it is usually worthwhile to repay the amount above the limit since it is very likely that the gross interest payable to the lender would be greater than the net return which could be obtained from a risk-free investment.
(b) Where a building society repayment mortgage is near the end of its term. In these circumstances, the effective rate of interest charged is generally very high as it is based on the amount of capital outstanding at the beginning of a year with no account being taken of the capital subsequently repaid during that year (this has a far greater impact at the end of a mortgage than at the start, especially in the case of a gross profile mortgage).

In the case of a bank mortgage, the above does not normally apply as interest is usually calculated after taking into account all capital repayments.

Despite it not normally being financially expedient to repay a mortgage early, many people prefer to do so from an emotional viewpoint. If this is the situation, it should be remembered that an individual's personal requirements are generally of prime importance, even to the point where the financial results would be adversely affected.

Before the final payment on the mortgage is made to a building society, whether by early repayment or otherwise, it should be remembered that it is often worthwhile to leave a nominal amount unpaid, for the following reasons:

(a) the building society will continue to store the title deeds free of charge;
(b) the individual remains a member of the building society and consequently may receive priority over non-members in the event of a mortgage famine if an additional loan is required in the future;
(c) if a further advance is required, the individual would not normally incur any legal fees.

However, against these advantages, a higher rate of interest is often charged for further advances.

General principles in choosing a mortgage

The following general principles will often apply in choosing a particular type of mortgage.

(a) If the individual's main requirement is to keep the monthly outgoings to a minimum, a repayment mortgage is often most appropriate. A gross profile mortgage is usually more suitable than a constant net repayment mortgage for a first time buyer who initially has no surplus income.
(b) A repayment mortgage is normally more flexible than the other types of mortgage. However, against this, if a person sells a property in the early years of a mortgage, only a small proportion of the capital would have been repaid, particularly with a gross profile mortgage. In addition, it may be necessary for the repayment of the mortgage to be delayed beyond that originally anticipated. (In the case of both endowment and pension mortgages, the policies can usually be continued if a new loan is subsequently arranged. Consequently, the mortgage would be repaid within the original term selected.)

(c) If a person is in poor health, he may not be able to arrange an endowment mortgage since underwriting would generally be required.
(d) Endowment mortgages may not be available to older persons and in the case of a pension mortgage, the amount of the loan may be restricted.
(e) The choice between a repayment mortgage and endowment mortgage will often depend on the individual's tax position. For a basic rate taxpayer, a repayment mortgage is frequently more suitable, while for an individual paying tax at the higher rate, an endowment mortgage is usually preferable.
(f) For a self-employed person or an employed person not in an occupational pension scheme, a pension mortgage is likely to produce the best results. However, as previously mentioned, these mortgages are usually more suitable for those persons who are able to predict their future with reasonable certainty.

Other mortgage considerations

Other matters regarding mortgages which should be borne in mind are as follows.

(a) The type of property may restrict the choice of lender or method of mortgage repayment. This includes timber framed houses and older or 'listed' buildings.
(b) The Consumer Credit Act does not apply to any loan, regardless of size, if used to finance house purchase. However, the Act is applicable in all other cases with regard to loans of £15,000 or less, except where the loan is required for property improvements or repairs and there is an existing mortgage which was originally taken out with the same lender for property purposes.
(c) Building societies are required to show the Annual Percentage Rate (APR) of interest in all advertisements and personal quotations. This rate is calculated according to a statutory formula and is designed to show in a single figure all the different elements of the cost of a mortgage. It is therefore important to compare APRs rather than interest rates when considering a mortgage as this is likely to provide a more reliable indication of the total costs involved (although banks are only required to quote the APR for mortgages which fall within the Consumer Credit Act, the APR is also frequently shown for other loans).
(d) It is often possible for an individual to arrange a remortgage. This can then be used to repay an existing mortgage and provide additional capital for home improvements etc. However, the amount used for purposes other than repaying the existing mortgage might be treated as a further advance and consequently may attract a higher rate of interest. (Some building societies charge a higher rate of interest on the entire amount of the remortgage.)
(e) On a remortgage, mortgage interest relief is only available for that part of the loan replacing the original loan for purchase of the property. Tax relief on interest on a previous loan for home improvements will be lost. Also the MIRAS scheme only applies to a loan used to replace another loan which was used solely for house purchase. A remortgage that is replacing loans, only part of which are eligible for tax relief, will also fall outside the MIRAS

scheme. In this situation a separate claim will be necessary for income tax relief on the qualifying part of the loan.

(f) If an individual should have financial problems in meeting his mortgage repayments, it is generally advisable to inform the lender as soon as possible. Very often a temporary arrangement can be made to assist the borrower over a difficult period.

Mortgage variations

The following are types of mortgage which have been recently developed and are generally variations of repayment, endowment or pension mortgages.

(a) A fixed interest mortgage can be arranged whereby the rate of interest charged remains constant throughout the mortgage term, or for the first few years only, regardless of movements in the general level of interest rates. This type of mortgage can be suitable where a borrower considers that interest rates are likely to rise on average over the term for which the rate of interest is fixed.

(b) Low start or deferred payment mortgages provide for deferment of part of the interest or capital payments in the early years, the payments rising either in steps or at the end of an agreed period. Unpaid interest is added to the debt so that the overall cost will be higher. Another form of low start mortgage involves an endowment or low cost endowment policy on which the premiums rise in steps over a five-year period.

(c) LIBOR mortgages have their interest rate linked to the London Inter Bank Offered Rate for three-month loans between the major banks. Due to the short term nature of the rate, the interest on the mortgage is likely to fluctuate more than with a building society loan, although in most cases interest is only adjusted quarterly.

(d) Unit-linked mortgages are endowment based but instead of being on a with profits basis, growth in the policy is linked to the performance of one or more selected investment funds (see Chapter 8). The policy is reviewed at intervals to check the performance of the fund. If it falls short of that deemed necessary to produce the required amount, the level of premiums will be increased. However, in this case, care must be exercised to avoid the policy becoming non-qualifying, otherwise a tax charge may arise when the proceeds are received.

(e) Unit trust mortgages provide for repayment through the accumulation of units in a regular unit trust savings plan (see Chapter 3). Interest only is paid on the loan during the mortgage term, together with monthly contributions to the regular savings plan. The plan will be reviewed at intervals to check that the savings rate is adequate, or to release capital if the performance of the underlying funds is greater than that assumed at the time the mortgage was arranged.

(f) PEP mortgages are also interest only loans with the capital repayment deferred to the end of the mortgage term. A PEP (see Chapter 5) is taken out each year with a view to accumulating sufficient capital to repay the mortgage. Due to the favourable taxation treatment of PEPs, this type of mortgage can be particularly advantageous.

(g) Foreign currency mortgages are simply loans in a foreign currency such as
     Swiss francs, German marks, etc. Interest is payable at the rate prevailing in
     the country concerned. Such loans are often superficially appealing as
     interest rates in many countries are lower than those in the UK. However,
     the risk of currency loss should not be overlooked, i.e. the exchange rate
     between the selected currency and the pound sterling will vary, so that the
     sterling value of the debt will increase or decrease accordingly. The sterling
     value of the interest payments will also vary to the same extent.
         A further variation of this form of lending is the ECU (European Commu-
     nity Units) loan, which represents a basket of currencies. As a result, the risk
     from exchange rate fluctuations in a single currency is reduced.

It should be remembered that unit-linked, unit trust, PEP and foreign currency
mortgages carry a greater risk that the capital accumulated at the end of the
mortgage term may not be sufficient to repay the loan. However, if the underlying investments perform well, then either the overall cost will be less, or the
return at the end of the mortgage term will be greater than originally projected.

Raising income from the home

Elderly home-owners have a choice of methods of raising capital or generating
income through the mortgage or deferred sale of their property. The main types
of scheme are described below.
    Apart from raising capital or generating income needed by the home-owner in
retirement, these schemes can often be advantageous in inheritance tax planning.
This is because the mortgage or deferred sale causes a reduction in the person's
estate with any capital raised not necessarily remaining in the estate.
    Whether it is worthwhile for an individual to arrange one of these schemes can
be decided only after all the circumstances have been considered. These will
include the health and age of the person, whether there are any close relatives and
whether other resources are available. In any event, before an arrangement is
made, professional advice should be obtained with regard to both the financial
and legal consequences.

Home income plans
The basis of these schemes is for the home-owner to be granted a mortgage on his
home and the loan used to purchase an annuity. This will provide him with a
monthly income for the remainder of his life or, in the case of a joint husband and
wife plan, until the death of the survivor. At that time, the mortgage will be
repaid either from the sale proceeds of the property or from other sources.
Consequently, the benefit of the capital appreciation on the home will be
retained.
    Before payments are made to the home-owner, two deductions are normally
made. These are interest payments on the mortgage and basic rate tax on the
income element of the annuity.
    The operation of these schemes is considerably simplified when the MIRAS
system applies, as the deduction for mortgage interest is made net of basic rate
tax.
    In order to obtain tax relief on interest on loans up to £30,000 arranged under a
home income plan, the following conditions must be satisfied:

(a) the home-owner must have attained the age of 65 or, in the case of a joint scheme, both annuitants must have reached this age;
(b) a minimum of 90% of the loan must be applied to purchase an annuity (the remaining 10% can be taken in cash where permitted);
(c) the loan must be secured on property in the UK or Eire;
(d) the property on which the loan is secured must be the only or main residence at the time the interest is paid.

The income element of the annuity is normally paid after deduction of basic rate tax. However, it is possible for a non-taxpayer to arrange for the annuity payments to be paid gross without the deduction being made. In addition, he will obtain the benefit of tax relief on mortgage interest. Higher rate taxpayers will need to make a claim for tax relief at the higher rate on interest payments but will be assessed for higher rate tax on the income element of the annuity payments.

Other considerations with regard to home income plans are as follows.

(a) The home must be a freehold or long leasehold, have no tenancies and be in reasonable condition.
(b) It is preferable for the property to be free of all mortgages. Consequently, any existing mortgages should be repaid before a home income plan is arranged.
(c) Like the annuity, the loan interest rate is normally fixed with the result that the home-owner will usually know the amount of income which will be provided by the plan throughout his lifetime, subject to changes in tax rates.
(d) It is often possible to increase a loan once the plan has been in existence for a number of years by way of a top-up mortgage.
(e) Apart from any contribution made by the company offering the home income plan, the home-owner would be responsible for the legal costs etc. involved in arranging the scheme.

The income produced by arranging a home income plan will mainly depend on the following factors:

(a) the amount of the annuity purchased;
(b) the age of the home-owner when the plan is taken out (the older the person or persons concerned, the greater will be the annuity);
(c) the tax position of the home-owner (individuals not subject to tax and higher rate taxpayers will obtain the greatest benefit);
(d) whether the annuity is arranged on a single life or joint life basis;
(e) the level of interest rates at the time the plan is effected;
(f) whether the whole amount of the loan is used to purchase an annuity or whether a part is taken in cash;
(g) whether the annuity is taken out on a capital protected basis in order to reduce the loss in the event of early death.

The market for home income plans is dominated by two organisations — Allied Dunbar and Abbey National. Both companies require a minimum age of 70 at entry for a single home-owner, although Allied Dunbar stipulates a minimum age of 73 for women for some of its plans. In the case of a joint plan, each person must have attained the age of 70 with the combined minimum age being 150. If a house is inhabited by a married couple, both schemes require the plan to be arranged on a joint life and last survivor basis.

The main differences between the Allied Dunbar and Abbey National schemes are as follows.

(a) Allied Dunbar grants mortgages up to 80% of the value of the home with the minimum loan being £15,500 and the maximum usually £30,000. There must also be a difference of at least £6,000 between the value of the property and the amount of the loan. The minimum loan from Abbey National is £15,001 and the maximum 65% of the value of the home or £30,000, whichever is the less.

(b) If the home is sold and another purchased, both Allied Dunbar and Abbey National allow their schemes to be transferred to another property. In the case of the Allied Dunbar scheme, this will have no effect on the net income. However, in the case of the Abbey National scheme, it is necessary to take out a new mortgage at the then quoted rate of interest. This may be higher or lower than the original mortgage.

(c) Both the interest rate charged and the annuity paid by Allied Dunbar are lower than with Abbey National. Although this would not normally be of particular relevance, it would be important if it was necessary for the mortgage to be repaid early, e.g. if the individual moved to an old people's home. Consequently, in the case of the Allied Dunbar scheme, he would be left receiving very low annuity payments.

The following example based on terms offered by Allied Dunbar illustrates the increase in net spendable income by arranging a home income plan.

Example 20

A woman aged 75 obtains a mortgage of £30,000 (75% on a house valued at £40,000). No cash is being taken, and the annuity is on a non-capital protected basis.

Income tax rate	*Nil %* £	*25%* £	*40%* £
Annual gross annuity	3,705	3,705	3,705
Less: Basic rate tax on income element	–	234	234
Net annuity	3,705	3,471	3,471
Less: Mortgage interest net of basic rate tax relief	1,856	1,856	1,856
Less: Higher rate tax on income element of annuity	–	–	140
Plus: Higher rate tax relief on mortgage interest	–	–	371
Increase in net spendable income	£1,849	£1,615	£1,846

Before a person makes a final decision to proceed with a home income plan, the following matters should be borne in mind.

(a) Where there are no capital resources other than the home itself, it would be necessary for the property to be sold on the death of the individual (or individuals, in the case of a joint life plan) in order for the outstanding loan to be repaid. Therefore, the home could not be left to children or other dependants.

(b) Once a contract has been completed, there is no scope for an individual to change his mind and encash the annuity.

(c) When the individual dies, the annuity will cease. Consequently, if his death should occur immediately after effecting the contract, his beneficiaries would just be left with an outstanding loan and no compensating benefit. As a result, a home income plan is not normally suitable for a person in poor health.

Despite this, if the home-owner was prepared to receive a lower net income, he could choose a capital protected annuity so that in the event of his early death, only part of the loan would be repayable. Under the Allied Dunbar scheme, 25% of the loan is repayable if death occurs within the first year, 50% in the second year and 75% in the third year. In the case of the Abbey National scheme, an amount is returned to the estate equal to the excess of the purchase money over the total gross annuity payments made.

(d) The annuity payments can affect the eligibility for means-tested benefits such as housing benefit and income support (age allowance, however, would not be reduced since the interest paid on the mortgage would exceed the taxable income received). Consequently, the advantage of increased income from a home income plan can partially be lost by the reduction in other benefits.

Home reversion schemes

A further method for a home-owner to raise capital from his home is to enter into a reversion scheme. Under these contracts, the property is sold for approximately half its value, depending on the age and sex of the person concerned, with the home-owner normally being allowed to live in the home rent free for life. The property would then revert to the buyer on the death of the occupant (or occupants). Usually it is required that the capital raised be invested in an annuity for life, either on a single or joint life basis.

A major disadvantage with these schemes is that the home-owner usually loses the benefit of any future capital appreciation on the home.

Variations on the home reversion scheme include:

(a) *instalment reversion* where the property is sold in stages over a ten-year period;

(b) *50% reversion* where the owner retains a half share in the equity of the property;

(c) *variable income* where instead of a lump sum, the individual receives an income for life which varies with the value of the properties in the scheme's residential property fund.

As with home income plans, the annuity payments can affect eligibility for means-tested benefits but, in addition, may also affect age allowance.

Roll-ups and draw-downs

A recent innovation from some building societies is that of loans to elderly home-owners, requiring no interest or capital repayments during their lifetime. A mortgage is taken on the home with interest at a commercial rate being added to the debt at yearly intervals. Redemption of the mortgage is required on the death of the occupant (or occupants).

The purpose of such loans, known as roll-ups, is to raise capital without a charge on the income of the borrower. Roll-up loans do not generally qualify for tax relief on mortgage interest (see page 83) and therefore there is usually no restriction on the use of the capital raised.

Because of the roll-up of interest, the loan is normally limited to about 30% to 40% of the value of the property. In the event of the accumulated loan and rolled-up interest amounting to more than approximately 70% of the value of the property (as revalued periodically), it will be necessary for interest payments to be made or the capital sum reduced. Consequently, great care is required before a decision is taken to roll-up interest as, for example, a loan with interest rolling-up at the rate of 13½% pa will more than double every five and a half years, or at 10% pa, approximately every seven and a quarter years.

A development of the roll-up scheme is that of draw-downs. With this facility a loan is approved up to an agreed amount determined as above; the borrower then 'draws-down' capital as required, with interest being calculated only on the amount borrowed.

Roll-ups and draw-downs will not have any adverse effect on age allowance but may affect eligibility for housing benefit and income support.

12. Providing for school fees

Next to purchasing a house, the cost of educating children privately is likely to be a family's largest financial commitment, with current school fees for one child up to £7,500 pa or even more in some cases.

There is no magic formula in providing for school fees. Each case must be considered individually with the purpose of ensuring that the necessary monies become available on the required dates in order to pay the fees. School fees provision is therefore very much an investment problem, but with due regard being given to the taxation consequences of any plan.

However, before a school fees scheme can be properly considered, the individual's asset and income position will need to be assessed, together with the general overall situation.

Assessing the situation

Before embarking on the private education route, a proper assessment should be made to decide whether this is possible at all. Therefore, a detailed schedule should be produced to show the estimated funds required to pay the school fees, together with the dates when they fall due, with allowance being made for future increases (these usually exceed the rate of inflation) and extras. After this schedule has been prepared, it will be necessary to consider the possible sources of funds from which the school fees can be paid. These sources may be broadly classified as (a) capital; (b) income; and (c) other. In practice, it will often be necessary for at least two of the above sources to be used in order to provide the funds required.

If a decision has been reached to educate a child privately, the following matters should be taken into account before a school fees scheme is implemented:

(a) the choice of school;
(b) the possibility of the child not attending the chosen school or any other private school;
(c) the possibility of the child changing to a different school mid-stream;
(d) death or incapacity of the child;
(e) the prospective increase in costs due to inflation, government action, etc.;
(f) the possibility of abolition of private education;
(g) deterioration in the parents' financial circumstances;
(h) death of the parents.

If it is intended for the child to attend university or other further education, provision should also be made for parental contributions to student maintenance grants to cover living costs during term-time (the annual contribution payable would mainly depend on where the student lives and the income of the parents, unless the student is classed as independent).

Funding from capital

Apart from paying school fees directly out of capital as and when they fall due, the following are the four principal methods by which capital can be applied for school fees purposes:

(a) school fees composition schemes;
(b) educational trusts;
(c) fixed interest schemes;
(d) temporary annuities, etc. used to fund suitable life policies and savings plans.

School fees composition schemes
School fees composition schemes are essentially deferred annuity contracts, i.e. they allow a lump sum to be paid in advance which will be less than the total fees to be funded. The main characteristics of school fees composition schemes are as follows.

(a) The size of the discount which the school is able to offer will largely depend on the length of the period before the fees become due and the level of interest rates at the time the lump sum is paid.
(b) As the school would have obtained the status of an educational charity, the scheme could be particularly attractive to a higher rate taxpayer, since he would not be liable to either income tax or capital gains tax arising from the investment of the lump sum by the school. Furthermore, if the lump sum was paid by a parent or guardian and a trust was declared under Section 11 of the Inheritance Tax Act 1984, this would not be a transfer of value for inheritance tax purposes (a Section 11 trust enables parents and others in restricted circumstances to make dispositions for the education, maintenance or training of a child without liability to inheritance tax). The practical implications of declaring a Section 11 trust are considered later under educational trusts.

    However, if the payment was made by any other person, a chargeable transfer would arise, although this may be within his annual exemptions or the nil rate band, currently £118,000.
(c) One of the main advantages of school fees composition schemes is that they are simple to formulate and convenient to operate. Against this, a major disadvantage is that they are often inflexible. Therefore, the following matters, which may be open to negotiation, should be investigated before a scheme is arranged:
    (i) the position if the child does not attend the school (normally a repayment would be made but on unattractive terms);
    (ii) the position should the child leave the school or die before his education has been completed;
    (iii) the position if the advantages relating to educational charities should be abolished.
(d) The competitiveness of a school fees composition scheme will depend to a large extent on the rates offered at the particular time. Consequently, a quotation in accordance with the individual circumstances should be obtained and the investment return in percentage terms compared with other possible alternatives.

Educational trusts

Educational trusts are themselves independent versions of composition fees schemes operated by schools and therefore many of the above comments will also generally apply to educational trusts. However, as far as the basic operation is concerned, it is the trust rather than the school which will purchase the annuity from an insurance company. The annuity instalments will be made payable to the school and sent via the trustees to meet the school fees for the child concerned (these fees can be provided for on a level basis or to increase each year at a fixed rate).

The following are some of the more important practical differences between school fees composition schemes and educational trusts.

(a) Although school fees plans arranged through educational trusts still lack flexibility, this is less so than with composition schemes due to the following factors.
   (i) The school to which the fees are to be paid need not be nominated until shortly (normally at least one month) before the first payment becomes due. As a result, the problem of the child not attending a school previously nominated is largely overcome.
   (ii) There is usually a facility to switch funds from the benefit of one child to the benefit of another. However, this option will only be relevant if there is at least one other child undergoing private education.
   (iii) If the child should die before the termination of the school fees plan, the amount paid into the plan, less any school fee payments already made from the plan, is usually guaranteed to be repaid under the trust deed. However, although the repayment is generally made with interest, this interest is normally below market rates.
(b) The inheritance tax position of school fees plans using educational trusts may also be different from school fees composition schemes and will depend both on whether the lump sum payment is made by the parent, and if so whether he declares a Section 11 trust, and also on whether the right to surrender the plan is retained.

   If payment was made by the parent or guardian and he did not wish to use his annual exemptions for school fees purposes, he could declare a Section 11 trust in which case the payment would not be deemed to be a transfer of value for inheritance tax purposes. However, under the trust, the benefits of the plan are held for a specified child and consequently cannot be used for another child or returned for the parent's own use. Therefore, even where the right to surrender the plan has been retained, the amount payable on surrender would be required under the terms of the trust to be applied for the education, maintenance or training of the child concerned.

   If a Section 11 trust is not declared, the payments arising under the plan can normally be used for the benefit of a different child provided sufficient notice is given (usually a minimum of one month).

   In the case of any payer other than a parent or guardian, a transfer of value for inheritance tax would arise. If the right of surrender was waived at the outset, any liability would arise at the start of the plan. However, if the right to surrender was retained, the chargeable transfer would not be deemed to arise until the time when the first term's payment of school fees was made (the amount of the transfer would be equivalent to the surrender value of the plan at that time).

Where a donor gives the money to the parent who then takes out the plan as bare trustee for the child, the gift would be treated as a potentially exempt transfer.

Fixed interest schemes
Fixed interest schemes are provided from the purchase of suitable fixed interest investments such as gilt-edged securities, corporation stocks and national savings certificates. It may also be possible to make use of any existing investments. The purpose of the scheme is to ensure as far as possible that the investments mature shortly before the necessary funds are required to pay the school fees.

The choice of the particular investments will very much depend on the net returns provided after taxation has been taken into account and the suitability of the maturity dates of the investments so as to coincide with the dates when the school fees fall due.

Fixed interest schemes offer the following main advantages.

(a) The investment returns provided are often competitive compared to other methods of school fees provision, but this will depend on market conditions at the time.
(b) The schemes are generally very flexible with the investments not being restricted for education purposes if circumstances should change.

The main disadvantages of fixed interest schemes are as follows.

(a) In order to prepare a worthwhile scheme, considerable time may have to be involved in making the detailed calculations etc. required.
(b) The schemes are generally cumbersome in operation particularly as:
    (i)   the investments will usually produce relatively small amounts of income which would then need to be reinvested and declared for taxation purposes;
    (ii) in practice, it is often not possible to purchase suitable investments which mature shortly before the time when the termly school fees become due. As a result, two courses of action are usually open, neither of which is ideal.
        Firstly, an investment could be purchased which matures sometime before the school fees are required, in which case the investment proceeds would normally be temporarily reinvested.
        Alternatively, the investment purchased would mature after the date when the school fees were due so that it would become necessary to sell the investment before maturity. Consequently, the exact sales proceeds would not be known in advance.

Temporary annuities, etc. used to fund suitable life policies and savings plans
Capital may also be applied for school fees purposes to purchase a temporary annuity or other suitable funding medium which will provide the required amounts to pay the premiums for appropriate life policies. The maturity proceeds from the life policies can then be used to pay the school fees. Unit trust and investment trust regular savings plans and regular investments in personal equity plans can be funded in a similar way. (The main types of life policies which may be suitable for this purpose, unit trust and investment trust regular savings plans and a series of personal equity plans are discussed later in this chapter.)

Funding from income

Unless the school fees are paid directly out of income as they fall due, it will usually be necessary for the payments to be spread over a period longer than the period of education. It is therefore normally worthwhile, wherever practicable, for appropriate action to be taken at the earliest possible date, not only to prevent the payment period extending beyond the time the child leaves school or university, but also to minimise the cost involved.

Consideration should also be given to the position should the main source of income cease. This could arise if the provider was to die early, become disabled or be made redundant.

The following are the principal methods of planning school fees out of income:

(a) life assurance schemes;
(b) unit trust and investment trust regular savings plans;
(c) a series of personal equity plans;
(d) deferred annuities through an educational trust.

Life assurance schemes
Although there are several different types of qualifying life assurance policies available, they all enable the proceeds to be received with no personal liability to income tax and capital gains tax provided that premiums are payable for a minimum period of ten years (or three-quarters of the term, if less, in the case of an endowment type policy). Accordingly, where premiums are started in sufficient time for them to be paid for the above period before the school fees commence, the policies outlined below would normally be most suitable.

(a) A series of endowment with profits policies maturing in successive years over the period of the child's education at a senior school. This method has the advantage of generally providing a competitive return, particularly for higher rate taxpayers, with scope to receive increasing maturity proceeds each year in order to cover the higher education costs due to inflation, etc.
(b) Flexible endowment policies where it is required to retain the option as to when the policy proceeds should be received. However, this flexibility does not come without cost, and therefore these policies are in general less attractive than the more normal endowment with profits policies.
(c) Unit-linked policies (such as maximum investment plans) using the tax free income facility available after ten years. Where a policy is used for school fees purposes, it is usually expedient that it should be linked to a stable fund rather than to a volatile fund.

Premiums in respect of the above policies can sometimes be arranged to start at a lower level than is normal, then rise in future years as, hopefully, the parents' income also increases.

Where there is insufficient time for premiums to be paid for the minimum qualifying period before the school fees fall due, it may be worthwhile to obtain loans from the insurance company against the surrender value of the policy in order to pay the school fees. The loans would then be repaid out of the policy proceeds at maturity.

It is therefore important at the outset to obtain a positive commitment from the insurance company that loans will be made together with the relevant terms and conditions.

If there are any existing life assurance policies, it may be possible that these could also be used for school fees provision. (It may also be possible to use a personal pension policy and take the benefits from age 50 in order to provide capital and income for the payment of the school fees. However, this would not normally be advisable unless the individual was able to make use of the higher contribution limits in order to catch up and provide for his retirement at a later date.)

An important advantage of using life policies as a method of providing for school fees is that if circumstances should change, the policies can be applied for other purposes without any loss being suffered. In addition, the death benefit provided would normally be available to pay the school fees should the parents die prematurely.

Unit trust and investment trust regular savings plans
These plans, which were discussed in Chapter 3, represent direct investments into unit trusts and investment trusts on a regular (usually monthly) basis. They have many of the characteristics of unit-linked life policies investing in equities, although the taxation position is different. As no life cover is provided, consideration should be given to effecting a separate term assurance policy in order to safeguard the future provision of fees in the event of the early death of the parents.

Unit trust savings plans provide even greater flexibility than unit-linked life policies and may be terminated at any time without penalty. They are also likely in many cases to produce results superior to those of a life policy investing in the same unit trust (see Chapter 8). However, it is generally expedient for the savings plan to be linked to a general unit trust rather than to a more volatile trust. This should reduce the risk of the plan having a very low value at the time the monies are required to pay the school fees.

Allowance should be made for capital gains tax which may arise on the sale of the units or investment trust shares.

A series of personal equity plans
As stated in Chapter 5, a UK resident aged 18 or over may invest up to £4,800 pa in a personal equity plan (PEP). The investments of a PEP must be in ordinary shares in UK incorporated companies quoted on a UK stock exchange or dealt with on the Unlisted Securities Market. However, a person is allowed to invest up to £2,400 pa into unit trust and investment trust plans, with the normal tax advantages applicable to PEPs. Like unit-linked life policies and regular savings plans, it is preferable that the choice of underlying investments should be conservative so as to reduce the risk of the PEP having a very low value at the time the school fees become due. A separate term assurance policy should be considered as life cover is not provided under the PEP.

A series of PEPs is a very tax efficient method of providing for school fees since there is no tax to pay either on capital gains or on dividend income. Consequently, if an individual decides to arrange a unit trust or investment trust regular savings plan, this is likely to be more advantageous within, rather than outside, a PEP. However, as previously mentioned, any PEP should normally be regarded as a medium to long term investment.

Deferred annuities through an educational trust
Under this scheme, premiums are usually paid monthly until the final term in which the fees are needed with each premium purchasing a guaranteed level of fees provided by way of a deferred annuity arranged through an educational trust. This method may be useful for higher rate taxpayers where there is only a short period before the school fees commence.

Funding from other sources

Apart from meeting the costs of school fees from his own capital or income, the following are other sources which may be available to a parent.

(a) Dispositions from a grandparent or other relative. If the disposition was to be by way of a lump sum, it may be appropriate for an accumulation and maintenance trust or a discretionary trust to be formed. The trustees could then make the necessary payments from the trust at the relevant times.

(b) From the parent's company. Where the parent is a director of a private company and has a credit balance on his director's current account, it may be possible to withdraw this for school fees purposes.

(c) From loans. Although there are several methods by which borrowings can be made to pay for school fees, the interest on the loan would not normally be allowed as an expense for tax purposes. However, the following ways may be particularly suitable in the appropriate circumstances.

   (i)   If the parent owned his own business, it may be possible for him to increase his drawings and then arrange a loan to replenish working capital. Tax relief would then be obtained indirectly on the amounts withdrawn to meet the school fees.

   (ii) If the parent could not afford the cost of both personal pension contributions and school fees, it may be worthwhile for him to pay the contributions and then arrange a loan under the pension policy. As a result, tax relief would effectively be allowed on the contributions against his highest income tax rates payable even though relief would not be obtained on the loan interest paid.

   (iii) If the parent lived in a house with no mortgage or only a relatively small mortgage, it may be possible for him to move house and obtain a larger mortgage up to £30,000 with tax relief allowed on the interest paid.

(d) By moving to a house with a lower value. If this was done, capital could be released for the payment of school fees. However, if this was the only possible resort available to the parent, he may consider that the private education route was not worthwhile.

Conclusion

For many parents, considerable sacrifices will have to be made in order to send their children to private schools. These sacrifices, however, can often be mitigated by making the best use of the facilities that exist in the given circumstances. In particular, it should be remembered that:

(a) while best results will generally be achieved by early action which should be taken as soon as possible after the child is born, even a late contribution would usually be worthwhile;

(b) a well-designed scheme will have a considerable amount of in-built flexibility — this is of the utmost importance due to the uncertainties that may lie ahead.

13. Wills

Intestacy

Although many people delay in making a will, the consequences of this can be very serious. If a person dies without having made a will (approximately 65% of the population do this), his estate will be distributed according to the laws of intestacy, subject to post-death variation (see Appendix 3). The main disadvantages of dying intestate are as follows.

(a) The estate may not necessarily be distributed in accordance with the individual's wishes.
(b) The appointed administrators may not be those whom the individual would have chosen.
(c) It may take longer for the estate to be distributed. When a will has been made, an executor can take up his duties immediately after the death occurs.
(d) The costs may be greater.
(e) There may be an unnecessary inheritance tax liability.
(f) Children will receive capital automatically at the age of eighteen; it may be the individual's wish that capital should be paid at a later age.
(g) A testamentary guardian cannot be appointed for young children.
(h) Trusts may arise under an intestacy which can produce complications, including statutory restrictions on the trustees' power to invest and advance capital. These restraints might be particularly onerous where the estate has shares in private companies.

The need for professional advice

In order to avoid the danger of having a will which does not reflect the intentions of the testator, or having a will which proves to be invalid, it is essential that its wording should be clear and precise. Consequently, it is generally advisable that the will should be drawn up by a solicitor and other professional advice obtained where appropriate, e.g. to minimise inheritance tax. In this way, the following common mistakes should be avoided:

(a) failure to dispose of all the estate, resulting in partial intestacy;
(b) specific gifts that are free of tax could dissolve the residuary estate;
(c) gifts being made to witnesses or their spouses (these are legally ineffective and therefore the person concerned would not be able to receive his or her legacy);
(d) alterations being made to the will at or before the time it is signed without being authenticated and therefore having uncertain validity;
(e) no consideration being given to the possibility of a beneficiary dying before the testator;

(f) failure to consider the effects of the testator's divorce and/or remarriage;
(g) being unaware of a dependant's rights to make a claim against the estate if reasonable financial provision has not been made for him;
(h) failure to appreciate that the word 'children' includes legitimate, illegitimate and adopted children but not normally step-children.

Important matters before drawing up a will

The following are some important matters which should be attended to before a will is drawn up.

(a) Consideration given to the disposal of the body on death, including the bequest of any particular part for scientific research, etc.
(b) Agreement obtained of the persons to act as executors and trustees.
(c) If there are young children, consideration given to the appointment of a guardian (and his consent obtained) to cover the event of the testator's early death. This is particularly important if only one parent is still alive.
(d) An estimate made of the value of the estate by calculating the market value of assets and deducting any liabilities. A list of these assets would also be desirable. (Appendix 4 is a detailed 'dying tidily' log which should be completed and filed with the individual's private papers.)
(e) Preparation of a list of the persons (including charities) to benefit under the will, showing any particular assets to be passed to specific beneficiaries.
(f) Trust provisions regarding beneficiaries, including the powers given to the trustees.
(g) Consideration given as to whom the assets should pass if a beneficiary dies before the testator.
(h) Where a testator owns property overseas, it is preferable that this should be dealt with by a will drawn up under the terms of the local law. Care is required that it should not inadvertently be revoked when making a new UK will.

Executors

The responsibility of an executor is to carry out the wishes of the deceased and deal with the distribution of his estate. This can involve arranging the funeral and generally taking over the deceased's affairs, including being responsible for the payment of all taxes due. The executor should also take immediate possession of any valuables in order to secure their safety and should arrange insurance where appropriate. Although his responsibility commences from the time the deceased dies, it will still generally be necessary for the will to be proved and his appointment confirmed by a grant of probate.

The choice of an executor, who may also be a beneficiary, is very important as a considerable amount of work and responsibility may be involved. The following matters should be borne in mind before an appointment is made.

(a) It is often advantageous for co-executors to act such as the spouse (or if not alive, a friend or relative) together with a person in professional practice, e.g. an accountant or solicitor.

(b) An executor should preferably be younger than the testator.
(c) It is often worthwhile to include a substitute executor in the event of the appointed executor dying before the testator or being unwilling or unable to act.
(d) If the will includes a trust, it will usually be expedient for the trustees to be the same persons as the executors. The testator should ensure that the executors know his wishes and can be relied upon to carry them out.
(e) The will can be written so that the final decision as to the distribution of the estate is postponed until after the death itself. The executors can then make a decision based on all the circumstances. This type of will (known as a discretionary will) is only suitable if the testator is confident of the executors' judgement.

Variations and disclaimers

At the present time, a beneficiary can effectively redirect any of the assets received under a will to another person within two years of the deceased's death. This is effected by means of a written variation with an election being made to the Inland Revenue within six months of the date of the variation.

Variation of a will can be particularly appropriate where the deceased may have gifted the entire estate to his widow without having made use of the inheritance tax nil rate band, or where the beneficiary does not wish to receive the inheritance. A variation is also possible under an intestacy.

While similar in many respects to a variation, a disclaimer has several important differences. These would include the following.

(a) Under a disclaimer, the beneficiary can merely disclaim or waive his entitlement without making any election to the Inland Revenue. Accordingly, the terms of the will or intestacy would need to be examined in order to discover who benefits in lieu. In the case of a variation, the assets can pass as agreed, e.g. a widow who has benefited under her husband's will can effectively rewrite it to benefit the children.
(b) A disclaimer must relate to the whole gift, whereas a variation can be made either in respect of the whole or only part of it.
(c) In the case of a disclaimer, the beneficiary must not have received any previous benefits from the gift, e.g. receipt of income. However, for a variation, this has no relevance as any benefit received is treated as belonging to the beneficiary up to the date of the variation.
(d) Although both a disclaimer and a variation can be made at any time within two years of the deceased's death, it will only be made retrospective to that time in the case of a disclaimer.

Variations and disclaimers can be very helpful in both capital gains tax and inheritance tax planning mainly due to changing circumstances, especially tax, and to the testator not always being aware of the wishes of the various beneficiaries. However, that said, their use would arise less often if the will had been properly prepared at the outset. They should also not be regarded as a substitute for proper estate planning.

Due to the increasing use of variations as an inheritance tax avoidance device, the Government has stated that legislation might be introduced in 1990 in order to counter abuse.

Other matters

Other matters with regard to wills which should be borne in mind are as follows.

(a) The will should be kept in a safe place such as in a bank or with a solicitor and the executors advised of its location.
(b) Marriage (or remarriage) will automatically revoke a will unless it states that it was made in expectation of that particular marriage.
(c) Divorce (i.e. decree absolute) automatically disinherits the spouse from receiving any defined interest unless the will specifically states that this should not happen. In the same way, it prevents the spouse from acting as executor or trustee as appointed by the will.
(d) The will should be reviewed at regular intervals (say not less than every five years) in order to take into account changes in the testator's circumstances and in tax legislation.
(e) If a person wishes to alter his will, this is usually possible by way of a codicil. However, in almost all cases it is preferable for a new will to be made which would reflect the required changes.

Note: This chapter has been written based on the law in England and Wales. It should be remembered that the position may be different in Scotland and Northern Ireland.

14. Trusts

Trusts, in various forms, have been in existence for centuries. However, the concept is strange to many people and the uses of trusts, particularly following recent changes in tax legislation, are not widely appreciated. The principal purpose of this chapter is to discuss some of the terms of English trust law, the differences between the various types of trust, and the uses to which the more common forms of trust can be put.

What is a trust?

A trust is a separate legal entity, usually set up with a formal document or under a will. Trusts are often referred to as 'settlements' and for all practical purposes the two words are interchangeable. There are five main constituents of a trust:
(a) the settlor – the person who sets up the trust, usually by gifting assets to;
(b) the trustees – the people (usually two, three or four in number) in whose names the assets are registered and who control them in accordance with the terms of;
(c) the trust document – the legal document which instructs the trustees how to administer and distribute;
(d) the trust fund – the assets of the trust, including the original property given to the trustees, and assets transferred to the trustees subsequently, the capital growth on the assets, and any income retained by the trustees on behalf of;
(e) the beneficiaries – the people, whether specifically named or not, who can benefit from the trust fund under the terms of the trust document.

Thus, although the trustees have legal ownership of the trust assets, they have no personal interest in them, unless they are also beneficiaries of the trust.

Trusts are used in a wide variety of situations, including charities, employees, pension schemes, life assurance policies and the maintenance of historic buildings. However, this chapter is limited to the use of trusts for the financial benefit of an individual's family and friends.

The settlor
The settlor often wishes to dispose of capital for the benefit of the members of his family, but for practical reasons may not wish them to have outright control of the capital. Examples of this are as follows:

(a) the settlor does not wish to lose control of the capital;
(b) the beneficiaries might be children or young adults;
(c) the settlor may not know specifically who he wants to benefit;
(d) the beneficiaries might not have the experience, time, or ability to look after the capital;

(e) the settlor might wish to protect the capital in the event of a bad marriage, a death or a bankruptcy.

The settlor can himself be a beneficiary of a trust, but there are no tax benefits in this case. Indeed, there can be tax disadvantages, particularly in connection with the reservation of benefit rule.

The trustees

Although the trustees have to administer and distribute the trust fund in accordance with the terms of the trust document, in modern trusts they are usually given very wide discretionary powers. It is therefore important that trustees are chosen carefully. The settlor cannot directly impose his wishes on the trustees, but in practice he can strongly influence them by:

(a) making himself a trustee (normally the first named);
(b) writing a 'wish letter' to the trustees at the time of setting up the trust;
(c) reserving to himself the power to appoint new trustees, and sometimes to remove existing trustees.

Although trustees have to act unanimously, where votes on a company's share register are concerned, these are exercisable only by the first named trustee.

The role of a trustee can sometimes be onerous, particularly in the cases of larger complex trusts or where trustees might have to make difficult choices in dealing with beneficiaries who are close members of the family. For this reason, the appointment of an independent professional trustee can often be advantageous. Unless they are professionals, it is not usual for trustees to be paid for acting as such.

The trust document

Trusts can be set up either during the settlor's lifetime or under the terms of a will on death. Trusts set up during lifetime are often referred to as 'settlements', those under a will as 'trusts'.

It is not essential to have any written trust document at all. However, without this, the trustees are extremely limited in the way they can act, and doubts can arise in later years as to what the settlor intended. For maximum flexibility, it is advisable to have a modern form of trust document drafted by a solicitor who has a good working knowledge of trusts.

Trust documents tend to be lengthy and are often difficult to understand. Much of the text is of a technical nature and deals with the various powers given to the trustees. As a guide, the legal costs involved in setting up a trust often range from £250 to £1,000, depending on complexity and the variations required from standard documents.

Depending on the type of trust (see below), a good modern trust document will generally give the trustees wide discretionary powers including:

(a) the extent to which a potential beneficiary will benefit from the trust, if at all;
(b) the age at which a beneficiary will benefit;
(c) the power to invest the trust fund in any form of investment, whether or not producing income, including the purchase of a house for a beneficiary;
(d) the power to set up subsidiary trusts for beneficiaries;
(e) the power to borrow and lend.

Unless the trustees act fraudulently, they are usually protected from any personal financial liability.

The trust fund

A trust is often set up with a nominal amount of say £100, and further capital is usually gifted subsequently. The trust fund consists of two elements:

(a) capital – the original and subsequent gifts, plus any growth on the assets;
(b) income – income arising on the capital assets. Except in the case of interest in possession trusts (see below), if income is not distributed to beneficiaries, it is accumulated in the fund, usually by way of transfer to capital.

As mentioned above, the trustees are usually given extremely wide powers to invest in any form of asset. These can include land, life assurance policies, shares in family companies, paintings and overseas assets. In some cases, there may be restrictions on the particular type of asset in which an investment can be made, e.g. building society accounts.

The beneficiaries

Other than in specific types of trust, e.g. those set up under The Married Women's Property Act 1882, there is no restriction on who can be a beneficiary of a trust. The person does not need to be specifically named in the trust document, but does need to be in a specified class of beneficiary, e.g. grandchildren. However, in some cases, it is possible to add a beneficiary where he was not originally included. Many trust documents provide for substitution, so that in the event of a beneficiary dying, his children acquire his interest in the trust fund.

Depending on the type of trust, trustees are often given the maximum flexibility in deciding to what extent, if at all, a potential beneficiary should benefit from the trust fund, both in terms of annual income and capital.

Where appropriate, children can benefit from trusts from the day they are born, often with significant income tax advantages. It is usual to defer the age of majority for trust purposes from 18 to 21 or even 25.

Tax position of trusts

Setting up a trust

Recent changes in tax legislation have made it extremely cheap in terms of tax to set up a trust. It may not be necessary for capital gains tax to be paid on the transfer of certain assets to a trust (see Chapter 10) as the trustees would in these cases be deemed to acquire the assets at the original cost to the settlor. Stamp duty on gifts has been abolished (apart from a nominal 50p in some cases). The present inheritance tax legislation is comparatively liberal and the exemptions reasonable. In the larger cases, where tax liabilities do arise, they are likely to be substantially less than they would ultimately be if no action was taken.

Provided gifts are not deferred until too late in life (at least seven years before death), a husband and wife can dispose of substantial amounts of capital, even more so where business assets are concerned, without paying large amounts of inheritance tax. By the use of trusts, they can often at the same time keep effective control over the assets.

The trust
(a) Inheritance tax (IHT) – The extent to which there is a liability to IHT on the creation or during the life of a trust depends upon the particular type of trust (see below).
(b) Income tax – Generally, when a trust has been created, income which arises from the assets put into trust is treated for all purposes as the income of the trustees. This is completely separate and independent of their own personal tax affairs, and that of the settlor. The main exceptions to this rule are where the settlor has included himself or his wife as a beneficiary, and where income is distributed to the settlor's children while they are under the age of 18 and unmarried.

The tax liability on the income of the trust again depends upon the type of trust. However, where a beneficiary has a right to income, the trust will pay tax at the basic rate (25% in 1989/90). If the beneficiary himself is liable to tax at the higher rate (40% in 1989/90), he will be responsible personally for the extra tax on his trust income.

If the beneficiary has no right to income, but its amount is determined at the discretion of the trustees, the trust pays tax on its income at 35%. However, where income is distributed, it is deemed to have suffered tax at 35%, and if the beneficiary himself is liable to tax at below 35%, he can recover the excess. Thus, a child who does not have any other income, can recover the whole of the tax suffered by the trust on the income distributed to him to the extent of the single person's tax allowance (£2,785 in 1989/90). If the beneficiary pays higher rate tax, the extra tax is payable on the income received.

(c) Capital gains tax – Trustees are liable to capital gains tax on realised gains (less losses), subject to both indexation and an annual exemption (normally the first £2,500 of any gains in a year). The rate of capital gains tax depends upon the particular type of trust but basically the gains of trustees are chargeable to capital gains tax at the same rate as they pay income tax. As mentioned earlier in this chapter, it may be possible for a gain arising on the transfer of specific assets into a trust to be deferred. Similarly, it may be possible for a gain arising on specific assets leaving a trust, which is also subject to a tax charge, to be deferred.

Types of trust

There are five main types of trust which are described below:

(a) interest in possession trusts;
(b) voluntary settlements;
(c) accumulation and maintenance settlements;
(d) discretionary trusts;
(e) bare trusts.

Interest in possession trusts (also known as life interest or fixed interest trusts)
General description   In broad terms, an 'interest in possession' is defined as a right to receive the income arising from trust assets. Thus, an interest in possession trust is where the income arising on the trust capital is payable to a named beneficiary, the life tenant, usually for his lifetime. The beneficiary may

also have the use of the property within the trust if, for example, a house was settled upon trust giving the beneficiary the right to occupy it for his lifetime. The capital remains under the trustees' control and on the death of the life tenant (or early termination of his interest), the capital can pass to other beneficiaries (the remaindermen) as specified in the trust document (or, if the trust document permits, to those nominated by the life tenant).

The trustees are often given a discretionary power to advance capital to the life tenant.

Uses   Interest in possession trusts are most suited where beneficiaries are over the age of 25 years and where a settlor does not wish to pass outright ownership of assets to them, but wishes the beneficiaries to enjoy the income on the assets. Such trusts are particularly useful:

(a) where shares in family companies are involved, since any voting rights remain with the trustees;
(b) where the settlor considers the beneficiary might not want the responsibility or be able to look after the capital;
(c) where the settlor wishes to protect the capital in the event of, say, a bad marriage or the premature death of a son or daughter;
(d) where the settlor wishes to remove an asset from his estate and yet does not wish the beneficiary to be entitled to the capital until his (the settlor's) death;
(e) where the settlor wishes to create an IHT free fund payable on his death, which can be used by the beneficiaries to pay the IHT due, or to replace the IHT paid from the estate.

Tax position
(a) Inheritance tax — Transfers by an individual into an interest in possession trust do not attract a charge to inheritance tax on the making of a gift, provided that the settlor survives seven years from that time. Similarly, on most transfers from interest in possession trusts (such as the life tenant surrendering his interest in favour of another individual), no charge arises if the transferor survives seven years.

On death of a life tenant, a charge to IHT arises as the life tenant is deemed to own the underlying trust assets on which he has been receiving income. On such occasion, tax is chargeable at the full rate.
(b) Income tax — The trustees pay income tax at the basic rate, either direct to the Inland Revenue (for example on rental income), or by deduction at source (on dividends etc.). After deducting expenses, the trust income is added to the beneficiary's other income, and if he is liable to the higher rate of tax, the beneficiary pays the extra tax. If the beneficiary does not have sufficient income to cover his personal tax allowance, he can obtain a tax repayment.
(c) Capital gains tax — The rate of capital gains tax for this type of trust is 25% and generally the first £2,500 of gains made during a tax year are exempt.

Voluntary settlements
General description   Any settlement made without consideration, including a settlement which an individual makes for his own benefit by transferring assets to trustees, who then pay the income to him during his lifetime, with the capital remaining in trust, normally for his children.

Uses　Voluntary settlements are used when the individual wishes to protect himself from wasting his own capital or where he does not want the responsibility of managing it. Voluntary settlements can be particularly useful if the settlor is non-resident for a period.

Tax position　Although no IHT liability arises on the transfer of funds to the trustees, or from the trustees to the settlor, there are no tax advantages in such trusts. The settlor is assessed to tax on the trust income and gains as if he continued to own the trust assets. In addition, the settled property remains part of the settlor's estate for IHT purposes.

Accumulation and maintenance settlements
General description　Accumulation and maintenance settlements are normally established for the maintenance, education and benefit of children or grand-children under the age of 25, including those not yet born. While the children are under that age, the trustees may be able to accumulate income, i.e. add it to trust capital, or it can be used to pay the children's living expenses (such payments would normally be made to a beneficiary's parent or guardian while the children are minors). Capital may also be advanced to a beneficiary at the discretion of the trustees. Trustees can be given complete discretion over the allocation of both capital and income between beneficiaries while they are under the age of 25. Thereafter, trustees can retain control of the capital, paying only income to a beneficiary, but reserving the right to advance capital to him at any time.

Uses　These settlements are mainly of use to a parent or grandparent who wishes to benefit his issue under the age of 25, both during their minority and in later years. They are also very beneficial in tax planning, for example where a grandparent wishes to provide funds to meet school fees, or where a parent wants to give to his children shares in the family company, but does not know at the time which children will take an active interest in the company. Accumulation and maintenance settlements provide maximum flexibility, without the IHT charge normally associated with interest in possession or discretionary trusts.

Tax position
(a) Inheritance tax — A gift by an individual into an accumulation and maintenance settlement is treated in the same way as an outright gift to another individual and qualifies as a potentially exempt transfer, i.e. no IHT is chargeable on the gift if the settlor survives for seven years. These settlements are also not liable to tax when a beneficiary becomes entitled to capital or income and are not subject to a ten-year charge as in the case of discretionary trusts (see below).
(b) Income tax — Income is subject to both basic rate tax and additional rate tax (currently 10%) in the trustees' hands. However, when income is distributed to beneficiaries at the trustees' discretion, it carries a tax credit of 35% which, depending on the tax position of the beneficiary, may be recoverable, either in whole or in part, or further tax may be payable. Where a beneficiary is specifically entitled to income, e.g. where he is over the age of 25, the trustees are liable only to basic rate tax, with an equivalent tax credit to the beneficiary.
(c) Capital gains tax — Until such time as the beneficiary is specifically entitled to income, the rate of capital gains tax for these types of trusts is 35%, i.e. the

rate equivalent to the sum of the basic rate and the additional rate. Once a beneficiary becomes entitled to income, e.g. at the age of 25, the rate of tax on the underlying capital is 25%. The first £2,500 of gains made during a year are generally exempt from tax.

Discretionary trusts
General description A discretionary trust is one set up for a number of designated beneficiaries or classes of beneficiaries, in which distributions of capital and income during the trust period are entirely at the discretion of the trustees. The trustees have no obligation to distribute income to all beneficiaries and, subject to certain restrictions, any income not distributed can be retained in the trust fund.

Uses Discretionary trusts are very flexible and can be used in a number of different situations, including the following:

(a) where a settlor wishes to give away capital to his family but does not know at the time who he wants to benefit;
(b) where the settlor wishes one class of beneficiary to receive income, e.g. grandchildren, but another class to receive capital;
(c) where one spouse wishes to pass capital to the next generation, but wants the surviving spouse to have the opportunity of receiving income and/or capital if required.

Tax position
(a) Inheritance tax — Although discretionary trusts are the most flexible type of trust, they are the least favourable for IHT purposes. Subject to the amount of any previous gift, the creation of a discretionary trust attracts a charge to IHT if the value of the assets gifted exceeds the amount of the nil rate band, currently £118,000. A further charge, generally at very low rates of tax, may be made on capital distributions from such settlements or on each tenth anniversary of their existence. The latter (generally known as the 'periodic charge') is subject to a maximum of 6% of the capital value of the trust.
(b) Income tax — Income is subject to both basic rate tax and additional rate tax in the trustees' hands. However, when income is distributed at the trustees' discretion to beneficiaries, it carries a tax credit of 35% which, depending on the tax position of a beneficiary, may be recoverable either in whole or in part, or further tax may be payable.
(c) Capital gains tax — The rate of capital gains tax for discretionary trusts is 35%. The first £2,500 of gains made during a year are generally exempt from tax.

Bare trusts
General description Assets transferred to a bare trust are held by trustees for a named beneficiary who has an absolute and unconditional title to both the capital and the income. In effect, the transfer is an outright gift with the trustees holding assets in name only; the beneficiary can insist at any time that the assets are transferred to him.

Uses   Generally, a bare trust is used when an individual wishes to make a gift to a minor child, an overseas beneficiary or an elderly beneficiary who has difficulty in managing his own affairs.

Tax position
(a) Inheritance tax — Assets held in bare trusts are deemed for IHT purposes to belong to the beneficiary and offer no additional tax advantages over outright gifts.
(b) Income tax — The income on the assets is assessed on the beneficiary and taxed at his appropriate rate of tax. Tax difficulties can arise when a parent transfers assets into a bare trust for his own children if they are under age 18 and unmarried.
(c) Capital gains tax — Gains of trustees will be assessed on the beneficiary and taxed at his appropriate rate of tax.

Non resident trusts

A popular way of holding investments is via a non resident trust. Its inheritance tax treatment is the same as for a resident trust but it has capital gains tax advantages and also sometimes income tax advantages.

Tax position
(a) Income tax — If the settlor or his wife cannot benefit from the trust, foreign income can be accumulated free of UK income tax by the trust.
(b) Capital gains tax — For capital gains tax purposes, a settlement will be non resident if the trustees, or a majority of them, are not resident in the UK and the administration of the trust is carried out abroad. The effect of such non residence is that disposals of assets by the trustees which would normally be subject to capital gains tax, would only give rise to a liability on the beneficiary in the following case. If the beneficiary is resident in the UK and receives payments of capital out of the trust which broadly represent capital gains, he would be liable to capital gains tax. Therefore, if the trustees reinvest such gains, whether in UK assets or overseas assets, it is possible to defer capital gains tax indefinitely (it is also possible to entirely avoid capital gains tax if the beneficiary whom it is desired to benefit ceases to be resident and ordinarily resident in the UK and then receives such payments of capital out of the trust).

It is seldom advisable to set up a non resident trust, unless substantial tax savings can be achieved, as its administration must be in a tax haven in order to avoid local tax. Management expenses also can be very high.

Trusts and life assurance policies

Life assurance policies are frequently set up in the form of a trust in order to provide a fund outside the estate of the settlor to pay IHT on his death. Usually the settlor will pay all the premiums. If the premiums are large, to ensure they are PETs where they are paid to an accumulation and maintenance settlement or interest in possession trust, the cash should be gifted to the trustees who should pay the premiums. Where the assured is the settlor, a fund can be built up outside his estate with no tax payable on his death. At that time, the fund can be used by the beneficiaries to pay IHT, allowing the assets of the estate to be distributed intact.

Where the trust is in the form of an interest in possession trust, it will often provide that any proceeds can be advanced to the beneficiaries absolutely to enable the tax to be paid. If the trust is in the form of an accumulation and maintenance settlement, the power to advance capital, before or after the beneficiaries attain age 25, will generally provide sufficient flexibility to enable any policy proceeds to be used to fund the payment of inheritance tax. However, the trustees of neither trust can compel the beneficiaries to use the monies to pay IHT, nor can the trustees pay it on behalf of such beneficiaries.

Modern day use of trusts

Modern trusts are normally very flexible and are used for a wide variety of purposes. A large proportion of the country's wealth is held upon trust, for example pension funds and unit trusts. Family trusts have played an important part in personal financial planning for a considerable time and with today's complex tax legislation, they are now even more useful.

Family trusts are used for many purposes in tax planning, but their principal purpose is not in tax mitigation, but the retention of wealth within the family and the management of capital and income for beneficiaries. However, significant tax advantages are usually available.

There is generally a trust suitable for most situations but, before creating a trust, it is usually essential to seek professional advice from an adviser who is experienced in current trust law and taxation.

Appendix 1. Personal financial planning questionnaire

Date

1. Personal details

Name (in full) (Mr/Mrs/Miss)

Address   Date of birth

Occupation   Retirement age

Name of spouse (in full)   Date of birth

Occupation   Retirement age

Are you and spouse both UK residents?

Are you and spouse in good health?

Do you/spouse smoke?
If yes, please give details.

2. Family details

Names of children	Date of birth	Married or single	Ages of grand-children
(i)			
(ii)			
(iii)			
(iv)			

Are any children or grandchildren likely to marry shortly?

3. Requirements

Are you concerned to:
(a) Increase net income   YES/NO

(b) Increase value of assets   YES/NO

(c) Reduce potential inheritance tax   YES/NO

(d) Improve or provide a pension   YES/NO

(e) Other requirements (please specify)

What is your attitude to risk (on a scale of 1 to 5)?

Cautious = 1   Adventurous = 5

How experienced are you in respect of investments carrying risk?

Inexperienced = 1   Experienced = 5

4. Assets (estimated current values)

	Self £	*Spouse* £
House (private residence)		
Other houses, flats, etc.		
Business or share of partnership		

Investments (please give details separately):
(a) Bank deposit/current accounts
(b) Building society accounts
(c) National Savings
(d) Guaranteed income bonds/guaranteed growth bonds
(e) Fixed interest securities
(f) Ordinary stocks and shares (equities)
(g) Unit trusts
(h) Investment bonds
    (Please give details of withdrawals being taken)
(i) Private companies
    (Please state approximate % holdings
    including related holdings)
(j) Other investments

Chattels:
(a) Car/caravan/boat

(b) Antiques, jewellery, etc.

(c) Special items (e.g. works of art)

(d) Other domestic items

Other assets (please specify)

5. Liabilities

	Self £	*Spouse* £
Mortgages on: (a) Private residence		
(b) Other property		
Bank: (a) Overdraft (b) Loan accounts		
Other loans/credit cards		
Taxation		
Other liabilities (please specify)		
Do you anticipate any substantial capital expenditure? If yes, please give details	YES/NO	YES/NO

6. Gifts

Please give details, values and dates of all material gifts made by you
or spouse within the last seven years

Note: Please include details of any inheritance tax paid and exemptions used.

7. Trusts, settlements and inheritances

Are you/spouse a beneficiary of any trust?   YES/NO
If yes, please give details.

Are you/spouse likely to benefit in the future under any will?   YES/NO
If yes, please give details.

Are you/spouse a settlor or trustee of any trust?   YES/NO
If yes, please give details.

8. Wills

Have you and spouse made wills?   YES/NO
If yes, please state main provisions.

9. Income (please state gross income)

	Self £	*Spouse* £
Earned:		
Remuneration		
Business profits		
Pension:		
State		
Former employer(s)		
Self-employed pension/personal pension policies		
Other (please specify)		
Total earned income		

	Self £	*Spouse* £
Investment:		
Bank deposit/current account interest (grossed up)		
Building society interest (grossed up)		
National Savings		
Annuity and bond income:		
Taxable		
Non-taxable		
Fixed interest securities		
Ordinary stocks and shares (equities)		
Unit trusts		
Trust income		
Private companies		
Other (please specify)		
Total investment income	———	———
Total income	———	———
	═══	═══

Do you/spouse anticipate any substantial increase or
decrease in income?   YES/NO
If yes, please give details.

10. Expenditure

	Self £	*Spouse* £
Mortgage interest		
Bank interest:		
Overdraft		
Loan accounts		
Other charges		
Total expenditure	———	———
	═══	═══

Do you/spouse anticipate any substantial increase or
decrease in expenditure?   YES/NO
If yes, please give details.

11. Mortgage (if applicable)

Is mortgage repayable by:
  Capital and interest method

  Endowment policy

  Self-employed pension/personal pension policy

  Company pension arrangement

  Other method (please specify)

Name of building society, bank or other lender

Year of commencement

Original term

Outstanding mortgage £

Interest % payable

12. Life policies, permanent health policies and purchased life annuities

(a) Life policies

Date of commence-ment	Name of company	Life assured (and contractor if different)	Sum assured	Type of policy, e.g. whole life, endowment	With profits, without profits, unit-linked	Net premium payable (annual)	Term of policy (years)	To whom proceeds payable

(b) Permanent health policies

Date of commencement	Name of company	Name of insured	Benefit payable	Deferment period	Type of policy, e.g. level, index-linked	Previous renewal premium	Termination date	Special provisions

(c) Purchased life annuities

Date of purchase	Name of company	Purchase price	Gross annuity	Capital element	Income element	Term, e.g. life, no. of years	Type of annuity e.g. joint life and last survivor

13. Retirement provision

Employer's pension scheme (if applicable)
(a) What date did you commence with present employer?

(b) Are you a member of employer's pension scheme?   YES/NO

(c) What is the pension scheme retirement age?

(d) What is anticipated level of pension benefits on retirement?

(e) Does pension scheme provide for capital sum and widow's
        pension on death before retirement?   YES/NO
     If yes, at what level?

(f) Are you entitled to pension benefits from
        previous employments?   YES/NO
     If yes, please give details.

Self-employed pension/personal pension policies (if applicable)
(a) Have you made any self-employed pension/personal
        pension contributions?   YES/NO
     If yes, please give details.

(b) What are the current annual contributions payable
        and to which companies?

(c) Have you any unused relief available in respect of the
        previous six tax years?   YES/NO
     If yes, please give details.

(d) At what age do you anticipate taking pension benefits?

Does spouse have own pension arrangement?   YES/NO
If yes, please give details.

14. Other information

Please give details of any relevant information not already stated in this questionnaire.

Appendix 2. Minimum retirement ages for certain occupations

Retirement ages have been agreed by the Inland Revenue for self-employed persons or persons not in an occupational pension scheme in respect of the following professions and occupations.

Profession or occupation	*Retirement age*
Athletes (appearance and prize money)	35
Badminton players	35
Boxers	35
Cricketers	40
Cyclists	35
Dancers	35
Divers (saturation, deep sea and free swimming)	40
Footballers	35
Golfers (tournament earnings)	40
Jockeys — flat racing	45
— national hunt	35
Models	35
Motorcycle riders (motocross or road racing)	40
Motor racing drivers	40
Non-commissioned royal marine reservists	45
Rugby league players	35
Speedway riders	40
Squash players	35
Table tennis players	35
Tennis players (including real tennis)	35
Trapeze artistes	40
Wrestlers	35

Note:
The concession to take pension benefits at an early retirement age may be withdrawn if the individual changes his occupation but continues to contribute to the same policy. Therefore, when a change of occupation arises before benefits are taken, it may be worthwhile for the old policy to be made paid-up and a new policy effected for subsequent contributions.

Appendix 3. Distribution of an estate under an intestacy

A summary of the position in respect of the distribution of an estate under the laws of intestacy is shown below. It should be noted that the position in England and Wales differs in some respects from that in Northern Ireland and considerably so from that in Scotland.

ENGLAND AND WALES

If deceased dies leaving:

Persons who benefit:

1. *Spouse* but no issue, parent, brother or sister, nephew or niece

   1. *Spouse* takes everything absolutely.

2. *Spouse* and *issue*

   2. (a) *Spouse* takes £75,000 absolutely
      Plus personal chattels (car, furniture, pictures, clothing, jewellery, etc.)
      Plus life interest (income only) in half of residue.

      (b) *Issue* takes half residue on reaching age 18 or marrying before that age
      Plus, on death of spouse, the half residue in which the spouse had a life interest.

3. *Spouse*, no issue, but parent(s) or brother(s) or sister(s) or nephew(s) or niece(s)

   3. (a) *Spouse* takes £125,000 absolutely
      Plus personal chattels
      Plus half residue absolutely.

      (b) Parents, but if none, then brothers and sisters (nephews and nieces step into their parents' shoes if the latter are dead) take half residue.

4. *No spouse*

   4. Everything is taken by:
      (a) Issue; but if none:
      (b) Parents; but if none:

If deceased dies leaving:	Persons who benefit:
	(c) Brothers and sisters (nephews and nieces step into their parents' shoes if the latter are dead); but if none:
	(d) Half-brothers and half-sisters (or failing them, their own respective issue); but if none:
	(e) Grandparents; but if none:
	(f) Uncles and aunts (cousins step into their parents' shoes if the latter are dead); but if none:
	(g) Half-uncles and half-aunts (or failing them, their own respective issue); but if none:
	(h) The Crown.

Notes:
(a) 'Issue' is defined as children (including illegitimate and adopted children), grandchildren and so on. However, it does not include step-children.
(b) Where part of the residuary estate includes a dwelling-house in which the surviving spouse resided at the date of death, the spouse has the right to have the dwelling-house as part of the absolute interest or towards the capital value of the life interest under 2(a) and 3(a) above.

NORTHERN IRELAND

If deceased dies leaving:	Persons who benefit:
1. *Spouse* but no issue, parent, brother or sister, nephew or niece	1. *Spouse* takes everything absolutely.
2. *Spouse* and *issue*	2. (a) *Spouse* takes £75,000 absolutely Plus personal chattels (car, furniture, pictures, clothing, jewellery, etc.) Plus half of residue where only one child survives and one-third of residue where more than one child survives. If a child of the intestate predeceases him leaving children of his own, the surviving spouse takes the same share as if the child had survived the intestate.
	(b) *Issue* takes half or two-thirds of residue depending on whether one child or more than one child survives the intestate.

If deceased dies leaving:	Persons who benefit:
3. *Spouse*, no issue but parent(s) or brother(s) or sister(s) or nephew(s) or niece(s)	3. (a) *Spouse* takes £125,000 absolutely Plus personal chattels Plus half residue absolutely. (b) Parents, but if none then brothers and sisters and half-brothers and half-sisters, who are all treated equally (nephews and nieces step into their parents' shoes if the latter are dead) take half residue.
4. *No spouse*	4. Everything is taken by: (a) Issue; but if none: (b) Parents; but if none: (c) Brothers and sisters and half-brothers and half-sisters, who are all treated equally, (nephews and nieces step into their parents' shoes if the latter are dead); but if none: (d) Next of kin; but if none: (e) The Crown.

Notes:
(a) 'Issue' is defined as children (including illegitimate and adopted children), grandchildren and so on. However, it does not include step-children.
(b) Where part of the residuary estate includes a dwelling-house in which the surviving spouse resided at the date of death, the spouse has the right to have the dwelling-house as part of the absolute interest under 2(a) and 3(a) above.

SCOTLAND

Where a Scottish domiciled person dies intestate, certain rules come into operation which are intended to make provision for the surviving spouse and any issue of the deceased — these are known respectively as Prior Rights and Legal Rights. (Legal Rights also apply where the deceased person has left a valid will, and cannot be extinguished by that will.)

Prior Rights

The aim of Prior Rights (which take precedence over Legal Rights) is to ensure, where possible, that the widow/widower is left with a furnished house and a reasonable amount of money. These rights can only be claimed by a surviving spouse.

Divorced spouses have no claim on the deceased's property unless they benefit under a will.

Where a couple, not married to one another, have been cohabiting, the surviving partner may attempt to establish a claim by obtaining a Declarator of Marriage from the Court of Session (this may prove difficult to achieve). If successful, this would mean that the partner could then be treated as a spouse.

The following assets are affected by Prior Rights:

(a) the dwelling house;
(b) the furniture;
(c) money.

The dwelling house

The surviving spouse is entitled to ownership of the house in which he/she resided prior to the death of the other spouse and which was owned by the deceased. In certain circumstances, the spouse must take the value of the house in money instead of the property itself. This will usually be where the house forms part of a larger property, e.g. a farm and farmhouse. If the deceased owned more than one house at the date of death, the spouse has the choice, provided he/she lived in both regularly.

The value of the interest receivable in the house must not exceed £65,000. If it is worth more than this, the spouse is entitled to £65,000 in money in lieu.

The furniture

The surviving spouse is entitled to all the furnishings in a house up to the value of £12,000. The furniture, e.g. tables, chairs, beds, cooker, fridge, etc must have been owned by the deceased outright at the date of death and not held simply under a hire-purchase or credit agreement.

Personal items such as jewellery do not fall into this category. The right to the furniture is separate from the right to the house. Therefore, if the surviving spouse takes money instead of the property, this will not affect his/her right to furnishings.

Money

The surviving spouse is also entitled to a sum of money in addition to any money he/she received in lieu of the dwelling house. Where the deceased is survived only by a spouse but no children, the entitlement is £35,000. If there are surviving children, the entitlement is limited to £21,000.

Legal Rights

These are the rights that may be claimed by a surviving spouse and/or children, and are claimed out of the moveable part of the estate (property which can be moved — not land and houses). The amount granted under this right is dependent upon whether the deceased is survived by a spouse only, or by children only, or by both.

(a) If the spouse alone survives, his/her Legal Rights will amount to one half of the remainder of the moveable property after deduction of the debts, funeral expenses, a proportion of the expenses of administration and Prior Rights of money and furniture.
(b) If only children survive, they will be entitled to one half of the moveable estate divided equally between them. If the deceased parent has already

given a child a substantial gift during his/her lifetime, its value at that time may be offset against that child's entitlement to Legal Rights.
(c) If both the spouse and children survive, then the moveable estate, less Prior Rights so far as taken from the moveable estate, is divided into equal parts. One-third goes to the widow/widower, one-third is divided between the children and the remaining third is divided as part of the free estate (see below).

Note:
If a testator dies leaving a mortgaged house where the mortgage is secured by an insurance policy, the value of the policy has to be apportioned between the heritable and moveable estates for the purpose of calculating the Legal Rights entitlement.

Division of free estate

The remainder of the property (the free estate) is divided in the following manner.
  Everything is taken by:

(a) Issue, but if none:
(b) Parents and brothers or sisters (half to parents, half to brothers and sisters). If there are no parents, the brothers and sisters take the balance and if there are no brothers and sisters, then the parents take the balance. If there are no brothers and sisters or parents:
(c) The surviving spouse, but if none:
(d) Uncles and aunts or their descendants, but if none:
(e) Grandparents, but if none:
(f) Brothers and sisters of grandparents or their descendants, but if none:
(g) Remoter ancestors of the intestate, generation by generation successively, but if none:
(h) The Crown (if no relations can be found the Crown takes the estate as ultimate heir).

Notes:
(a) In Scottish law, 'issue' is defined as children (including illegitimate and adopted children), grandchildren and so on but not step-children (this is the same situation as in England and Wales and in Northern Ireland).
(b) In applying the rules relating to Prior Rights, Legal Rights and the division of the free estate, it should be noted that issue are entitled by representation to take the share of a parent who has died.

Appendix 4.   Dying tidily log

This log should be completed and filed with your private papers. Your next of kin (e.g. wife or husband) should be informed of its contents and location. This should assist considerably with the administration of your estate when the need arises.

INFORMATION RE ESTATE AND ASSETS OF:

Name

Address

Date of birth

National Health Number

National Insurance Number

---

1. Will

Date

Location

Executors — names, addresses, telephone nos.

Funeral wishes (e.g. burial, cremation, name of cemetery and plot number)

2. Professional advisers etc. (please state name, address and telephone number)

Doctor

Dentist

Solicitor

Accountant

Bank

Stockbroker

Insurance broker

H.M. Inspector of Taxes

    District

    Reference No.

Others

3. Assets

Main residence

Address

Ownership: sole, joint or as tenant in common

Subject to or free from mortgage

Mortgagee or lender

Address

Reference No.

Other properties

Address

Ownership: sole, joint or tenant in common

Subject to or free from mortgage

Mortgagee or lender

Address

Reference No.

Business or share of partnership

Investments (please state if held jointly)
    (a) Bank accounts and building society accounts
        Name and address of bank/building society

        Type of account

        Account No.

    (b) National Savings

    (c) Guaranteed income bonds/guaranteed growth bonds

    (d) Fixed interest securities

    (e) Ordinary stocks and shares (equities)

    (f) Unit trusts

    (g) Investment bonds

    (h) Private companies
        (state approximate % holdings including related holdings)

(i) Other investments

Assets held in trust

4. Liabilities

Bank overdraft arrangements

Loans

Other liabilities

5. Gifts

Please give details, values and dates of all material gifts made within the last seven years

Note: Please include details of any inheritance tax paid and exemptions used.

6. Pension and life assurance policies etc.

Name of Company	*Policy Number*	*Type of Policy*	*On whose life*	*Sum Assured*	*Names of Beneficiaries (if applicable)*	*Names of Trustees (if the policy is written subject to a trust)*

7. **Location of valuables**

(a) Property deeds

(b) Stock and share certificates, unit trust certificates, National Savings certificates, building society passbooks, etc.

(c) Pension and life assurance policies, etc.

(d) Contracts (e.g. hire purchase agreements, loan agreements, general insurance policies, etc.)

(e) Safe deposit box (if any)

(f) Safe deposit key (if any)

(g) Personal papers (e.g. birth certificates, marriage certificate, partnership agreement)

(h) Passports

(i) Bank statements

(j) Others (please specify)

8. Notifications required (in addition to those mentioned in earlier section)

    (a) Employer (state name, address and telephone number)

    0(b) Membership of occupational pension schemes (including former employers)

    (c) Department of Social Security

    (d) Deeds of covenant ceasing on death

    (e) Standing orders and direct debits

    (f) Credit cards/charge cards

        Name and address   *Number*

    (g) Trusteeships, executorships and guardianships held

    (h) Memberships of clubs and associations (please state name, address, membership number, etc.)

        Professional/trade associations

        Clubs

        Other organisations (e.g. AA, RAC)

(i) Honorary offices held

(j) Contracts

	With whom held	*Renewal date (if appropri- ate)*	*Where kept*
Hire purchase or loan			
General insurances			
House			
Contents			
Car			
Other general insurances			
Other contracts			

(k) Licences etc.

   Road fund licence (registration number and date of expiry)

   MOT certificate (registration number and date of expiry)

   Driving licence (serial number)

   TV licence (date of expiry)

   Other licences (please specify)

(l) Others

9. Other information

Please give details of any relevant information not already stated in this log.

Appendix 5. Keeping up to date

Keeping up to date with the constantly changing investment, pensions and life assurance markets, etc., as well as changes in legislation, is extremely time-consuming. Therefore, it is necessary to be very selective in the reading material chosen. The following list is intended as a guide.

Reading

Daily reading
(a) Good quality national newspaper*;
(b) Financial Times*;
(c) Literature from:
   Stockbrokers;
   Unit trusts;
   Insurance companies.

Weekly reading
(a) Investors Chronicle;
(b) Money Marketing*;
(c) Financial Adviser;
(d) Money Week.

Monthly reading
(a) Money Management*;
(b) Planned Savings;
(c) Pensions Management;
(d) BESt Investment;
(e) Offshore Adviser.

Reference

Weekly reference
(a) Money Management Rateguide;
(b) Planned Savings Rateguide.

Quarterly reference
The Savings Market (published by Planned Savings).

Half-yearly reference
Investment Fund Index — Investment Trusts (published by Centaur Communications Ltd).

Annual reference
(a) Personal Financial Planning Manual (by Robson Rhodes) (published by Butterworth & Co (Publishers) Ltd);
(b) The Unit Trust Year Book (published by Financial Times Business Information);
(c) The Investment Bond Year Book (publised by Financial Times Business Information);
(d) Executive Pensions Handbook (published by Financial Times Business Information);
(e) Personal Pensions (published by Financial Times Business Information);
(f) Allied Dunbar Tax Guide (by W.I. Sinclair) (published by Longman Professional);
(g) Tolley's Tax Guide (by Arnold Homer and Rita Burrows) (published by Tolley Publishing Co Ltd);
(h) Butterworths Yellow Tax Handbook (published by Butterworth & Co (Publishers) Ltd);
(i) Whillans's Tax Tables (published by Butterworth & Co (Publishers) Ltd).

Permanent reference
(a) Occupational Pension Schemes — Notes on approval (issued by the Inland Revenue Superannuation Funds Office);
(b) Memoranda issued by the Inland Revenue Superannuation Funds Office and the Occupational Pensions Board;
(c) Investing for Beginners (by Daniel O'Shea) (published by Financial Times Business Information);
(d) Investing in National Savings (issued by The Department for National Savings);
(e) Allied Dunbar Capital Taxes and Estate Planning Guide (by W.I. Sinclair and P.D.Silke) (published by Longman Professional);
(f) Working Abroad — The Expatriate's Guide (by David Young) (published by Financial Times Business Information);
(g) Retiring Abroad (published by Financial Times Business Information).

Courses (where suitable)
The professional adviser would also find it useful to attend courses (where suitable), and, where possible, to have occasional meetings with stockbrokers, investment fund managers or their marketing representatives, pensions specialists, and life assurance company inspectors/consultants. The individual seeking advice would benefit from the knowledge which the adviser gains in this way.

Notes:
(a) It is appreciated that an adviser would not normally have sufficient time for all the above reading even if he was to specialise full time in personal financial planning. Nevertheless, if he is involved in providing this advice, he should at least attempt to carry out the essential reading, etc. denoted by *.
(b) In order to gain maximum benefit from meetings with stockbrokers and investment managers, it is often worthwhile for the adviser to visit them at their own premises. Where this can be arranged, he would be able to see them in their working environment with the result that a better assessment can usually be made of their expertise etc.

Index

AWAKEN

NORTHERN WITCH #2

By K.S. Marsden

K.S. M

The Northern Witch Series

Winter Trials (Northern Witch #1)

Awaken (Northern Witch #2)

Printed by CreateSpace, an Amazon.com Company

Copyright © K.S. Marsden 2018
Edited by: Lesley Anne Neale
Cover by: Shazin Arefin

ISBN-13: 978-1721251377

ISBN-10: 1721251375

4

Chapter One

Mark spent most of his first class looking at the back of Damian's head. Damian was still the mysterious 'New Guy', after moving up from London a few weeks ago. He was certainly the odd-one-out at their school in the little Yorkshire town of Tealford.

It wasn't Mark's fault, that Damian was conveniently sitting two rows in front of him. So, every time Mark zoned out of what Mr Black was telling them about the proper formation of rhyming couplets, Mark's eyes drifted back to Damian.

His hair was a dirty shade of blond, with highlights. And, Mark knew from their rare make-out session that it was also really soft to touch.

"… Mark?"

"Wha?" Mark panicked as the teacher called his name.

Mr Black looked less than impressed. "How many lines in a sonnet?"

Mark racked his brain for a moment. "Fourteen."

"Correct, and you will all be writing your own sonnets…" Mr Black turned back to the class and continued to summarise their next piece of coursework.

Mark had learned some new rhymes recently, from his witch-of-a-grandmother and her coven. He idly wondered if spells had the same rules as English class.

At the end of last term, Mark had embraced being a witch, started his training, and even faced a demon that had been fighting to possess Damian.

Mark hadn't *won* against the demon, but it had still been one hell of an adventure. And it wasn't over; the demon had claimed a place in Damian's soul, but its presence was immature. It was weak, a ghost unable to hurt anyone for now.

Mark and Nanna just had to wait until it was substantial enough to expel.

Until then, Mark was tasked with keeping an eye on Damian. With which, he had no problem at all.

His gaze automatically shifted towards his ward. Taking in the lightly-muscled shoulders and arms, and the chiselled cheekbones as Damian turned his head to follow their teacher's movements.

No, watching him was no problem at all.

*****

After class, Mark headed to the bus, when he was stopped by his best friend, Harry.

7

"Hey, I've hardly seen you all day," Harry said, falling into step beside him. "D'you want to come 'round tonight? My Mum's cooking her infamous stew, and I need witnesses in case I'm poisoned."

Mark chuckled at the thought of Mrs Johnson's bad cooking, which they'd all experienced at one time or another.

"Usual deal, we'll stop for pizza when we take you home."

"Sorry, can't. I've gotta work on my magic with Nanna tonight." Mark replied, "And tell her how today went, of course."

"Cos that won't take five minutes." Harry muttered, almost too low for Mark to hear.

"What?"

"Ne'ermind. Have fun with your witchy-voodoo thing. See you tomorrow?"

"Unless they miraculously cancel school." Mark replied, thinking of the snow day they'd had last term. Looking out at the grey torrential rain, he sighed. "Fat chance that'll happen again."

"Right, see ya." Harry said pulling his hood up, before he hurried to the bus that circled the villages to the south.

Mark jogged through the rain, as his west-bound bus pulled up. The rest of the students crowded around it, keen to alight the bus and into the warmth. Mark fidgeted at the back of the group, waiting to be able to get on too.

Filing onto the already-crowded bus, he saw a familiar figure sitting alone.

"This seat taken?" Mark asked.

Damian looked up, a slow smile creeping across his lips. His bright blue eyes gleamed with good humour. "Dunno, mate. I was saving it for someone special." He chuckled at his own joke, and moved his rucksack out of the way, so Mark could sit down.

"I guess you'll have t'settle for me." Mark countered. "How was your first day at school with… y'know…"

"My new friend?" Damian snorted. "I can't even tell he's there, most of the time. I think I was more concerned when I forgot where my tutor room was, and walked right into the girl's changing room."

"You didn't?"

"Yeah, I don't think the girls minded." Damian grinned, as he remembered the scene.

Mark could just imagine it, the hot 'New Guy' bursting in, when everyone was in a state of undress. The thought brought a flush of warmth, creeping up his neck, and Mark changed the subject.

"Do you want'a come up to mine? I'm practising magic tonight with Nanna, I know she'd want to see how you're doin'." Mark offered. "Then you could always stay for dinner."

Damian shrugged, "I wish I could. I promised my aunt I'd go straight home. I spent so much time with you over Christmas and New Year, she thinks I'm avoiding her."

Mark sighed, he wanted to feel sorry for Damian's aunt, but he couldn't. He'd enjoyed every minute he got to spend with Damian, even if the majority of the time was spent under the watchful eyes of Mark's parents and Nanna.

"Have you told her yet?" Mark asked.

"What am I supposed to say? 'Hey, Aunt Maggie, I'm possessed by the demon that killed my parents. What's for dinner?'" Damian rolled his eyes. "She'd have me locked up or seeing a therapist in a blink."

"We could get Nanna to tell-"

"No, that'd be even worse!"

"How?" Mark asked, wondering how on earth it could be worse than being considered crazy.

"Dunno, but it would." Damian admitted. "It's just best coming from me."

"Fine." Mark fell into silence, staring down the aisle of the school bus, the worn carpet a revolting brown colour from all the wet feet.

"I'll see you tomorrow." Damian said, as he pushed past Mark. His bright blue eyes filled with an ever-questioning doubt.

"Sure." Mark replied.

Mark's weren't the only eyes to follow Damian as he left the bus. He was still the mysterious new guy, and good-looking to boot; it was only natural that Damian stirred the curiosity of the other students.

10

Mark sighed and waited for his stop, the windows already darkening as the familiar Yorkshire countryside rolled along. After years of taking this route home, it was all like clockwork. Left turn as the old bus chugged up the hill. And then home.

Once outside, Mark sprinted through the freezing cold rain, up to the old farmhouse. Out of habit, he headed to the right-hand side of the house, where the warm light of his Nanna's kitchen drew him in.

"Get that bloody coat off, you're getting water everywhere!"

Mark had barely stepped into the kitchen, when his Nanna barked at him. He huffed and shrugged off his heavy coat, hanging it up on the wooden coatrack.

Nanna was pouring hot water into the teapot, and preparing the tea-tray - like clockwork.

Mark heard a rumble and a crash coming from further inside the house, and he glanced suspiciously at the closed door. "What's that?"

"Nuthin' to bother yourself with." Nanna replied curtly. "How was your first day back at school?"

Mark shrugged. "Same old boring things. Every teacher thinks they're the first ones to tell us about the importance of our exams. I mean, they don't really start for another four months, and I'm already fed up with GCSEs."

Nanna tutted and poured the tea. "And how's your boyfriend, Damian?"

"Nanna!" Mark nearly choked on a biscuit, feeling a flush of red creeping up his neck.

"Too soon?" Nanna asked airily. "Don't know what's wrong with you boys. Fine, how's your *friend*?"

Mark felt a smile tug at his lips as he thought of Damian. Damn, he'd only known him a couple of weeks, and he was already hung up on him. He took a sip of scalding hot tea, as he tried to feign a neutral expression. "He's fine. No sign of the demon, yet. How long is it supposed to take?"

"It's still early days. There's no set rule, but it could be anything from a few weeks to a few months. Some weak demons never get strong enough to possess their victims."

Mark gave a low whistle. "Please tell me the demon we faced at Christmas wasn't weak." He still had nightmares about the monster in the flames, towering over him, threatening to kill him. If that was considered weak, he didn't want to cross a strong demon.

"Trust me, he's got enough clout about 'im." Nanna replied. "He's definitely powerful; but until we know *which* demon we're dealing with, we won't know how strong the bugger is."

"Well, I promise to continue keeping a very close eye on Damian, whilst we wait." Mark said, almost keeping a straight face.

"I'm sure you will." Nanna chuckled and hit him with the back of her hand as she passed. She walked over to her bookshelf and pulled out a particularly thick volume. "Right, let's crack on with your training."

"I read about some really cool spells, where you can invoke elements and spirits…" Mark stopped as Nanna set the book in front of him, his early enthusiasm quickly fading. "Healing? Mum's a nurse, why would I ever need this?"

"In my experience, sixteen-year-old boys attract injuries like flies on s-"

"Nanna!"

"On top of which, your boyfriend – sorry, *friend* – is possessed by a demon. I imagine a few healing spells will come in handy." Nanna rummaged through her draws, "Denise brought me a lovely batch of camomile; I think I've left it upstairs. Get started with the healing paste."

Mark watched as Nanna disappeared, then dutifully got up and gathered the listed materials. The door to the living room rattled, and there was another clatter behind it. Mark jumped at the noise and looked at the door suspiciously.

Glancing, to make sure Nanna hadn't come back downstairs, Mark slowly pushed on the door handle…

The door was suddenly wrenched out of his hand, as a wild wind bashed it back against its hinges. Cold, heavy rain battered against his bare face and arms, as the gale howled.

Mark was faintly aware of a ginger streak darting through his legs. It took all his effort to lean into the

13

wind, and pull back the door, fighting to get it back into its frame. Once it clicked back in place, everything went very quiet and very still. Mark gasped for breath, his pulse racing.

"Mark, why haven't you started the healing spell?" Nanna's voice came from behind him.

Mark turned, suddenly aware of his soaking school uniform, that clung to his frame. "Nanna, why's there a storm raging in the living room?"

"No reason." Nanna said dismissively. "Now Denise grew this camomile in her garden this spring, she always produces good qual-"

"Nanna, Tigger was in there." Mark said sharply, pointing to the poor, distressed house cat, who stood by the Aga. His ginger coat was drenched and he looked a bedraggled mess.

Nanna's smile dropped, and she sighed. "It's nothing, just a spell that got out of hand. It'll blow itself out eventually. Proof that even the best of us lose concentration sometimes."

Mark waited to see if Nanna had anything else to say on the matter; or at least suggested something they could magically do to stop the storm; but she didn't.

He muttered to himself and, trying to ignore his damp clothes, Mark pulled the heavy book towards him, and started following the instructions.

It was all fairly easy, no more difficult than when he helped his Dad with homemade soup. After half an hour, Mark had produced a very dull-looking paste.

"Finished. I think." He announced. "It doesn't look like much."

Nanna closed her latest edition of Cosmopolitan. Setting the magazine on the kitchen table, she came to inspect her grandson's handiwork. She dipped her finger in the grey-green paste and smiled. "It looks as it should. You've done a good job."

"But it's just herbs," Mark protested, "It's not really magical."

"Just because herbs are natural and normal, doesn't mean they don't have healing properties. Most medicines and drugs are derived from naturally occurring substances." Nanna replied. "You should take this book home and read about the different herbs. Knowledge will always be useful."

Nanna proceeded to scoop the paste out and put it in one of her many spare jars. "Freshly-made stuff works best, but it's always wise to keep some pre-made healing paste ready, just in case of emergencies." She said, as she screwed the lid on tightly, before picking up a marker pen and labelling it clearly. "Don't want this getting mixed up with my home-made pesto..."

Mark chuckled. There was more rattling from the storm in the living room, but it did sound like it was losing strength. He wondered what spell Nanna had been doing – and when *he* would be allowed to learn something cool like that.

"Right, off with you. I'm sure you've got piles of GCSE homework." Nanna shooed.

Mark rolled his eyes, less than thrilled at the prospect of the trigonometry exercises he had on top of drafting a sonnet for English. "Oh, before I forget, can I borrow the horses this weekend?"

"Sure, why?"

"If it's not raining, I wanted to show Damian the area. It's always much more fun on horseback." Mark said, thinking of Nanna's two horses. One was young and sprightly; the other was a plodding old cob, perfect for looking after Damian.

Nanna eyed him warily. "And does Damian think this is a good idea?"

Mark shrugged, "We talked about it a few times. He didn't sound too keen, but that's just because he's never done it before."

"Mark..." Nanna's warning broke off, as she thought better of it. "Fine, make sure you put Lulu's boots on; you know she's accident-prone."

"Will do, thanks Nanna!" Mark drank the cold remains of his tea, before grabbing his school bag and coat. "See you later."

Chapter Two

The following morning, Mark met Harry before class. Harry was always early on Tuesdays, taking part in orchestra practise. His fingers were red from playing the guitar, and he looked vaguely annoyed with the whole thing.

"What's wrong?" Mark asked, hesitantly. When it came to the school orchestra, Mark knew that it didn't take much to get Harry ranting.

"Nuthin'." He muttered. "I missed my alarm this morning, so I've been rushing round, missing breakfast, just so I can get to this bloody novice, flat-noted session. It's so bloody boring now, I don't know why I bother."

"Because it's the only musical outlet this school provides..." Mark supplied. If there was one thing he knew about his best friend after all these years, it was how much he enjoyed music. "Here, I've got a bag of crisps somewhere."

17

He rummaged through his bag and pulled out a bag of cheese and onion. Not the best substitute for breakfast, but with any luck it would distract Harry from complaining any further.

Harry readily took the bag and tucked in. "So how was the voodoo session?" He asked through a mouthful of crisps.

"Yeah, it was good." Mark replied half-heartedly. "Nanna showed me how to do this healing paste; so y'know, really handy stuff."

"Uh-huh." Harry sounded unimpressed.

Any further discussion was halted by the shrill ringing of the bell, announcing the first lesson of the day was about to start. Students started to drag their feet to their classrooms, and Mark filed into History class, already struggling to focus.

Mrs Green greeted them all routinely, thankfully not expecting a response this early in the day. She started to drone on about the Elizabethan Era, and how they should have all drafted their coursework on the political pressures surrounding Queen Elizabeth I.

Her monologue was broken when the classroom door opened.

A familiar girl let herself in. It wasn't an unusual occurrence for Michelle to arrive late, and Mark watched with little interest.

"Later than usual, Michelle." Mrs Green stated.

The girl stood, looking unimpressed and disinterested. When it became clear that she wasn't going to supply a response, or an apology; the teacher motioned for her to sit down.

As Michelle passed Mark, he noticed the scruffy coat, with frayed edges, and patches that were no longer waterproof. Her frizzy brown hair hung down around her face, as it usually was; but Mark noticed the dark shadows under her eyes. Were they new? Or had he just never paid this much attention before?

He recalled what Nanna had said last month, when he'd reported that Michelle carried a troubled aura about her. Nanna wanted him to make the effort to get to know her, to socialise, to see if there was anything in his power to make things easier for her.

Michelle noticed him staring at her, and she shifted her chair with a sickening screech of its metal legs. She turned away from him and huffed pointedly.

Mark inwardly sighed, he doubted that Michelle would spare him the time of day. He didn't need to magically read her aura, to tell that she was trying to repel all attention.

Mark spent the rest of the lesson trying to concentrate, as Mrs Green continued to read the points they were expected to cover. Names, facts and dates began to blur, and Mark looked down at his notebook, filling it with notes that made no sense.

The bell rang, and Mark was glad to put the History work aside for another day. He glanced over to Michelle, who hurriedly shoved her stuff into a black rucksack.

"Hey, what're you doing later, Michelle? D'you fancy joining us at dinner?" Mark asked, hurrying to get all the words out before he lost his nerve.

Michelle paused in what she was doing and turned slowly to look at him. Her brow creased, and the look of disgust on her face was clear. "Erm, no..." She said, stating the obvious, continuing to look at Mark as though he were an idiot.

Mark's earlier courage completely fled under the pressure of Michelle's gaze, and he only relaxed after she swung her bag on her shoulder and left.

"What was that about?" Harry's voice came.

"Nowt." Mark shrugged. "I just... I thought I'd be friendly, y'know, last year in school and everythin'."

"Friends with *her*. You know, I heard she got arrested for drugs, and stole a police car from the station." Harry chuckled, swinging his rucksack onto his shoulder and 'accidentally' hitting Mark. "Get a shift on, we'll be late."

Mark snorted, "You don't believe that crap."

"Nah, I only believe in witches and demons, in this little town." Harry replied, continuing to laugh at his own hilarity.

Mark sighed, it was going to be one of those days.

*****

The cafeteria was quickly filling up, the constant rain forcing everyone to huddle in the hall, filling up the round tables that had been dutifully rolled out for dinnertime.

20

Mark had managed to get out of his last class as soon as the bell rang, and was already sat down with his plate of chips and lasagne. A few of his classmates shared the table, including Harry and his girlfriend, Sarah.

The couple only had eyes for each other and were in some deep, private conversation, which always made Mark feel left out. He wondered if he would experience that intense connection, now that he had Damian in his life. But who was he kidding, he didn't even know if Damian was even his boyfriend, never mind the rest.

At that moment, Damian walked into the cafeteria, and Mark's eyes locked onto him, as he queued for food with the other students.

Damian received a lot of curious and admiring looks, and Mark couldn't blame them. His dark golden hair looked decidedly dishevelled, framing his perfect face. Sharp cheekbones, and brilliant blue eyes; it was inevitable that wherever Damian went, he was made to stand out. He was tall, and physically fit from years of playing football, and he even made the drab school uniform look good.

"You look like you want to jump on him." A voice drawled behind him.

Mark felt a familiar red flush of embarrassment creeping up his neck. He hadn't meant to be caught staring. He turned to face his accuser, and saw Dean hovering by his shoulder.

Mark had never considered the ever-annoying Dean as one of his friends, but as the only two openly gay students in Tealford High School, they were often lumped together in social circles. Well, *three* gay students now, thanks to Damian.

"Which is totally fine, I can't blame you." Dean continued, "Just no sex in the cafeteria, the teachers don't like that."

"Dean!" Mark blustered, the flush of embarrassment taking over completely. "Sod off!"

Mark watched as Dean huffed and turned away. He was unbelievable sometimes. His mention of sex had been too much. Mark had never thought about sex... OK, he thought about it a lot, but being 'the only gay in the village' meant that it was purely fantasy. Something he didn't expect to be real until he moved away for college, perhaps. But, now he had a sort-of-boyfriend... the thought suddenly made him very nervous.

"Hey."

Damian's voice made him jump. Mark looked over, to see Damian slide into the chair next to him, wedging his tray onto the busy table.

"What's got you all flustered?" Damian asked, with that sweet, unsure smile.

"Nowt." Mark replied quickly, "Just some nonsense. How's school been this morning?"

Chapter Three

When the weekend finally rolled around, Mark had managed to persuade Damian to hack out with the horses in the countryside. Damian had been strangely reluctant to put his life in the hands of a half-tonne beast, with a mind of its own, but Mark's enthusiasm had eventually won him over.

Mark's Dad dropped them off at the yard at ten o'clock in the morning. The rain was holding off, though grey clouds still sat heavily above them. As Mark got out of the car, he was hit by the familiar, warm smell of horses. Damian clambered out after him, looking less-than-convinced.

"I'll pick you boys up about twelve." Mark's Dad said, before rolling up his window and driving away.

Mark turned to face Damian, keen to see his first impression of the place. Unfortunately, Damian looked like he wanted to chase down Mark's Dad for a lift home.

"We're going riding for *two hours*?" Damian asked, his voice miserable.

"Nah, by the time we've tacked up, gotten ready; untacked and mucked out; we'll be lucky to be in the saddle for an hour." Mark replied, shrugging.

"Mucked out?" Damian echoed faintly.

"C'mon, it'll be fun." Mark insisted, as he started to walk down to the yard.

The stable yard was a relatively small business. There were a dozen airy stalls in an American barn, keeping the horses in an enclosed space, away from the harshest of the winter weather. The owner was one of Nanna's friends, a down-to-earth woman who kept her old Shire horses in perfect luxury. She rented out the rest of the stables.

She glanced up, sparing the lads a brief nod, as she led her huge, lumbering horse to a paddock behind the house.

"That's massive." Damian hissed, his eyes wide, as they followed the gentle giant.

Mark chuckled, "S'fine, you're riding summat much smaller. Come and meet Holly."

Without wasting any more time, Mark led to one of the first stables in the barn. A very hairy head poked over the top of the stable door. The horse looked as wide as it was tall, and had lop-sided brown and not-so-white patches covering its body. Its gentle brown eyes gazed at them lazily, and its stubby little ears only lifted when Mark pulled a treat out of his pocket.

"Wow, it looks very chilled." Damian commented, daring to reach out and stroke the coarse hair on the horse's muzzle. "Is it doped?"

"*She*." Mark stressed. "No, this is her normal, steady self. Holly is pretty relaxed about everything. She'll look after y-"

Mark broke off, as his coat was grabbed and sharply yanked, the collar digging into his throat and making him choke. He spun around to look accusingly at a tall brown horse, who stood with her ears pricked, the picture of innocence.

"Hmph, and this is Nanna's other horse Lulu."

Mark noticed Damian's hand hesitantly reach out to stroke her, too. He quickly pushed his hand out of the way of Lulu's teeth.

"No! No, er..." Mark snapped, suddenly feeling guilty. "Sorry, Lulu is a temperamental little madam. Very funny about strangers. I wouldn't touch her unless absolutely necessary."

Damian looked like he was going to say something, but just shrunk back, and put his hands in his pockets.

"C'mon, we'll get their gear." Mark said, leading to a secure cabin outside the airy barn.

Inside, there were rows of bridles hanging on the wall, above corresponding saddles and tack boxes. Mark showed Damian the best way to carry Holly's tack, and proceeded to dump them in his arms.

"This is heavy." Damian grumbled, moving his arms to try and make it more comfortable. "It won't hurt the horse?"

"Nah," Mark replied, as he grabbed Lulu's gear. "With your weight on top of them, the saddle is a minimal addition."

When they returned to the horses, Mark expertly removed their rugs, brushed them, and tacked them up. He gave a running narrative of what he was doing and why, to try and help Damian understand. By the end of it, Damian was still wearing that less-than-thrilled expression.

Mark inwardly smiled, he knew he'd cheer up once they got going. This first bit was always boring, but necessary.

Eventually Mark got Holly and Damian to the mounting block, both suited and booted, and ready to go. Damian was borrowing Mark's velvet show hat, and very much looked the part. Until he got on.

"Shit, it's moving." Damian swore, as Holly shifted her weight, getting used to her rider. His hands gripped the pommel of the saddle as tightly as his padded gloves would allow.

"Well, yeah... she is alive." Mark commented, trying not to roll his eyes. "Wait here, while I get Lulu."

"You can't leave me alone!"

Mark chuckled at the stress in Damian's voice. He knew that the ever-obedient Holly wouldn't move an inch, until she was told to. Mark gracefully swung up into Lulu's saddle, and picked up the rope he'd clipped to Holly's bridle.

"Let's go. You're gonna love this."

Without waiting for a response, Mark nudged Lulu into a nice energetic walk, and headed to the track at the back of the yard. He waved at the yard owner as they passed; she stood watching with her massive shire beside her, then grinned at Damian.

Damian's blue eyes were bright with worry, but he soon settled into the comfortable, plodding pace of his horse.

Mark led the way up the familiar track, turning left and letting his horse climb the sharp ascent. He heard Damian swear behind him, at the change of direction, and shouted to lean forward and let Holly do all the work. His own horse, Lulu, had her ears pricked forward and happily stomped up the hill like a mountain goat.

As they crested the top, the wind whipped the breath out of him, and Mark paused to take it all in. He would never tire of the Yorkshire countryside that was his home. The rolling hills criss-crossed with ancient stone walls. White snow still hugged the crevices, the last remnants of winter. The small, gnarled trees that dotted the landscape, tough enough to survive the weather. The sky was filled with dark-grey clouds, the wind chasing them across the horizon.

"Wow."

Mark turned to Damian, their horses halted side-by-side. The lad had a look of wonder, as he gazed out at the scene.

"We don't have this in London." He commented. "I mean, you see pictures and stuff; but this is something else."

Mark stamped down the temptation to say 'I told you so', and tightened his grip on the reins. "C'mon, we'll ride down to the river. A shame it's not summer, we could've gone in."

"You're kidding, right?"

Mark just chuckled, and got the horses moving again. Swimming in the river could be fun, especially with certain company. His mind drifted back to last month, when he'd saved Damian from the snowstorm. Damian's clothes had been soaked through, and clung to his athletic frame...

Mark's attention snapped back to the present, as his horse sharply leapt aside. Lulu's ears were flat back and her muscles tense, and Mark hurried to steady her before she bolted.

"What's happening?" Damian's voice was laced with panic.

Mark looked around them, trying to find the source of Lulu's unease, but there was nothing he could see that would upset the horse. Perhaps it was the scent of a predator, that spurred on such a violent reaction; but Mark had never seen anything bigger than a fox up here.

"Dunno, it's fine now." Mark answered, finally turning in his saddle, when he was sure his horse wasn't going to take off. He looked at Damian, whose bright blue eyes were wide with fear, and his hands gripped the front of the saddle again. Good old Holly looked remarkably relaxed. The little mare ignored Lulu's antics, and was quietly grazing, waiting for her rider's next command.

Mark sighed, maybe they should turn back now, before he scared Damian off horses forever. And, he had to admit, before he scared him away completely.

Mark looked at their surroundings. They had left the main track, to take a shortcut to the river. There was nothing but grass underfoot, and rough bushes hovering low to the ground.

Mark looked closer, through the dead-looking thorns at his side, and saw a lump of stone. It was pockmarked and worn from hundreds of years in the elements, but its shape was too geometric to be accidental.

It wasn't unusual to come across the remains of old buildings up here, but Mark had never spotted this one before. He-

He thought he heard a voice, deep and constant, reverberating through the air. Mark couldn't make out what the voice was saying, the words deformed, and lost to time. Everything about him went still. The wind dropped, and the birds were silent. Mark strained harder, sure he could understand the voice, if he just tried hard enough...

His horse suddenly squealed with fear, and reared, throwing Mark off balance. He tried to pull himself straight in the saddle, but Lulu was blinded by panic, and bolted.

Mark felt the air shift around him, he thought he heard his name being shouted, and then with a heavy thud, everything went black.

Chapter Four

Mark cracked open his eyes, wincing at the bright light. His head hurt, it felt like someone was stabbing the back of his skull with a fork.

"Wha' happened?" He groaned, starting to shift his weight, but stopped. He was lying on something soft, the material coarse and itchy against his skin.

Mark slowly looked about him, and groaned again as he saw the hospital bed. He was in an open ward, and he could see another half a dozen beds, mostly vacant. In a couple of the beds, older chaps were sitting, reading their newspapers. This was not how Mark had planned this day would go.

"You're awake, again?"

Mark relaxed at the familiar sound of his Dad's voice.

"What happened?" Mark repeated.

"You fell off your horse and hit your head – good job you had your helmet on." His Dad replied, sitting on the hospital bed, making it dip under his weight. "You gave poor Damian the fright of his life. He kept his cool, though. He called the ambulance and us."

Mark raised his hand to his head, and winced when he touched a tender spot. The skin under his jaw was sore, too, where the hat's harness must have dug in. "How long was I out?"

"Not long. Damian said you were awake as soon as he finished on the phone, but you weren't exactly... lucid."

"Oh no, what did I do?" Mark groaned, a familiar nervous blush crawling up his neck.

"I think what you were saying was probably more embarrassing." His Dad said, with a knowing smile. "But I'll leave that for you boys to discuss."

"Where is Damian?"

"He went to get coffee, with your Mum, while we wait for the results of the CAT scan. The doctors wanted to make sure there wasn't any swelling in your brain."

Mark chewed over that. Damian had stayed in the hospital for him; it was a faint silver lining to this whole episode.

"What happened up there?" His Dad asked, breaking through his thoughts. "Damian said everything was fine, and then Lulu went mental. He didn't feel he knew enough about horses to offer an explanation."

"Everything *was* fine. I don't..." Mark paused, recalling something. "We rode away from the track, and came across some stone ruins. I thought I heard... there was a voice. I couldn't understand it, but I suddenly felt unnerved. Maybe Lulu was affected, too. Do you think it could be magic-related?"

His Dad looked uncomfortable. "I don't know, you'd have to ask Nanna; that's her area of experience."

Mark sat, gazing at his Dad. It occurred to him that, although he accepted magic, he never seemed to embrace it. Growing up, Mark had never questioned it – that was just the way his Dad was. But now that he was learning witchcraft from Nanna, he wondered again why his Dad had never taken it up.

"Dad, why..."

Mark was interrupted by the return of his Mum and Damian, nursing cardboard coffee cups. They both looked visibly relieved to see Mark sitting up in bed.

"How are you feeling, sweetie?" His Mum asked, gliding over to his side.

"Sore. Embarrassed. And sore." Mark listed briefly.

His Mum chuckled and shook her head. "Well, we just saw Doctor Reed in the corridor. She said that your results have come back clear. She'll be here shortly to officially discharge you."

Mark looked from her, to Damian, who kept his eyes firmly on the floor.

Mark's Mum must have noticed, and she less-than-subtly coughed to get her husband's attention. "Shall we go for a walk?"

"You've just been for a walk." Mark's Dad replied, his voice tired.

"Yes, I *realise* that, dear. Still, we should *go* and make a start on the paperwork." His Mum suggested.

When her husband still didn't take the 'hint', she grabbed his arm and physically dragged him away from the ward, letting the boys have their privacy.

"Really smooth, mum." Mark muttered beneath his breath, as he watched his parents disappear around the corner. Privacy was an illusion in this open ward, with other patients sitting only a few metres away. The other men still looked engrossed in their newspapers, so this was the best they were going to get.

"I'm so sorry about today, that did not go how I planned." Mark said, his words rushing out into the silence.

Damian finally looked at him, his blue eyes bright with pain. "When you fell... all I could think was 'not again'." He said quietly.

Mark paused, Damian's words slowly sinking in. Damian had been a cursed soul, and had left London after his parents, and grandmother had died, and his best friend ended up in a coma; all within a short space of time. Mark remembered how he had been suicidal after his aunt was nearly involved in a fire last month. And he felt guilty for not remembering sooner.

"Damian... I never thought... I'm sorry, I didn't realise how this would affect you." Mark apologised in a rush. The riding accident had been exactly that – an accident. He hadn't planned it, and nothing could have stopped it; but he still felt a stab of responsibility. "You didn't have to come to the hospital."

"I had to make sure you were alright." He replied, moving from his frozen stance, to sit on the bed next to Mark.

Damian's hand was so close to his, that Mark could feel the warmth emanating from him. He felt a sudden urge to reach out and lace his fingers through Damian's.

"Mark..." Damian's lowered voice broke through his train of thoughts. "Do you think that *he* is responsible? I thought that the curse ended when he got his way."

Mark shook his head, "No, it shouldn't be possible. Nanna said that he would be weak, whilst the possession is in its infancy." *Unless... he's started to awaken*. Mark shivered at the thought, but didn't say it aloud.

Damian took a deep, steadying breath, "Well, I really want to say that I've had worse dates, but this one was an epic disaster."

"Date?" Mark echoed, suddenly feeling light-headed at the simple phrase.

"Yes, why, do you Northerners have a different term?" He teased.

Damian glanced down at the bed, and moved his hand, until it rested on Mark's. As they touched, Mark felt an electric surge rush across his skin. Mark lifted his hand and intertwined his fingers with Damian's. His pulse raced.

"No, I... I think I like the term 'date'." Mark stammered.

"Next time, can we do normal date-stuff? No horses or hospitals. Maybe the cinema?" Damian suggested, lightly.

Mark bit back the urge to grin and jump out of the hospital bed. Next time, there was going to be a next time! He coughed to clear his throat. "Deal."

Chapter Five

Mark was under strict orders to rest for the remainder of the weekend. Monday morning rolled round again far too quickly.

Mark was both excited and anxious about seeing Damian again. Yes, they'd agreed to go on a second date, but maybe Damian would think differently, now he'd had time to sleep on it.

Mark didn't have to worry. As the school bus trundled down the dark lanes, Damian sat next to him, completely relaxed, biting back a smile, as he purposefully rested against Mark's side, in this cramped space.

Looking into his blue eyes, Mark could see that Damian still wanted him in his turbulent life.

Once they arrived at school, Mark noticed a familiar figure charging towards him.

"Mornin', Harry." Mark said with a yawn.

"Mornin'? I'll bloody *mornin'* ya." Harry huffed. "Why did I have to learn from my mum, that you ended up in hospital this weekend?"

"Oh." Mark stopped in his tracks. "I meant to text you on Saturday, but I got home and fell asleep. The rest of the weekend was a bit of a blur; Mum said I had classic signs of concussion."

Harry's mardy expression didn't change.

Mark sighed, "It really wasn't that exciting. I fell off Nanna's horse, got a bit of a sore head, and a bruised ego, as well as a bruised ar-"

"You fell off in front of Damian?" Harry asked.

Mark nodded, unwilling to say it out loud, again. He wondered how long the embarrassment would pain him.

"Oh, well that makes it better." Harry replied, his voice lightening to his normal, amused tone. "It serves you right, mate, dragging 'im up to the horses. Anyone could see Damian didn't want to go."

"I thought once he was up there, he'd change his mind." Mark argued, "And to be fair, he did... until everything went to hell. So, you're saying the potential demon activity was karma?"

"Yeah, guess so." Harry grinned, "Tell me again, in detail, you fell on your-"

Mark groaned, "Can you go back to being angry with me?"

"Nah, this is much more fun." Harry elbowed Mark, and started to walk towards the school building. "What actually happened up there?"

"No idea. One minute everything was fine, the next there's this weird voice I can't understand and this creepy feeling of a void. Then Lulu freaked out, and I ended up on the ground."

Harry chewed it over, and Mark was happy to see he was taking it all seriously. "Do you think it could be Damian's..." He broke off and looked at the oblivious students around him. "...friend?"

Mark shrugged, "I don't know, I lost consciousness pretty fast. It could have been... his friend."

Harry blew out a breath. "This whole 'friend' thing is awkward. Doesn't it have a name?"

"I'm sure it does, and we'd love to know it, because that might be the first step in getting rid of it." Mark replied, sharper than he meant to.

"Huh, I think I'll call it Bob." Harry replied.

"Bob? You can't go and name a de- name it Bob!"

"What would you rather have? Fred? Daisy? Lucy Satan Sataniel?"

Mark couldn't help it, he laughed. "OK, you win. Bob."

"I always win." Harry gloated without a hint of modesty. "So, on with your story. Bob scared your horse, and you fell off in front of your new fella?"

Mark rolled his eyes, looking for a way to change the topic. "Have you finished Mr Black's homework?"

39

"The sonnet? Yeah, pretty much." Harry replied. *"There was a man from Donegal, who only had one-"*

"That's really not a sonnet." Mark snorted a short laugh. "I *dare* you to hand it in."

*****

After the school bus dropped him off at the end of the lane, Mark hurried up the drive.

Nanna seemed to have anticipated his arrival, and was locking the door. She waved at Mark, her car keys in hand. "Jump in, we're off to investigate."

Mark obediently clambered up into Nanna's ancient Land Rover. Nanna had got the car when she was a newly-wed; it was even older than Mark's Dad. Nanna always swore that her careful maintenance of the car kept it running; but Mark couldn't help but wonder if there was a little magical aid, as the engine purred to life.

Mark gripped the arm-rest, as the car sped and bounced down the road, much faster than when his Dad drove. He remembered why he rarely travelled with Nanna. "So, what are we investigating?"

"I want to witness this mysterious stonework, and creepy voices." Nanna replied calmly. "There's nothing in this world that could scare Lulu, so I want to see what upset my horse."

Upset the bloody horse, yeah. "I'm fine, thanks for asking." Mark muttered.

They pulled up to the yard in record time, as the sun was setting behind the hills.

"Come on, then." Nanna stated, starting to march towards the darkening countryside.

Mark sighed, grabbing a torch from the messy foot well, and jogged to catch up. The ground was rough and uneven underfoot, and Mark was soon struggling to keep up, even with the torch's light bobbing in front of him.

"You alright there, slow coach?" Nanna teased.

"Not all of us can see in the dark." Mark replied, bitter that he was being outpaced by someone four times his age.

"Hmph, I suppose I should teach you that spell soon." Nanna replied, as she turned down towards the river. "Whereabouts were you when everything went wrong?"

"About fifty metres ahead."

Nanna marched onwards, her cardigan flapping in the cold wind.

Mark cast his torch around, trying to spot something familiar. Everything looked different in the night. The track and the surrounding bushes had become grey shadows.

"Here. It's here." Mark called, fixing his torch beam on the rugged bush, with the hint of stonework underneath.

"Well, that looks like a whole lot of nuthin'." Nanna came back, to hover by his elbow. She closed her eyes, concentrating. "I don't sense owt, can you?"

Mark focused on the slab of stone. There were definitely no voices, no mysterious chanting haunting his thoughts. Mark tried to notice what else was different, and it finally occurred to him that there was nothing oppressive in the air around them. It was as fresh and free as any evening. "No, nothing. I didn't make it up, I promise."

"I know, lad, don't get in a tizz. It could be any number of factors that stirred the power – the daylight, the time of the year, or the rotation of the moon... it could even have been the proximity of Damian and his demon. Do me a favour, and make sure you keep him away from this spot, until we work out what's going on." Nanna knelt down, getting a closer look at the age-worn stone. "I'll contact the coven, find out if anyone has any historical info that can explain it."

Chapter Six

It was raining for the rest of the week. The dreary, never-ending drizzle was starting to make Mark feel claustrophobic, stuck inside, with no reprieve.

If there was someone even unhappier about the weather, it was the poor Southener, Damian.

"It never stops!" He grumbled again, as they hovered in the crowded student lounge during break time.

Every other student of Tealford High School had the same idea, preferring to squeeze into the dull little room, rather than battle the rain to venture out into the expansive grounds.

Mark shrugged, he couldn't promise that things would get any better until summer – and even that was chancing it.

"I haven't been able to play football since I came here." Damian continued to complain, "I'm getting withdrawal symptoms."

"Have you thought any more about trying out for the school footie team?" Mark asked. "They train inside, too."

"I dunno..." Damian sighed.

"Well, they're still totally shit. You might not win any league tables, but they could definitely use your help."

Damian chuckled at his comment. "Sure, I'll think about it. In the meantime, I have other plans. What are you doing Friday?"

"Nuthin'." Mark replied, a bit too quickly. He bit back his smile, "No plans, why?"

"Well, I figure we need to replace the memory of last weekend's atrocious date with something more fun. Still fancy going to the cinema?" Damian asked. "I mean, we don't have to, if you don't want to. It's just, there's the new Ryan Reynolds film..."

"Ryan Reynolds?"

Damian shrugged, trying to look casual. "I like a man that makes me laugh."

"And his looks have nothing to do with it?"

"What can I say – it's a bonus." Damian replied, finally cracking a smile.

Mark laughed at his expression.

"What's so funny?"

Mark turned to see his best friend pushing through the crowd, to stand next to him. Behind Harry, Sarah hovered, looking curiously between Mark and Damian.

"Nuthin' special. We were just planning a trip to the cinema on Friday." Mark explained.

"Oh, awesome, I haven't been for ages. What time are we meeting?" Harry asked.

"Ahm." Mark cast a glance towards Damian, stuck for words.

Luckily, Sarah caught up quickly, and punched Harry's arm.

"Hey, what was that for?"

"Friday night at the cinema? They're organising a date, you daft sod!" She stated, not worrying about keeping her voice down.

Realisation dawned on Harry's face. "Ooh, sorry mate..."

Mark felt a heated blush creeping up his neck, at the awkward moment - in the crowded room. Well, if anyone at school didn't know he and Damian were dating, they would now. It would probably be the highlight of gossip for the rest of the term.

"No, it's OK." Damian spoke up, trying to resolve the issue. "Why don't the four of us go, it can be like a... a double-date."

"Oh, Damian, thank you; but you don't have to." Sarah replied, smiling at his offer.

"I'm serious, it'll be fun." Damian insisted. "I've never done one before."

Mark silently mouthed 'thank you' to him, he'd have to find a way to make it up to Damian.

*****

Friday evening rolled around too quickly.

Mark couldn't work out if he was nervous, or excited. Which was crazy, this wasn't the first time he would be hanging out with Damian. They'd even shared a few passionate kisses, so there wasn't that to worry about, either.

As Mark changed his clothes for the fifth time, opting for a simple grey shirt and skinny jeans, Mark realised that this would be the first time he was on a real date. The first time he was spending time with Damian, where he was in unknown territory.

When he thought back, all that time spent at his house, and even the unsuccessful outing with the horses last weekend; Mark had at least the benefit of home advantage.

His worries spiked as he got a text, saying that Damian and his aunt were waiting outside for him.

Mark jogged downstairs, checking for the umpteenth time that he had his phone and wallet. He stopped at the sound of a wolf whistle, followed by his Dad's laughter.

"Oh, you look so handsome, Mark!" His Mum cooed, getting up from the settee to give him a hug, but changing her mind, mid-motion. "Have a good time tonight."

46

"Thanks." Mark mumbled, as he struggled to remember how to put his shoes on. "See you later."

He grabbed his best black coat and headed outside, where a modest Corsa hatchback stood waiting. Mark climbed into the passenger seat, smiling nervously at Damian in the back seat.

"Thanks for the lift, Miss Cole."

"No problem, Mark. And please, call me Maggie. Miss Cole makes me sound so grown-up."

"Sure thing." Mark replied.

The car fell into uncomfortable silence, as Aunt Maggie drove down the dark, winding roads. Eventually, there were signs of the relatively-urban area of Tealford, as street lamps started to light their way, and the houses crowded together.

When they pulled up in the busy cinema carpark, Mark thanked Maggie again.

Jumping out, he saw Harry and Sarah hovering by the entrance, waiting for them.

"Wow, Harry's on time. That's like, a sign of the apocalypse." Mark joked.

Harry scowled at him. Luckily, his arms were wrapped around Sarah, and couldn't physically retaliate.

"Let's go, I don't want to miss the trailers." Damian laughed, slipping his hand casually into Mark's.

Mark's pulse raced again, at the simple contact. "Soundsgoodt'me." He blurted out. He was suddenly very aware of how coarse his hands were from working

47

on the farm; and why did they pick now to go all clammy.

*****

When the film finished, they made their way outside with the masses.

"That was fun. D'you guys want to get a drink?" Mark asked, as they stepped into the cold air.

"Ye-"

Harry started, but Sarah elbowed him quiet.

"Thanks, Mark, but we've gotta go catch our bus." Sarah replied, looking meaningfully at her boyfriend.

"Yes... we have to catch our bus..." Harry "Oh, next weekend, before I forget!" Harry rushed, "There's this thing on, y'know at the Hub? It's kinda important, and it'd be great if you guys could come."

Mark stared at his best friend, Harry was going very red in the face. Whatever this thing was, it was making him embarrassed, and probably stressed.

"What thing?" He asked.

"Just'a thing. Saturday night, six o'clock. You'll be there?" Harry asked, his words coming out in a quick stream.

Mark bit back a smile at his awkward evasion. "Yes, if it's important to you, I promise I'll be there."

Sarah bobbed on her tip toes, next to Harry, a ridiculous grin on her face. Obviously, *she* knew what the big deal was. Mark made a mental note to get it out of her later.

48

"Anyway, we'll see you guys at school, we can discuss details then." Sarah said, less-than-subtly dragging Harry in the direction of the bus station. "See you later?"

"Yeah, see ya." Mark answered, watching them walk away, looking the perfect couple.

"Just us, then." Damian said from beside him, winding his fingers around Mark's.

Mark gulped, a nervous blush creeping up his neck. "Y-yes. Only the best establishments, around here, of course..." He nodded towards the popular venue, further down the street.

"You've got a McDonalds up here?" Damian grinned, as he spotted the familiar golden arches.

"Yeah, fine dining at its best." Mark joked.

The fast food restaurant was typically busy for a Friday night, attracting its usual crowd of teenagers, young families, and the odd person in a suit.

Mark hesitated as he headed over, noticing a group of teens his age, perching on the tables outside, despite the damp benches. He recognised a few of them, including Michelle. Mark inwardly cringed. Since their brief interaction, she had been shooting death glares whenever he came near, chasing off any chance of speaking again.

Mark felt Damian sharply pull his hand away. He looked up to question the move, but Damian just pulled his coat collar up, and hurried into the building.

"Hey, you ok?" Mark asked, as he followed.

"Yeah..." Damian glanced warily at the group of teens, who stood staring at him. The glass walls of the restaurant stretched from floor to ceiling, and offered nowhere to hide. "They just give me a bad vibe."

Mark frowned, waiting for more of an explanation.

"They... they remind me of a group of bullies from back home." Damian admitted.

"Oh." Realisation dawned, as Mark recalled the parting of their hands, and the casual distance. "Y'know, nobody cares if you're gay, here."

Damian huffed, "From the guy that never had to deal with bullies."

Mark turned and watched Michelle and her friends, as they larked about outside. "Judging them just because they look like trouble?" Mark commented, only half-joking. "I mean, they probably have been banned from McDonalds, so they're not totally innocent-"

"They give me a bad vibe." Damian repeated. "I've learnt to trust my gut feeling with people."

Mark sighed, he always tried to avoid snap judgement of strangers, but even he knew his date night would take a dive if they discussed it now. Mark turned his gaze away from the group, and less-than-subtly shifted the topic to the film they'd just seen.

Damian visibly relaxed, and he was more than happy to discuss it in length. Especially the topless scene.

"Nothing compares to Deadpool, though." Mark argued.

"I don't know, there's a naked charity run in Van Wilder, which was pretty awesome." Damian replied, with a grin. Seeing Mark's confusion, he explained. "One of his earlier films, I found it in Aunt Maggie's DVD collection. She's got a surprisingly good taste in films."

"I'll have to come round, and we'll have a movie night." Mark suggested.

"Sure." Damian blurted out.

Mark couldn't tell if he was excited about a third date; or keen to secure another non-adventurous activity.

Damian glanced at his watch. "We should head out; Aunt Maggie will be here any minute."

Mark scooped up their rubbish and put it in the bin, and obediently followed Damian outside. The evening was cold, but at least the rain had stopped. The clouds parted enough to show glimpses of stars above. It was a very unextraordinary night, but walking along the quiet, dimly-lit paths with Damian, Mark felt there was something amazing in the air.

He shot a nervous glance towards Damian, who just smiled, and nudged him with his shoulder as they walked, playfully pushing him off balance.

"I really enjoyed myself tonight." Mark said, immediately kicking himself at saying something so bloody unoriginal.

Damian stopped walking and turned to face him. Mark was suddenly aware how close they were. The lamplight caught the sharp cheekbones and full lips, and Damian's bright blue eyes were fixed on his.

Mark hardly dared breathe as Damian raised his hand to graze the side of his face, his fingers tracing the corner of Mark's mouth, and across the rough skin of his cheek. Mark's skin was on fire from Damian's innocent touch. A shiver ran through him, and he couldn't hold back any more. Mark's hands bunched in the thick material of Damian's coat, and pulled him even closer. He leant in to kiss those full lips... and was interrupted by Damian's phone blaring out with Rag'n'Bone Man's husky singing voice.

Damian swallowed hard and fumbled to get his phone out of his pocket. "Aunt Maggie." He grumbled, the words coming out like expletives. Damian shot Mark an apologetic look, as he answered the phone. After a few rushed, embarrassed words, he hung up. "She's waiting for us outside the cinema."

Mark tore his gaze away from Damian's lips, and gave a disappointed sigh. "Perfect timing." He muttered, as the perfect romantic moment slipped away.

Chapter Seven

"Rise and shine, sleeping beauty!"

Nanna's voice broke through Mark's dreams, jerking him awake.

His eyes shot open, and when they finally focussed, they confirmed that Nanna was in his bedroom.

"Nanna! You can't... I'm too old for..." Mark stuttered, pulling his duvet up to his chin. "Nanna, haven't you heard of privacy?"

Nanna tutted. "It's nowt I ain't seen before. Dreaming about Damian?"

"Wha-?"

"You're sporting a lovely bit of drool."

Mark huffed and wiped his mouth, he *had* been dreaming about Damian, and this had been a very rude awakening.

"Come on, get up, we've got plans." Nanna stated, hitting the foot of the bed, to make her point.

Mark stifled a yawn and picked up his phone. "Seriously? It's eight o'clock in the bloody morning, Nanna. It's barely light out."

"Yet me and my friends have already been up for hours, discussing your mysterious ruins and voices. They wanted to go see for themselves. So up you get, boy."

"It's Saturday morn-" Mark broke off from his whinging and looked at Nanna. "Your friends? As in witchy friends?"

"Of course, who else?" She commented airily, knowing she'd caught his attention. She chuckled to herself, as she turned and left his bedroom.

Mark waited for Nanna to completely close the door, before he threw the covers back and pulled his slippers on. He glanced down to check that his pyjamas weren't too scruffy; he paused for a moment, deciding against the Batman dressing gown his Mum got him last year.

As Mark dashed downstairs, the smell of bacon wafted up to meet him.

True to form, his Dad was already on with making bacon butties, a staple of their Saturday morning routine. Mark's Mum was forcing coffee on two vaguely-familiar guests.

"Mark, you remember Denise, and her son Danny." Nanna waved her hand, as she made a quick introduction, "They come to our annual Winter Solstice shindigs."

Denise was exactly how Mark remembered her, the witch who looked stuck in the sixties. Her dress was bright and billowy; her hair, which had been bright red before, was now silver with green tips. She was nearly as old as Nanna, but had that same, youthful glow.

Her son was a stark contrast, all sharp lines and neatness. He looked more suitably dressed to go to the office, than walk through the countryside. He looked like he was only in his early-twenties, but had a mature air.

"Aye, that was one hell of a show last month!" Denise crowed, tackling Mark in a hug before he had chance to process what was going on. "That poor boy, getting lumbered with a demon. I brought my copy of *Dictionnaire Infernal*. Perhaps if we have time later, we can read up on which demon you're dealing with."

Mark spotted a huge hardback book on the table, its pages yellowed with age. Mark wasn't much of a reader, but he was suddenly curious what the book might contain.

Noticing his rapt attention, Nanna gave him a playful knock. "Later," she insisted. "Get some bloody clothes on, an' we might get out t'house sometime today."

Mark scowled a little. He was used to Nanna embarrassing him in front of his friends and family; but in front of other witches was a new and unpleasant thing.

"Fine, fine." Mark grumbled, heading back upstairs.

*****

55

Twenty minutes later, Mark was clinging for dear life, in the back seat of Nanna's Land Rover. Denise was in the front seat, gabbling happily away. Her son was relegated to the back seat. He maintained his calm appearance, but Mark spotted his white knuckles, as Danny clung to the seat.

Mark decided to allow himself a smidge of amusement... until Nanna hit a pothole that rattled his bones.

Not a moment too soon, they were pulling into the yard. Mark swore beneath his breath, as he unbuckled his seatbelt. He couldn't wait until he was seventeen so that he could drive for himself – which was an added bonus to never having to get into Nanna's car again.

Once outside, he was surprised to see the yard owner, waiting for them, her two Shire horses tacked up behind her.

"You're late." She stated.

"Sorry, Mary, some of us slept in." Nanna replied, shooting a glance at Mark. "Mary is letting us borrow her horses; much quicker to ride to the location."

Nanna made a quick introduction between everyone, then headed to the tack room. "Mark, you can ride Holly."

Mark couldn't hide his grimace. He *liked* Holly, he had nothing against her, but the placid cob was the equivalent of having a horse with training wheels.

"Wipe that look off y'face." Nanna chided, "If summat sets off the spooky experience you had, I'm the only one that can stop Lulu from getting upset."

Mark apologised and followed on to the horses. When they were all ready and on board, he tried not to grimace again, as everyone sat a foot above his head. Holly didn't mind being the runt of the pack, and the cob happily plodded along behind the huge Shire horses, and the tall, elegant Lulu.

At the head of the ride, Nanna nudged Lulu into action, and let the mare canter up the grassy tracks. Her hooves light and silent, compared to the heavy beasts that trailed behind her.

Mark forgot his worries, as he leant forward in his saddle, the cold wind whipping the breath from his lungs. As the powerful animal beneath him picked up her pace, Mark felt adrenaline surge through his body.

The ride was over too soon, as Nanna pulled to a halt, at the now-familiar overgrown section of land.

"Get over here boy and tell your story." Nanna called out, as she deftly dismounted.

It took a little longer for Mark's short-legged cob to reach the site, and he was the last one to dismount. He looked over at the other witches, who stood expectantly, ignoring the wind that tugged at their hair and clothes.

Mark repeated what had happened again. This must have been the hundredth time he had to explain what happened, but he still felt an embarrassed flush creeping up his neck as he got to the end and admitted he'd fallen off, knocking himself unconscious.

When he finished, Nanna crossed her arms, and looked at her friends. "So, did you find any history or stories about this place?"

"Nothing." Danny answered, "But that's hardly surprising. These hills are likely filled with traces of the past, but it's so isolated they may never come to light."

Mark raised a brow at how confident the young man sounded. His expression wasn't missed, and Denise elbowed him playfully. "Our Danny teaches at Tealford College. Local history is his speciality."

"Oh... how useful..." Mark commented politely. He wasn't surprised that Danny was a teacher and history buff, there was an air of a fuddy-duddy that seemed to fit that profession perfectly.

"Well, it was a long shot." Nanna commented, "Shall we begin?"

Denise and Danny seemed to know what she was talking about, as they nodded and started to move away from the stone ruin.

"Mark, take up the South point." Nanna said. When Mark just looked blankly at her, she sighed and elaborated her instructions. "Stand opposite me, about five foot from the stone. We're going to use the power of a circle, like we did at the Winter Solstice."

"Hopefully nothing as explosive." Denise chuckled from Mark's left.

Mark moved as directed, eyeing the other witches to make sure he was an equal distance from them. As he found the right spot, he felt a wave of power flow through him, both exciting and grounding him. He could get used to this, he thought, as the adrenaline started to spike in response to the bubbling magic.

After a few moments acclimatising to the rush of power, Mark pushed his senses forward to explore the other witches. Each of them was open to the connection, unable to hide their intentions and focus. Mark reached out to Denise, and felt the brush of her magic, which welled up with an intoxicating joy and life. When he turned his mind to where Danny stood on his right, there was something cooler, more logical, and more powerful than Mark had been expecting from the dull young fellow.

Finally, Mark turned his attention to Nanna. His senses couldn't even get close to her without being overwhelmed, her power something beyond his ability to read. With his eyes open, he could see her clearly, only a few feet before him; but when he closed his eyes, he was blinded by the brilliance of her. He shivered, it was easy to forget how strong his kooky Nanna was.

Nanna was murmuring words, and as she concentrated on the ruins, magic flowed into the circle. Mark could see it spark as it collided within the barrier they had created. The magic swelled and he could feel the pressure building, squeezing the breath out of him.

Within the circle of witches, the air began to thicken with grey smoke, that shuddered, as something tried to break through.

'Steady.'

Mark felt a stab of panic, as he remembered the battle with the demon last month. This was followed swiftly by the soothing word dropping into his mind. He recognised Denise's signature of magic, as it drifted into his chest and calmed him.

Slowly, a figure materialised. The outline of a young man, gradually sharpening, and coming into view. He wore a dull-brown tunic, the material coarse and well-worn. Beneath it, his shoulders were broad, and his arms thick from manual work. His dark hair hung in long tangles, and his bright-green eyes stood out distinctly. Mark shivered at the strange feeling of familiarity, as the young man looked at him.

Mark looked behind him and saw a low-slung stone building that flickered in and out of existence, as the vision blurred with reality.

The unknown man turned to face the building, releasing a shuddering breath as he did so. He gripped something in his hand, and seemed to be bolstering himself.

Mark shouted an intelligible warning, as he saw the man raise a knife.

The man paused, as though he heard him, but shrugged it off.

He brought the point of the knife to his forearm, cutting a symbol into his own flesh with three swift strokes. By the time he was done, he was trembling, and the bloody knife dropped from his hand, falling into the overgrown scrub.

The man's trembling abruptly stopped, and his broad shoulders straightened. His whole aura had changed, as he turned confidently away from the cottage.

Mark swore the man was looking directly at him. Mark's breath caught as he noticed the green eyes shift to black.

A knowing smile lifted the man's thin lips, and he raised his bloody arm.

"*Dī bag sage.*" The words hissed out.

Mark's attention pulled away from the vision, as he felt the magical connection with the other witches waver. The magic was sucked in like a black hole, compressing in the middle of the circle.

It suddenly exploded outwards.

Mark was thrown back several feet, landing heavily on his arse. He grunted as pain reverberated through his body. Swearing beneath his breath, he rolled to sit up, feeling new bruises as he did.

Mark glanced up and saw Nanna, Denise and Danny all looking shaken, but still standing. Great, it was just his luck to be the only one to end up on his arse.

Danny walked over and offered him a hand up. "Don't worry, kid. You've obviously still got a lot to learn."

61

"*Obviously*." Mark echoed bitterly, "I did only start last month."

Danny eyed him curiously. "You're the grandson of the Grand High Witch, and you only just started? How old are you, fourteen?"

"Sixteen." Mark replied, once he was back on his feet. He brushed the crushed grass off his jeans. "How old were you, when you started learning witchcraft?"

Danny shrugged. "I don't remember. My mother always included me in spellcasting."

Mark grumbled beneath his breath. He was quickly feeling like a dunce, when it came to his new status as a witch.

He kept his thoughts to himself and walked over to Nanna and Denise. The two older women stood with their heads together, discussing what they'd just seen. Both of them offered opinions, using names and expressions that went over Mark's head.

After a few minutes of standing like a numpty, Mark interrupted. "So... what does this mean? Did it tell you anything?"

"You have eyes, boy. You saw what I did." Nanna teased.

"I saw stuff, but it doesn't mean I can process it." Mark argued, thinking how unclear and unhelpful the vision had been.

"Fine. It looks like our demon, or another one like it, possessed someone who used to live here." Nanna looked over to Danny. "What's your estimate on the time?"

"By his clothes, I would guess early 14th century. Sorry I can't be any more precise." Danny replied, in knowing tones.

"Have you heard of any stories about this?" Nanna asked.

"No, not specifically." Danny answered with a shrug. "Back in those days, people saw the work of the devil in everything. Now that I know what I'm looking for, I can research it further, if you think it'll help our current situation."

"Denise?"

"Nothing. I don't recognise the symbol, but there are thousands of demons. We can start looking through the *Dictionnaire* when we get back. I could murder a brew." She commented, twisting her dyed hair around her fingers. Denise looking oddly carefree, to say they'd just invoked a vision of a demon who fought back across a gap of centuries.

Mark shivered, as a cold wind whipped across the barren hills. Now that the excitement was over, he was more than ready to go inside, drink tea, and hopefully talk magic.

Luckily, Nanna agreed, and led them back to the horses, who grazed happily a short distance away. The animals seemed unfazed by the powerful spell that had occurred nearby, and Mark assumed it was some of

Nanna's subtle magic that stopped them from wandering further away.

Holly was incredibly happy to be grazing, and the little coloured cob kept her head firmly on the ground, snatching up as much grass as she could. Mark struggled in vain to pull her head up, and on his fifth attempt, he finally got control. By this time, the others were all mounted on their tall, obedient beasts, and looked down at Mark, a hint of impatience at having to wait.

Mark felt an embarrassed blush creeping up his neck again, and he kept his eyes firmly locked on his horse, as he swung into the saddle.

Chapter Eight

The four witches all piled into Nanna's country kitchen, made warm and inviting by the hot Aga.

Nanna set out tea and biscuits, as everyone made themselves comfortable.

Mark felt four heavy paws land on his thigh, as their slightly-podgy house cat jumped into his lap. Tigger purred, sending calming vibrations through Mark's hand, as he stroked him. Mark quickly felt today's stress drop away, as the comforting warmth of the cat grounded him.

At first, he watched with keen interest, as Denise propped open the heavy tome that was the *Dictionnaire Infernal*. Each page of the book was covered in dense writing, with amazing illustrations that were supposed to depict the demons. A man with a horse's head, riding what appeared to be a giant rat; a grotesque stag with wings; a spindly-limbed monster that Mark couldn't

65

describe... each turn of the page brought more unusual and disturbing drawings.

"What were they on?" Mark muttered.

Denise chuckled beside him. "They're *representations*. The only way the artist could express something he couldn't understand." Denise tapped a drawing of a man giving birth to a pig, "Of course, that doesn't mean the artist *wasn't* on some loopy juice."

"Have you ever met a real demon?" Mark asked.

Denise glanced towards Nanna, before answering. "A few, over the years. You inevitably meet some of the blighters, in our profession. They're mainly middlin' creatures, nowt to get excited about."

"So, what do they *really* look like?"

Denise crossed her arms. "I thought you saw the demon in the fire last month, same as everyone else?"

Mark shrugged, "I figured the whole 'hell and brimstone' look was just for show."

"There aren't any set rules over what they look like. Some are almost human, others are part-beast. You have shape-shifters, and those that exist on a different plane and have to possess victims." Denise replied enthusiastically. "Oh, Nanna, do you remember that one in the nineties – couldn't make up her mind if she wanted to be a red dragon or a white wolf? And she ended up-"

"Being a fluffy lizard with that bright pink mohican?" Nanna laughed, as she recalled the demon. "She weren't much frightening after that."

Mark grinned at the mental image.

The rest of the morning devolved into Nanna and Denise trying to one-up one another with their stories of demons.

Mark found their tales amusing – most of them, he hoped were being exaggerated for the sake of the story – but he couldn't help thinking they were getting off track. What about Damian's demon? They were no closer to identifying it; or working out if it was linked to the demon in their vision.

Eventually, the two older ladies lost their steam for stories of old. Danny, who had been standing quietly in the corner, nursing a cold cup of tea for the last hour, finally moved.

"We best head off, mum gets mardy if she's late for her afternoon Bingo." He announced, grabbing their coats off the hook.

Denise scowled at him briefly, then shrugged. "I'd argue with the lad, but he's right. I'll see you soon, Nanna. Mark, why don't you keep hold of that book, it might make some interesting reading for you!"

"Thank-" Mark's response was interrupted when Denise pulled him in for a fierce hug. For a dainty woman, she was stronger than he expected.

Over her shoulder, he noticed Danny saying goodbye to Nanna. Or, at least Mark thought they were saying bye.

"… tell him, or at least teach him to protect himself."

Mark expected Nanna to chase Danny away with one of her trademark glares, but she actually appeared to be considering the young man's advice.

With a bustle of activity, Denise and her son left.

Mark looked expectantly at Nanna and waited.

The older woman took her time, unhurriedly clearing up the teapot and cups from the table.

"Well?" Mark asked, when it became obvious she didn't intend on starting a conversation.

"Well what?"

"You and Danny seemed to have a cosy little chat." He huffed. Tigger seemed to sense his stress and began purring in his lap again, his sharp little claws kneading Mark's thigh.

Nanna turned to face Mark, then glanced down at the cat. She sighed, "There's no need to get in a tizz. Danny was just suggesting that, with your closeness to the demon, you need to catch up on some defensive spells."

"Oh." Mark's flicker of anger was suddenly doused. If Danny was persuading his Nanna to teach him more spells, that was good news. Wasn't it?

"Yes." Nanna replied coolly, her lips pursed. "I think you'll like this one. Although Tigger might not be so keen."

She rummaged through the kitchen, putting seemingly random items on the table.

"As this is the first time conjuring the protection spell, it's best to cleanse the workspace, and encourage

68

balance. You're going to create a circle, similar to what we did this morning, but on a smaller scale." Nanna instructed, nodding towards the clutter. "You will need to connect the four points of the compass. The North is earth, the flowerpot of basil should do; the East is air, you best put an empty bowl there to concentrate the power; the South is fire, you have to light a candle; and the West is water, so a bowl of tap water will suffice."

Mark hurried to follow her commands, trying not to swear when he splashed cold water up his sleeves. "So... I'm not going to get knocked on my arse again, am I?"

"Only if you do it wrong." Nanna replied.

As Mark lit the candle, and moved it into place, he felt a strange calm settle over him. It wasn't heavy, quite the opposite, it felt like everything was lifted away from him. There was no stress, and no worry; all that was left was his steady breathing and the pulsing of power he was starting to recognise as his own.

"Wow, I could stay like this forever." Mark murmured.

Nanna chuckled at his reaction. "It's only so obvious because it's new. You'll get used to it."

Mark let the peaceful atmosphere lap over him, before remembering there was a reason for this warm-up spell. "What next?" He asked, a little reluctant to move on.

"Next, you need to gather herbs into one of the small hessian bags."

"More herbs?" Mark asked.

69

"More herbs." Nanna echoed. "Monkshood, sticklewort, fennel, and mugwort."

As Mark went through the well-stocked herb collection, he noticed Nanna grab a book from the shelf and place it open on the table.

"Now, you need to bind the spell to yourself with a drop of blood."

"Blood?" Mark recoiled at the idea.

"Stop being such a baby, it won't hurt." Nanna replied, handing him a thick needle. "Much."

Before he could overthink it, Mark stabbed the sharp point of the needle into the tip of his finger and winced. "Ow." He complained, feeling a little squeamish as a pearl of blood rose. He held it over the little bag and carefully let the blood drop onto the herbs.

Mark felt a wave of power emanate from the bag in his palm.

"Good." Nanna said quietly, stepping backwards. "Now recite the spell."

Mark looked down at the open book, where there was a handwritten verse on an ageing page. "Y'know this doesn't even rhyme."

"Are you here for the poetry? I thought you were interested in witchcraft." Nanna huffed. "When you create your own spells, they can be as rhyming as you like."

Mark paused, caught by the thought of creating spells of his own. It seemed a million miles away right now. He looked again at the book, and started to recite:

"Pure of heart, kind of soul;

"I seek the protective spirit.

"Hear my fears, mark them well;

"Bring one that will stop harm."

Mark felt the power in his hand start to vibrate, and it suddenly exploded out, sending goosebumps up his arm.

There was a yowl from Tigger, as the fat housecat ran out of the kitchen faster than Mark had seen his podgy frame go.

"Wha-?" Mark broke off, as he felt something nudge his leg.

He looked down, staring for a long while at a black and white dog that hadn't been there a moment ago.

"Where'd you come from, fella?" Mark asked, running his hand through the dog's thick coat. He was very friendly, but when Mark checked his neck, there was no collar or dog tag.

Nanna chuckled from the far side of the room. "It's always exciting to see what they look like for the first time." She watched Mark, as though waiting for something. "3...2..."

"Oooh." Mark clicked, looking from the bloody satchel of herbs, to the dog. "You're kidding me! That isn't... that can't be...."

"I thought you might like this one." Nanna said, still smiling. "He's just a spirit, that takes on a physical form whenever you need protection. They're different for each witch, matching their needs. This is one of the few spells where being a weaker witch gets a stronger result."

Mark was only half-listening, as he knelt to give the dog a good scratch behind his ears. "What does your protective spirit look like?" He finally asked, expecting Nanna to casually state that hers was a dragon.

Nanna shrugged, "I don't have one. Oh, I've tried, believe me, but the spell doesn't work for me. I'm too powerful; there are no weaknesses a spirit would need to protect."

Mark looked up at her, "You could have tried to sound humble, when you said that."

"Hmph, what a waste of time." Nanna nodded towards the herbs still clasped in his hand. "You should keep them with you at all times, for now. In a few weeks, he should be bonded to you enough that you don't need the herbs or spell to summon him."

"So, what now? I take him home to Mum and Dad?" Mark asked. He knew they had encouraged him to learn witchcraft, but he wasn't sure what his parents would make of a new family pet. It wasn't exactly a hamster, that he could hide under his bed.

"No, he'll fade away to the spirit plane when he's not needed. Simply relax your mind, let go of your fears."

Mark closed his eyes, to try to find that peaceful balance he had felt, when he called the corners. His breathing steadied, and his thoughts started to drift away.

He opened his eyes again, and grinned, noticing the dog had gone. "Now *this* is a cool spell."

Chapter Nine

Mark knew he was dreaming, but it was a very realistic dream. Normally, his dreams were surreal, like when he and Harry went canoeing in an over-sized guitar.

This time, he found himself up in the wind-swept moors, close to the river. As he walked to the peak of a hill, he knew what he would find: a rough little homestead with stone walls and a thatched roof. There was a warm glow in the windows, and Mark was drawn forward.

The heavy wooden door opened, letting out a blast of heat and light, as a young man left.

Mark recognised the shaggy brown hair, and the strong frame that spoke of a lifetime of physical work. The man looked straight at Mark, with the clearest, greenest eyes he'd ever seen.

It was the same man from the vision Mark and the other witches had invoked. Again, Mark was struck by familiarity, he felt like he knew him. Which was only cemented by the knowing gaze the young man locked on him.

A dog barked and ran past Mark, straight to the man. It was a black and white collie, just like the spirit he'd summoned. The dog was so excited to see the man, he couldn't decide whether to wag his tail or roll over. The dog attempted both, in a chaotic movement, wriggling on the floor with delight.

The young man laughed, and greeted the dog as an old friend.

Mark held his breath as the dog turned its warm brown eyes towards him. He felt a pang of jealousy – that was *his* spirit animal; how could he be so excited to see a man that was linked with a demon? Even if the young man was good-looking; and had no trace of a dark aura around him…

*****

When school started on Monday morning, Mark was keen to get there. He hadn't seen Damian or Harry since Friday, but he'd texted them after the witchy session on Saturday.

He'd got used to sitting next to Damian on the school bus, and he was surprised that he wasn't there. Damian had sent him a message last night to say he'd meet him at school instead. Mark wondered vaguely if he was ill, or perhaps having trouble with the demon –

Mark imagined the latter would feel awkward to put in a text message.

When he arrived at school, he saw Harry waiting outside, yawning widely, as he watched the other students move past with a typical Monday sluggishness.

"Hey, so what's this awesome bit of magic you had to brag about?" Harry asked, jumping straight to the point.

"Mornin' to you, too." Mark replied. He looked about the school grounds, that were still busy with students filing from the buses and unhurriedly traipsing to class. "This way."

Mark led over to the edge of the school property, where things were a bit quieter and where, he hoped, he wouldn't get in trouble for bringing an animal on site. He smiled at Harry's perplexed expression and pulled the bag of herbs out of his pocket. Mark hesitated for a moment, not actually sure how to summon his protective spirit; Nanna had said that he wouldn't need to speak the spell, but now Mark felt a wavering doubt. His fingers closed tightly around the rough bag, and he concentrated on bringing it forward.

"Nice dog." Harry said. He bobbed down to give the black and white dog a fuss. "So... you learnt to summon animals? That's kind of a cool spell, I guess."

"Not quite." Mark grinned. "He *is* the spell."

Harry looked between Mark and the dog, his mouth hanging, as he put two and two together. "You're kidding? That's awesome. Do you think Nanna would teach me that spell?"

Mark laughed as his best friend gave the dog a thorough scratch. He knew Harry had always wanted a dog, but his father had claimed an allergy to animal hair years ago, making a pet dog a no-go.

"What's his name?" Harry asked, chuckling as the dog stuck his cold nose in his face.

"Oh." Mark looked down at his 'protective spirit'. "I don't think he has one."

"Tsk, every dog needs a name." Harry stated. "I can think of one."

"No, you're not naming him Bob. Or Dave, or Boris."

"I was gonna say Luka." Harry countered.

"Luka... that's actually quite good." Mark commented, in surprise.

Harry shrugged. "It's the name I gave my imaginary dog when I was a kid." He replied sheepishly.

"Alright, Luka it is."

Mark glanced over his shoulder and noticed that the school grounds were empty, except for them. "Come on, we need to go, or we'll miss the bell."

He put the bag of herbs deep into his pocket and concentrated on releasing the spirit.

"See you later, Luka." Harry said, somewhat mournfully, as the dog faded into a wisp of smoke.

As they headed back to the main entrance, Harry was debating on whether his father would be allergic to a magic dog; but Mark started to tune out.

Smiling and laughing with a group of Tealford students, Damian was making his way towards the school, too. He seemed to feel Mark's gaze, and looked across the grounds, until he spotted him.

"And here's Damian." Harry muttered, with a sigh. "I'll see you inside, I need to find Sarah before she accuses me of neglect."

"Yeah, later." Mark replied, vaguely aware of Harry leaving his side, his eyes still fixed on his almost-boyfriend.

Damian said something to the other guys, and moved away from them, his new friends giving him hearty pats on the shoulder as he passed.

Mark felt an unexpected bubble of jealousy. He knew the other guys, and he knew they were all straight, none of them were interested in Damian the way he was. But... it was *his* Damian.

Damian walked across to them confidently, his tall frame graceful. Mark was struck again at the attractive well-defined cheekbones, and the glint of light in Damian's dark blond hair.

As he drew near, his previous confidence drained. He always seemed to be second-guessing himself, especially now, with his 'special friend'.

"Hi." Damian greeted, suddenly awkward again.

"Hi, so what's the big secret this morning?" Mark asked, watching the rest of the lads disappear inside the school building.

"I took your advice." Damian said, looking away with embarrassment. "I kinda tried out for the footie team this morning."

"Really? How'd it go?" Mark asked, suddenly nervous on Damian's behalf.

"Good. Very good. They were impressed." Damian replied, his cheeks reddening as he admitted it.

"So, they let you join the team?"

"Better than that, they want me to start as centre forward at their next game this weekend." Damian smiled uncertainly, "Coach said they might as well, 'cos even if I'm crap, I can't make the team any worse than it already is."

Mark chuckled. "I told you they were rubbish; did you think I was exaggerating?"

Damian brushed aside the comment, "The team seem really nice, too. Well, except for the guy that was centre forward before. I think his name was Eric? He's been demoted to second striker, so I guess it's only natural that he's a bit grouchy."

Mark watched Damian's face light up as he spoke of being on a football team again. Mark wanted him to be happy, wanted him to enjoy being here at Tealford; it looked like he'd been right that the sport was a key to that. He was rewarded with a warm, satisfied feeling, settling comfortably inside him.

The bell went, interrupting Damian as he gave a blow-by-blow account of the football try-outs.

They started to move towards the classroom; to start the boring part of their day.

"Will you come to my game?" Damian asked quietly. "It starts Saturday at three."

"I wouldn't miss it." Mark grinned, playfully shoving his shoulder into Damian's as they walked down the hall.

*****

The morning passed in a mind-numbing blur, with the only highlight being Harry's reading of 'his' sonnet in English class. He had agreed to put aside the dirty limerick, and instead lifted Julia Stile's sonnet from 10 Things I Hate About You, including a dramatic attempt at waterworks.

The whole class had laughed, and even the teacher had been unable to keep a straight face, so when Mr Black gave Harry detention, it was hard to believe he was being serious.

At dinner, everyone was still laughing about it, and people that weren't even in their class, came up to the table and shouted lines at them.

"I've gotta admit, I'm surprised you know that movie." Mark teased, "I'm even more surprised you know it off by heart."

"It's one of Sarah's favourites, she makes me watch it, like once a month." Harry replied, with a shrug. "We watched it last night, and she dared me to repeat it in class."

Mark chuckled. "Well, you definitely won that one. What's your prize?"

Harry wiggled his eyebrows, "Wouldn't you like to know."

Mark looked up, to see Damian enter the food hall. He was still the handsome new guy, but for the first time, he was surrounded by other people. Mark recognised some of the football team, and their followers. It was crazy that, even though they were shockingly bad, the football team represented the most popular people in the school. As a herd, they moved to get food from the dinner ladies, and drifted to their regular tables.

Damian laughed at one of their comments, then slowly extracted himself, claiming the seat next to Mark.

"Well, if you change your mind..." One of the lads said, gesturing vaguely in the direction of the footballer's table.

Damian brushed the offer away, turning his attention to his food.

Mark noticed that he was smiling easily, and his bright blue eyes looked relaxed. He looked... happy.

"What?" Damian asked, when he noticed Mark staring.

"Nuthin'." Mark replied, "I don't think I've ever seen you look so relaxed."

Damian's light mood stilled for a moment. "It's weird, I've lost so much, and the threat of... him, is still hovering. I thought I'd never recover after my parents died, but for the first time in months, everything seems to feel *right*. I've got you. And now... I've got friends and football... it seems surreal, but I'm happy."

Mark found himself leaning in, at Damian's honest declaration. When Damian mentioned that Mark was part of his new, positive life, Mark's heart thudded. All he wanted was to protect Damian, from the demon, from his grief, and from himself. His mind inevitable cast back to last month, when Damian had nearly died in a snowstorm, after seeing no possible other way to escape his traumatic life.

Mark had been lucky to find him and had been bound to him ever since by a sense of duty. Well, that and being completely infatuated with him.

"Mark?"

Mark heard his name vaguely, followed by a sharp jab to his ribs.

"Ow." He said, looking accusingly at his 'best friend'.

"You were ignoring me." Harry complained. "I asked you a question."

"And the appropriate response to that was to poke me?"

"It made me feel better." He replied indignantly.

Mark sighed. "Fine, what was your question?"

"Dean's having a party, wanna go?"

"Oh, yeah, sounds good." Mark replied immediately.

"I thought you guys didn't like Dean?" Damian asked, a frown creasing his brow.

"It's not like that, it's a love/hate relationship." Mark offered.

"Yeah, we love to hate him." Harry chuckled, earning himself a punch from his girlfriend.

"Stop being mean." She chided.

Mark bit back a smile, before he got punched as well. He looked across the hall, and saw Dean flitting between tables, chatting animatedly with the other students, and flirting with both guys and girls.

He turned to Damian, to answer his question seriously. "It's not that we don't like him, Dean is just really annoying. On the plus side, he throws the best house parties when his parents are away. Everybody will be there, including your new football buddies."

Damian looked thoughtful, "A party would be good. I haven't been to one since I left London."

Chapter Ten

By the time school finished on Friday, everybody was buzzing about the party. Even though term had only started a few weeks earlier, the students were keen to take a break from the monotonous cycle of coursework and study.

The rumours about what would happen at the party started to spread. Someone in Mark's science class swore that Dean had hired a rock band, because it turned out his cousin was a hairdresser for them on tour.

Someone else swore that Dean had ordered a dozen crates of champagne for the night.

A group of girls were giggling over the fact that Dean was going to bring someone from Hollyoaks as his date.

Mark knew the rumour mill was nonsense, but he still couldn't help getting excited. This was the first time he was going to one of Dean's parties with an actual date.

Mark pulled on his favourite jeans, and tried on a few shirts, before settling on one. He did a double-take in the mirror, when he realised it was the same shirt he'd worn to the cinema last weekend. He flushed red, as he dragged his top back over his head, tossing it onto his bed. What he wore had never bothered him before, so why was he freaking out over choosing a bloody shirt!

There was a knock at his door. "Yeah." Mark called, distracted as he rummaged through his remaining clothes.

The door opened with a familiar creak, followed by silence.

Mark turned, pausing when he saw Damian hovering in the doorway. He looked ridiculously handsome in faded jeans and a waistcoat, a look that Mark could never have pulled off. Damian also stood wearing a heated expression, his eyes fixed on Mark's bare torso.

"Y-you're early." Mark stammered. He was comfortable in his own skin, and he gave thanks for the years of farm work that kept him fit, with muscles concentrated on his shoulders and chest. It was still strange to have Damian stare at him with desire.

Damian snapped out of his trance, bringing his eyes up to meet Mark's; his usually bright blue irises seemed darker.

"I'm right on time." Damian countered. "I... there was something I wanted to tell you... I mean, talk to you about."

Mark waited for Damian to continue, but he'd fallen silent, his eyes slipping down, away from his face again. "Damian?"

"What? Oh yeah, it's not important." Damian replied, shaking his head. "I feel stupid even mentioning it, but Nanna told me I should share anything weird..."

When he fell silent again, Mark grabbed a smart black jumper, and pulled it on, waiting for Damian to carry on in his own time.

"I've been having strange dreams lately. About places and times that I've never seen, but they feel familiar. And war; there seems to be so much war and fighting..." Damian said, his voice barely audible. "I wake up, and I feel like I haven't slept; I've been exhausted all week."

"What?" Mark could feel a sense of guilt rise up in him. He'd been having repeated dreams about the mysterious green-eyed man from the vision. Having his handsome face haunting his dreams had been rather pleasant. All the while, his boyfriend had been silently suffering with nightmares.

"Yeah, it's been freaking me out." Damian said, running a hand through his hair. "At first, I thought it was a crazy one-off, but it's been non-stop... I didn't want to say anything because, y'know it's *just* dreams. But I feel like I'm going mad, I'm so tired, I'm snapping at poor

Aunt Maggie. I've never been an angry person, but now it's there, all the time. I've tried to hide it..."

Mark stood awkwardly in his room, whilst Damian unloaded his burdens. He felt unable to help, and his mind raced as he wondered what he should do, as a friend, and as a witch. Mark suddenly felt out of his depth, and wished he had an answer for Damian.

"Thank you, for telling me." Mark said, reaching out for Damian, and resting his hand on his arm, wanting any contact he could. "We can ask Nanna, I'm sure there's some spell that can help. Who knows, maybe it means the demon is strong enough to expel."

His optimism was so forced, Mark was surprised Damian didn't call him out on it. But Damian seemed distracted, his blue eyes were still dark, and drifted from Mark's gaze, lower to his lips. Mark felt his heart thud in anticipation, as he leant closer. He could feel the warmth radiating from Damian, and he kissed his soft lips.

Damian let out a gentle groan, his lips parting, and Mark felt his lithe fingers curl into his hair.

Mark felt all his worries slip away. Everything felt perfect in this moment.

"Boys!"

Mark jumped guiltily away, as his Dad's voice echoed through the house.

"If you want a lift to this party, we need to leave now. I'm not missing kick-off."

Damian was breathing hard, and stepped away from Mark. "We should... um, we should get going." He coughed.

*****

The party was already well underway when Mark's Dad dropped them off at Dean's house.

"Now remember boys: no drinking, no drugs, no tattoos, violence, or ritual sacrifice..."

Mark cringed, as his Dad gave the usual 'Dad-talk'. He pushed Damian out of the car, following as quickly as possible.

The house had once been an old barn, but Dean's parents had spared no expense in refurbishing it. Inside, it was a sharp contrast, with big airy rooms, and minimalist decor. Every time Mark came here, he was struck with the feeling of being inside an art gallery. Expensive, but cold.

On the other hand, there was plenty of space for parties.

"Want to get a drink?" Mark asked, as he noticed Damian hesitate.

"Yeah." Damian replied, his eyes scanning the crowd.

Mark led the way towards the well-stocked kitchen, "What do you want to drink? There's Coke, lager, wine? Or some cheap-looking... I think that's cider?"

"Just pop for me." Damian said, embarrassed.

"No, that's cool. I mean, I don't drink, not really." Mark replied in a hurry, grabbing a couple of cans of

Coke. If he was honest, he'd got drunk at Dean's last party, and didn't want to repeat the embarrassment. "I bet this is tame compared to the parties you had in London?"

Damian shrugged. "Depends on the attendees. Some were pretty chill, others were... not. But those tended to get closed down pretty quick before things could escalate."

They wandered through the crowded rooms, until they found Harry and Sarah near the source of music. Mark was slightly disappointed to find there wasn't a live band, or DJ. Instead there was a laptop with speakers, and a bunch of students hovering round, trying to add their favourite songs to the playlist.

Sarah was bouncing on her toes to the music, whilst her boyfriend stood sullenly at her side.

Mark knew that this really wasn't his best friend's scene. For Harry, listening to music only counted when it was a live gig.

Damian was eyeing the make-shift dancefloor, then looked towards Mark. He nodded towards the dancers. "Want to dance?"

Mark flushed red at the thought of trying to move his body rhythmically, with the pressure of his whole school watching. "Um, I don't dance." He mumbled.

Sarah overheard him and huffed, giving him a light punch on the arm. "Mark, when a hot guy asks if you want to dance – *you say yes*!"

Damian chuckled, and when he got no further with Mark, he held his hand out to Sarah. "Would *you* like to dance?"

"Yes!" Sarah said, very loud and clear. She childishly stuck her tongue out at Harry and Mark, as she passed them.

Mark watched, as Damian danced. It looked like it was perfectly natural for him, and he moved to the beat, as though it was a part of him. Sarah was right, he looked incredibly hot right now. Mark was torn between wanting to be up there with him; and being nowhere near, so he didn't look like a drunk giraffe by comparison.

"I'm new to the whole relationship thing. Will we get in trouble for this?" Mark asked Harry, only half-joking.

"Nah," Harry replied, taking a swig of his drink, "Looks like they're havin' too much fun to care."

They both stood, watching the dancing, getting much more joy from observing than taking part.

"Still on for tomorrow?" Harry asked.

Mark paused, trying to remember what they had planned.

"The Hub, in Tealford." Harry prompted.

"Oh yeah, tomorrow at six o'clock." Mark recalled, feeling guilty that he'd forgotten.

Harry looked nervous, an expression that Mark had never seen on him before – he didn't know Harry's face made that look.

"It... it's a new talent evenin'." Harry said in a rush. "Don't go tellin' everyone, but I'm performing."

Mark's thoughts all stopped, and he looked at Harry in surprise. "You are?"

"Yeah... I've been practising in secret, only Sarah knew 'cos I didn't want it to be a big deal."

Mark felt stung that his best friend was keeping secrets from him, but put on a smile. "No, that's awesome! I can't wait to hear you."

Harry grinned, visibly relaxing now that he'd shared his big secret. "And six o'clock sharp – I'm on early in the evening."

"I'll be there." Mark replied, nudging his best friend. He thought it was funny that the religiously-late Harry was nagging him about being on time. "Damian has his first footie game tomorrow afternoon, but I'll have plenty of time to get there – promise."

The party carried on into the night, with light, music and laughter pouring out of Dean's house.

Mark had lost track of Damian about half an hour ago, and he felt rather guilty for leaving him alone. Sure, Damian was now a fully-initiated Tealford student, same as everyone else; they might be dating, but surely Mark wasn't the only person Damian knew by now.

As he checked for him in the crowded rooms downstairs, Mark bumped into Dean. Literally. He hadn't seen him walking around the corner until it was too late, and he managed to knock Dean's drink all over his forearm.

"Enjoying the party?" Dean asked, pursing his lips at the spilt drink.

"Yeah, it's great. Sorry about your drink." Mark replied quickly, glancing away. He wondered if there was any way he could quickly end this conversation. He didn't want to be rude to his host, but he'd honestly been avoiding him all night.

"This is the very reason I don't drink the good stuff at a party – there's always a risk of spillage. How frightfully boring that it happened bumping into you." Dean said, gazing at Mark thoughtfully, his eyes red with a hint of bloodshot. "Y'know, by Monday morning, the rumour mills will have turned that innocent little sentence into something... scandalous. Drinks were spilled in a fit of passion!"

"Yeah right - everyone knows I'm with Damian now."

"All the more scandalous, then!" Dean effused, with a knowing wink. "Or maybe the rumours will turn it into a three-"

"Dean!" Mark snapped, "Seriously, is there nothing else on your mind?"

"What, like GCSE revision and my crummy after-school job? Why would I waste my time thinking about that dull stuff? You, my boy, need to learn how to relax." He replied, jabbing a finger into Mark's chest.

"I'll work on it." Mark tried not to roll his eyes. "Have you seen Damian?"

"Well yeah, I see him all the time. That boy is hard to miss."

"Dean, I meant have you seen him recently? Say, the last ten minutes?" Mark tried again, wondering if a drunk Dean could understand the parameters.

"Lost your lover already? If I were you, I'd handcuff that boy to me. If you want to borrow handcuffs, I've got some upstairs." Dean mused.

Mark sighed, knowing he wasn't going to get a straight answer out of him. Dean was a pain in the arse when he was sober, never mind now.

"Never mind. I'll see you later." Mark said, excusing himself.

"Ugh, you really are no fun. This is supposed to be a *party*. My party." Dean sighed dramatically. "Your boyfriend's outside, playing football with some of the others."

Boyfriend. Mark was really starting to like that word. Maybe Nanna was right, he should just embrace the fact that he and Damian were an item.

"Thanks, Dean."

Mark made his way to the back garden, which was a massive, landscaped extravaganza, fit for the Chelsea Flower Show. True to form, some of the party-goers were playing with a football on the biggest patch of grass they could find.

Mark smiled, it hadn't take long for Damian to fit in and find friends, even if he was a Southerner, and possessed by a demon. Mark idly wondered which posed the biggest hurdle. His eyes scanned over the crowd, as he tried to spot Damian's blond head in the dimly-lit garden.

Before he could spot him, Mark faltered. Something felt off; the world seemed to shift, and Mark was filled with the same oppressive feeling he'd had at the old ruins.

The rest of his schoolmates fell silent, looking around wildly, trying to pinpoint what was wrong.

The wind dropped, and everything was quiet and eerily still.

In the darkness, Mark thought he saw a grey mist rolling towards them. That wasn't unusual at this time of year, but as he pushed out his senses, he could read a black and pained aura. Something wanted revenge, it wanted to slake its bloodlust.

Even without witch-training, the other students began to sense something was wrong. Their primal instinct for survival kicked in, and people started to run inside, the night air now filling with shouts of panic.

Mark stood his ground, as everyone pushed past him, even though that little voice in his head was demanding he get in the bloody house – now. He took a deep breath, trying to gather his wits. Whatever it was out there was doing an awesome job of sending fear coursing through him.

Before he could even think to summon him, the black and white dog appeared at his side, nudging his hand with his cold nose. Luka stood calmly and quietly waiting, oblivious to the danger pressing closer.

Mark shuddered as the grey fog rolled in closer, spilling over the stone walls of the garden. He could see the snapping, snarling jaws, with black eyes hovering above; insubstantial beasts straining to break free and attack.

He racked his brains for a spell – any spell – that could be used. Nanna's emphasis on protection and healing didn't really offer anything to fight back against this threat.

Mark felt a nudging at his leg and looked down at Luka. Luka. He might be the key. Nanna said he was fuelled by Mark's fear – well, he should be super-charged right now.

"Attack." Mark commanded. When Luka turned his warm brown eyes questioningly, he tried again, "Stop them! Please, just help."

Luka started to nudge him more firmly, and when Mark didn't move, the dog grabbed his trouser leg and pulled in the direction of the house.

"No, stop – that wasn't what I meant!" Mark protested, as he stumbled off balance. "Luka, bad boy, stop!"

His pleas were useless, as the black and white dog relentlessly tugged at his trousers. As they neared the

French doors, they were flung open by Harry, who grabbed Mark by the arm and dragged him inside.

Harry and Sarah closed the doors and locked them, before they rounded on Mark.

"What the hell do you think you're doing?" Harry demanded. "You run *away* from the freaky ghost hounds, you nutter."

"I thought I could do something." Mark argued, breathlessly.

"What are they?" Sarah asked, her voice shaking.

Mark shook his head. "Dunno." He could still see the grey fog through the window, it churned and coiled mere metres away, inching closer.

The house was ripe with fear, the panic of the students almost tangible.

"You need to call Nanna." Harry insisted.

"On it." Mark agreed, pulling out his phone.

He waited impatiently as it rang for what seemed like an age, before his Nanna answered.

"Mark? You better have a good reason for this. I'm in the middle of watching Dirty Dancing..."

"We're being attacked by monsters." Mark interrupted.

There was a pause on the other end. "Well, that's not a poor excuse. What monsters?"

"A fog rolled in, and there was a dark aura." Mark reported quickly. "There are beasts in it. We're all in Dean's house, but I don't know if the walls will keep them out."

"No, probably not." Nanna replied.

"I tried to fight them off, but that didn't work."

"Are you mad? Mark, you need to protect the house. I'll be there as soon as possible."

Mark heard the clang of keys, and he could picture Nanna bustling through her house. "But how?" He asked.

"You've been practising nowt but protection spells." Nanna snapped. "You know what to do."

She hung up, and Mark was left under the expectant stares of his friends.

"I've gotta hold them off." He said, his stomach twisting in a sickening knot. "Where's Luka? And where's Damian?"

"Damian's *currently* in the living room with the rest of the footie team." Harry replied in an odd tone. "Luka set off that way, he looked like he knew what he was doing, so I didn't stop him."

Mark took a deep breath, trying to calm himself. It didn't help that the oppressive atmosphere sent his pulse racing, setting every nerve on edge.

"Right, can you guys check on the others, and... Damian..." Mark looked at them seriously. "Can you check his little friend isn't reacting to this? If it is... find a way to get him away from everyone, but stay safe."

Harry and Sarah exchanged a meaningful look, but nodded and followed Mark's instructions.

Mark jumped out of his skin as there was a rattle at the French doors. Whatever was out there was trying to get in.

The noise of scrabbling claws rang out against the brickwork, as it made its way along the building, searching for a weak point.

Mark swore inwardly. He mentally pictured the four corners, and slowly felt his panic diminish, and stopped choking him.

Right, now he just had to defend the house against monsters. Nanna always said a lot of magic came down to focus and intention.

Mark called the corners again, and with a deep breath he connected to the magic that thrummed at his fingertips.

Mark sent his senses out, feeling the power ripple gently. The positive energy broke through the evil aura, and Mark willed it to physically stop the beasts.

At first it worked, the creatures fell back, surprised at the barrier, but then they attacked with renewed vigour; the walls were shaking and the glass shattered.

Mark could hear his friends screaming, but he couldn't move. It was taking all his effort to hold that block, and he could feel the beasts hit the weakening defences again and again. He couldn't wait for Nanna. There was no time. There had to be another answer.

It happened without any conscious thought. Overcome with exhaustion, Mark dropped the protection spell. He could sense the beasts pause at the disintegrating barrier, then howl and surge forward.

More screams went up from the house.

"*Dī bag sage.*" The words fell from Mark's lips, as he concentrated on the beasts.

He felt the magic tear through him, leaving him trembling in pain. The creatures' snarls soon turned to whelps, and the dark fog contorted unnaturally.

Mark ended up on his knees, struggling for breath. He looked up, the malevolent aura that had surrounded the house was now recoiling. It was shifting, the pain-fuelled anger of the creatures had changed. They felt pain, they felt *fear*, and Mark was the cause. The magic that had conjured the beasts started to shudder, becoming unstable. There was a loud blast, and then everything was still.

Chapter Eleven

Mark's ears were ringing, and he jumped when someone grabbed his arm. He could see Harry speaking to him, and he shook his head, trying to hear the words.

Harry helped him to his feet, and together they staggered back into the main part of the house.

Other teens were starting to move, looking as shell-shocked as Mark felt. Some were staunching bloody wounds, or sitting patiently whilst their friends bandaged lacerations. Nobody bothered looking up as Mark made an entrance, they were all too pre-occupied.

Mark started to hear beyond the ringing, beyond the sobbing of students. There were lots of questions, but nobody had any answers.

"What happened?" Mark asked Harry quietly.

Harry looked at him in disbelief. "If you don't know, mate, I don't think anyone does."

Mark felt a vibration in his pocket, he pulled out his phone to find a message from Nanna. '*Out front. NOW.*'

Mark sighed and made his way to the front door. He hesitated in the doorway, looking out into the night. It was dark, but there was nothing unnatural about the darkness. The only scary thing left, were the headlights of his Nanna's Land Rover.

The silhouette of several people showed against the lights, as they made their way towards the house.

"Mum? Dad?" Mark rushed forwards at the unexpected sight of his parents.

"Are you alright, sweetie?" His Mum asked, checking his limbs were still attached, before wrapping him in a fierce hug.

"Yeah, what are you doing here?" Mark asked breathlessly.

"I thought it wise to bring a trained nurse." Nanna explained, "Is anyone injured?"

"Um, yeah. They're all inside."

Mark's Mum gave him a kiss on the cheek, and headed inside with her nurse's bag.

"What happened to the monsters?" His Dad asked, looking around, his confusion clear.

By the way Nanna looked, Mark was sure that she already knew. Could she sense the spell he'd used?

"I *told you* to protect the house – to leave the monsters to me." She said through gritted teeth.

"I'm sorry, I tried, but I wasn't strong enough." Mark felt a stab of guilt.

"Not strong enough? You have no idea, boy." Nanna muttered.

"Will someone fill me in? What happened?" His Dad demanded.

"Mark used dark magic." Nanna said quietly.

Mark's Dad blanched, and looked at him. Mark had never seen him look so scared, and he felt his guilt deepen.

"You..." Dad started in a shaky voice. "Where did you even learn such a spell?"

"I-in the vision, the man said it." Mark stuttered. "I didn't mean to use it, I didn't know it was *dark* magic."

"You said he'd never learn that side of witchcraft." Dad snapped at Nanna.

"Dad, it wasn't her fault." Mark argued, feeling suddenly irritated. "What's the big deal? It worked, it stopped whatever was attacking us."

"You have no idea, Mark. I knew it was a bad idea for you to become a witch." His Dad growled.

Nanna clipped her full-grown son around the ear, "Maybe he'd know the limits of magic, if you allowed me to give him a full training."

Mark felt his whole world rock. He thought his family had supported his choice to learn witchcraft. His Dad had never shown explicit interest, but Mark had never thought that he hadn't wanted him dealing with magic.

"Michael, go inside and help your wife. We'll deal with this later." Nanna said firmly, making it clear she wouldn't be questioned.

Mark watched his Dad reluctantly walk away from the brewing argument. "What's going on Nanna? What aren't you telling me?"

"That's a big old question, boy." She said, sounding tired. "Your Dad and I need to have a chat. Just know that there are different areas of witchcraft. Our coven is fuelled by nature, and the elements. We link with power that is created by life, and we treat it with the utmost respect. It's not always the quickest or easiest route, but we have to honour it.

"Then, there is dark magic. It is fuelled by pain, and demonic energies. It is powerful, and easy to tap into; which can make it hard to resist for witches that want to take the quick route to power. But it corrodes your soul, and it's easy to become addicted to it."

"I didn't know…" Mark replied quietly.

"I know…" Nanna sighed. "I'll explain more in time. Just… promise me you won't use that spell, or any dark magic again. I swear, everything we do is for your benefit, Mark."

Mark was surprised to see a private pain hovering in his Nanna's normally care-free expression. "I promise."

Nanna stood, staring at him; Mark wished she'd share the thoughts that were causing her such grief.

"I'm glad you're alright." She finally said, pulling him into a hug. "How was Damian and his demon tonight?"

"I haven't seen any sign of Bob." Mark replied, "Oh yeah, that's what Harry has nicknamed the demon. He and Sarah went to check on him during the attack."

"Well, get in there and find out if he's showing any signs of awakening." Nanna said. "Then we'll see about getting all your friends home."

Mark nodded. He could see blue lights in the distance, the emergency services were on their way. In the aftermath, it all seemed surreal now.

Chapter Twelve

Mark slept in late on Saturday, he was absolutely exhausted, and when he finally got up at midday, his limbs ached and pleaded to go back to bed. He lay in his tangled duvet, his mind running over everything that happened last night. He'd used a spell that had made his family flip out, but Mark felt strangely disconnected. It had *worked*, it had saved the day... even as the thought crossed his mind, it made his skin crawl. He'd caused those creatures immeasurable pain, something he never wanted to do again.

Mark checked his phone, and saw it was full of notifications. It looked like everybody at school had posted something on social media, retelling their version of events, and stirring up sympathy for their injuries. There were various theories over what happened, that their drinks had been spiked, or someone had got out the Ouija board. Ghosts and monsters were mentioned, and inevitably… magic. When Mark saw his name come up on a few posts he turned away from his phone.

When he went downstairs, the house was quiet. His Mum had gone to provide extra healthcare on her day off, for those that needed last night's bandages changing. Nanna was nowhere to be seen; and his Dad… well, Mark had never known him so quiet.

It was clear his Dad hadn't slept, with dark rings around his tired eyes. He simply looked at his son, saying nothing.

"Dad…"

"You stepped out of line, last night." Dad said, his voice rougher than normal. "You're grounded until further notice."

Mark frowned, "But Dad, I said I'd support Damian at his first football game; then Harry has a talent show tonight."

His Dad eyed him warily. "Fine, but I'm driving you to both, and then it's straight home."

"Dad, I didn't mean to upset you." Mark said. He could feel the disappointment radiating off him. "Dad, why… I thought you wanted me to be a witch."

His Dad took the time to inspect his almost-empty coffee mug, before he replied. "I want you to find your own path, Mark. That's what I've always wished for you. If you want to follow the family tradition and become a witch, I'm OK with that; but… I know the dangers involved, the risks you will run…"

"Dad, I'm learning as fast as I can. Besides, you're not a witch; you chose not to be one. Maybe in this Nanna knows best…" Mark's voice trailed off beneath the glare from his Dad.

"That's what you think of me…" He muttered, tapping his knee. "My mother is the Grand High Witch; I have seen more in my lifetime than you could imagine. Just because I wasn't the one casting the spells…"

"Why didn't you become a witch?" Mark asked.

"That's not important." Dad said with a shake of his head. He glanced at his watch. "We'll set off at half-two. I think you should work on your GCSE coursework until then."

Mark bit his tongue. It wasn't fair, he knew his Dad was keeping something from him, but couldn't figure out what it was. It seemed so out of character, Mark had always pictured his Dad as the pushover in the family. Now, he was worrying that Dad would put his foot down and stop his witchcraft lessons, just when he felt he needed them most.

Mark nodded and, only pausing to grab some dinner, he made his way upstairs, as his Dad continued to sit in stony silence.

*****

His Dad still refused to speak, as he drove them to the school football field. It was a very sparse affair, the pitch marked with faded white lines, and some very patchy nets strung up to a couple of rusty goalposts. Of course, there was no shelter for the players, or their fans.

107

It was a typical February day, with low-hanging grey clouds and a cold, interminable drizzle. Mark pulled up his fleece-lined hood, and headed to the small crowd that lined up at the side of the pitch.

"Hey, you guys made it!"

Mark turned to see that the nearest bundle of winter coat and thick clothes was Damian's Aunt Maggie. "Yeah, wouldn't miss it."

"Damian will be thrilled that you're here." Maggie said, her voice muffled by her scarf, but her eyes gleamed excitedly. "I still can't believe he's on the team – I was worried he'd never settle!"

Despite his dull mood, Mark forced himself to smile. "I've been telling him for weeks the school team could do with his skills. I thought kick-off was at three?" He asked, looking around at the lack of footballers.

"Oh, the other team has been running late, something to do with a flat tyre on their bus." Maggie replied, with a dismissive wave of her hand. "They messaged to say they were on their way."

"Shame they didn't let us know earlier, we could have waited inside." Mark's Dad said with a mild grumble.

"I'm surprised the Tealford team is looking in as good shape as they are. Partying 'til late last night – I heard something kicked off..." She mentioned, her eyes moving questioningly between Mark and his Dad.

"Damian told you about last night?" Mark asked warily, wondering if Damian had finally decided to be open with his Aunt.

"Not so much. He came in, looking completely shell-shocked." Maggie explained, "I didn't think it had been more than a few years since I went to a high-school party – have they changed that much?"

Ah, so Damian hadn't told her about the demonic pest. "It got... a bit chaotic. A bad crowd turned up." Mark said quickly, looking to his Dad and praying he didn't drop them in it.

"Kids these days." He eventually said in a tired voice. "You got dropped in at the deep-end, starting with a teenager."

"They're like a different species..." Maggie remarked.

Mark drifted away as his Dad and Aunt Maggie fell into a dull, grown-up conversation. After this morning's silence, it was a bit of a relief, to have his Dad distracted, and chatting normally with someone.

The other school's team finally turned up at half three, they jogged into the changing rooms with their kit bags, red-faced at their late arrival. By the time all players were on the pitch, it was quarter to four. Mark glanced at his watch for the umpteenth time, a ninety-minute game, plus a fifteen-minute half-time break... this would end about half five – he still had time to get to Harry's talent show at six.

Mark was immediately distracted from his worries, as he watched Damian, looking perfect in his footie kit. The bright red shirt and shorts hung loose about his athletic frame, and Damian jumped on the spot to keep warm. Mark had never seen Damian look so focussed, so at home.

The game started, and it wasn't long before the opposing team had stolen the ball from Tealford; scoring their first goal. Mark sighed, it had been a while since he had bothered watching his school team play, it was obvious they hadn't improved. They ran around with lots of enthusiasm, but it didn't translate into possession of the ball, or goals.

Except now they had Damian.

He managed to get the ball, and ran it up the length of the pitch, dodging the other players. It was mesmerising to watch the fluidity with which he moved.

A cheer went up from the fans, and Mark jolted. He'd been so busy watching Damian, it hadn't occurred to him that the ball hitting the net was a goal. Tealford's first real goal in months!

The amassed family and friends on the sidelines were quick to lighten up, daring to hope and get excited when their team got the ball.

Mark's pulse raced, as he got swept along by the rush. He cheered every time Damian took control of the game. His teammates had quickly learnt to pass to him at every opportunity, and soon he'd scored again.

The other school team quickly worked out he was the only player with talent, and started to block him, getting more desperate as time went on.

Damian was dribbling the ball between the defenders again, and with barely any hesitation, he shot, and he scored! The ball hit the net as the whistle went for half-time, with Tealford well and truly leading.

The thrill was cut short, as the defender failed to stop, his momentum and the wet grass throwing his late tackle off balance. Damian cried out as the studs hit his leg and knocked him to the ground.

"Damian!" Mark forgot there was a game in process and ran onto the pitch.

He was blocked by the coach, who gave him a warning glare as he headed to his fallen player.

After what seemed like an age of discussion between Damian and his coach, Damian started to get up, with the help of two of his teammates. The trio headed to the changing rooms, along with the rest of the team, for their half-time break.

Mark followed behind them, hovering outside the door with Aunt Maggie. They stood without speaking, waiting to hear that Damian was alright.

Eventually, the door opened, and the coach looked at them both.

"Damian's leg is hurt, it's not broken, but he's not going to play the rest of the game. I'd like him to go to hospital to get it checked, but he's refusing." The coach looked at Mark sceptically. "He's asking for you, Mark."

The coach stood aside, holding the door so Mark could go in.

"See if you can talk some sense into him." Maggie said, her voice shaking.

Mark nodded and went inside. It was a little warmer in the changing rooms than out on the field, but at least it was dry. Mark headed to the player's changing room, where the other lads were chatting excitedly. Despite their star striker getting injured, this was the first time they'd had a solid lead in a game, and they were obviously relishing the moment.

As Mark stepped in, they all fell silent. Their gazes were wary and, in a few cases, hostile. Mark had the distinct impression that he was trespassing.

"In there." One of the lads said, jerking his thumb towards another room.

Mark headed into a small room, empty except for the table, and a very pale looking Damian.

"You're hurt." Mark didn't need to ask, he could feel the pain radiating off Damian.

Damian tried to crack a smile, but it came out like a grimace. "I... want to finish my first game."

"You're mad." Mark stated. "You can't even walk on it."

"I know, but coach says it's most likely just muscle damage and bad bruising. And I thought... well, you've been learning healing spells with Nanna..."

"Oh no..."

"Please, Mark." Damian begged.

"Even if I could heal you, you'd only risk injuring it further if you played." Mark argued. "The coach is right, you need to go to hospital."

"Please..." Damian repeated.

Mark looked into those big, pleading blue eyes, and sighed. "This might not even work."

"I believe in you."

The words sent an unexpected warmth through Mark. He believed in him?

"Alright, leave your shin pad on for support." He mumbled, suddenly struggling to put words in a coherent order.

Mark took his gloves and leant over, wrapping his hands about Damian's calf. He tried to ignore how firm the well-defined muscle felt. Instead he tried to shift his focus to the areas that were giving off a signature of pain.

Mark closed his eyes and let himself connect to the magic around him. It was accompanied by the usual heady experience, but there was something new. The warmth that Damian had sparked now laced through his magic, making it stronger. Mark focused his power on the torn muscle and bruised flesh.

Damian shifted as his leg heated up, wincing at the pain.

Mark blocked it all out. He blocked out his concern, his guilt at causing pain and the pressure to succeed. All he was aware of was the spell, his magic coursing up and down the veins, knitting together the muscle fibres.

The spell came to a natural end, and Mark released the magic from his grasp, letting it sink away into the elements. He felt very disorientated as his senses rushed back to normal.

Mark looked at Damian hopefully. "Well?"

"It's sore." Damian confessed, as he gingerly swung his legs down from the table, and placed them squarely on the floor. He slowly stood up, testing his weight. "I... I don't think it's damaged anymore."

Mark let his senses run over Damian's leg. The signs of pain had faded greatly, and it looked almost normal. "I still don't think you should play on it. Aunt Maggie's here – even if you don't want to go to the hospital, she can drive you to my house, Mum and Nanna can check it's properly healed."

Damian dropped his gaze. "You don't understand, I have to play. I need to prove to myself, and *him*, that this is where I belong. That I will fight to be happy after everything that's gone on."

Mark's resolution wavered as Damian hinted at the trauma he carried. They had never really spoken about his parents, beyond the fact that they'd died in a car crash last year; nor of his grandmother, who had a heart attack after taking him in.

Mark told himself that he was waiting for Damian to feel confident enough to discuss it, but if he was honest, the topic scared him. It seemed too big, and too terrible a thing to lose so much of your family; and to know that the demon who had caused it was currently hitching a lift with him.

"Fine, you win. Just be careful, I don't know if I can fix you up again."

"Oh, believe me, those guys won't be able to get anywhere near me." Damian replied with a hint of cockiness, leaning in towards Mark.

Everything else vanished when their lips met. Mark would never get tired of kissing Damian, of running his hands through Damian's hair, the strength with which Damian kissed him back...

"Boys! Now is not the time!" The coach's voice broke through the haze. "If I have to put the cold hose on you two, I swear I will..."

Damian pulled away first, looking rather sheepish. "Sorry, coach."

"Sorry, coach." Mark echoed, then grinned at Damian. "Now you've gotta persuade him to let you play!"

After passing the curious and judging eyes of the rest of the football team, Mark ended up outside. He shivered as the drizzling rain stopped pretending, and came down for real. Despite the weather, the buoyant mood of the spectators remained high, when they saw their star player walk out, without a hint of a limp.

They cheered every time he got the ball, and even Mark joined in, whooping like an idiot when Damian scored ten minutes later.

Tealford's defences were still shoddy, and the opposing team managed to get a couple more goals in the second half, the ball flying past the rather stunned-looking Tealford goalie.

But Damian was right, every time he had possession of the ball, no one could even match him. He moved with grace and determination, shifting the ball out of reach with practised ease.

The whistle blew for full-time, and everyone went wild, running onto the pitch and jumping with excitement. They had won!

Even the coach had lost his professional demeanour, and was hugging Aunt Maggie, and every other person in arms' reach.

Damian was lost in a sea of players and well-wishers, and Mark had his work cut out for him, trying to push through. Even at a distance, he could sense an aura of pain rippling from Damian's leg, a sharp contrast to the big grin plastered on his face.

Damian's blue eyes locked onto Mark, and he headed his way through the crowd.

"You should rest that leg." Mark said, then immediately kicked himself for sounding such a buzzkill.

Damian looked a little sheepish. "Thanks again for fixing it. You have no idea how much this means to me."

As they stood close together, Mark could still feel the elation rushing through him; and Damian was practically glowing from adrenaline. As Damian parted his lips, but failed to follow up the comment, Mark wondered if he was going to kiss him. Their stolen kisses had been reserved for when they were alone. Snogging in front of the two football teams and their follower was a scary prospect.

Mark wondered if Damian was thinking something similar, as he gave a secret smile, looking around at the crowd.

"We're celebrating at the local pizza place. Want to come?"

Pizza and Damian, it seemed like the perfect evening. Mark sighed, "I would, but I've gotta get to Harry's thing tonight. Next time?"

Damian looked a little deflated. "No, sure, that's fine. You guys have fun."

Mark looked at his watch again, cringing at how late it was. "I really have to go. I'll text you later?"

Damian's reply was drowned by the chanting footballers who swept him back into their ranks.

Mark watched him disappear into the crowd, wishing he'd just kissed him, or maybe gone to the pizza party; the rest of the world be damned.

"Mark." His Dad snapped, pointing at his watch.

*****

Mark jogged down to their car, his Dad in tow. As the engine started, Mark checked his watch again. They could still make it, if they got a shift on.

His Dad pulled the car out gently, and as he drove down the road, Mark was silently cursing his Dad's steady driving. For the first time, he wished for Nanna to be behind the wheel.

As they drove, they hit patches where there was a mobile signal, and Mark was inundated by texts and voicemails from Sarah and Harry. They were all along the same theme – asking where the bloody hell he was. Mark sighed, and tried to reply, but the signal dropped again, leaving the message in limbo.

They hit a patch of traffic as they got to Tealford, and Mark stopped watching the clock on the dashboard, as it ticked past 18:00.

Mark grit his teeth as his Dad circled the nearby car park, at an excruciatingly slow pace. As soon as he stopped the car, Mark jumped out and ran for the Hub.

A man on the door stopped him, asking for his ticket. Mark swore beneath his breath and pulled out his wallet. "How much?"

"Fiver." The guy replied. "No discount for missing the first two acts."

Mark felt his stomach drop. He made his way inside, already knowing what he would find.

At the far end, a middle-aged woman was on stage, crooning along to a background track; her song replayed by the speakers set around the room. There were some tables, that were half-full; and a dancefloor that was completely empty. There was a crowd of people by the bar, and more hanging around a familiar figure.

Mark headed towards Harry, trying to work out what he could say to apologise.

Sarah spotted him before Harry did, and the smile fell away from her face. She moved to intercept him, resting a hand on his arm, her eyes searching for the life-threatening injuries that must have caused him to be delayed.

"Sarah, I'm sorry, Damian-"

Sarah snatched her hand away, her look of disappointment clear. "Harry was brilliant, it's a shame you missed it." She said coolly, stepping aside to let him pass.

Mark's already-sizable guilt increased. He'd known Sarah for years, and for the normally happy, bubbly girl to be so cold... he'd never known her so upset.

He went over to the crowd of people surrounding Harry and waved to get his attention. His best friend was obviously deep in conversation, missing the gesture.

"Hey, Harry..." Mark grabbed his sleeve, when he got close enough to him.

"Mark, do y'mind? I'm busy." Harry replied, shrugging out of his hold.

Mark felt something cold and sharp pierce through him. This was *his* Harry, his best friend... He shuffled backwards, not knowing what he was supposed to do, or what was the right thing to say to fix it.

"Sure... sure... I'll see you at school." Mark eventually said, chickening out.

Chapter Thirteen

School rolled round on Monday, far too quickly for Mark.

He'd never been in this situation before, where he didn't want to see his best friend. They'd had their arguments and squabbles over the years, but never had Mark felt so casually dismissed. Hadn't he tried to get there?

The situation played over and over in his head for the rest of the weekend. He couldn't have left Damian's game early. It wasn't his fault that it had run late. It wasn't his fault that he'd missed Harry's performance. It wasn't... No matter how many times he told himself that, he didn't believe it.

Mark got to school first, and despite the rain, he hovered in the yard, adamant he was going to talk to Harry and fix it all. Some of the other students gave him weird looks, as they ran into the dry building, but he didn't care.

Eventually, Harry's bus pulled up, and he hurried through the grey rain, heading straight past Mark without a word.

"Harry!" Mark grabbed his coat, stopping him in his tracks.

"What?" He demanded.

"What do you think? I wanted to apologise for Saturday." Mark said, exasperated. "Damian's game overran, I couldn't rightly leave mid-play."

"Damian? No, of course you couldn't, you'll bend over bloody backwards for 'im." Harry snapped. "And he's jus' playin' you."

"I don't-"

"Sarah caught him snoggin' Michelle on Friday night."

"What?" Mark asked, sure he'd heard Harry wrong.

"He's cheating on you, mate."

"No, that's not right." Mark replied, thinking back to Saturday, and their passionate kiss. "He's gay."

"So, you're calling my girlfriend a liar?" Harry fumed. "You trust Damian more than Sarah? You don't hardly know him. He could be bi, for all we know."

"No, but Sarah might say something out of spite, after I missed your gig." Mark said, immediately regretting his words.

Harry shot him a lethal look, and snatched his coat out of Mark's grip. "Screw you."

Before Mark had time to react, Harry stormed into the school, without a backward glance.

Mark hurried to get to class before the bell rang, he didn't need marking as tardy on top of everything else. He told himself that he was being paranoid, but every student he passed watched him. Some looked wary, others were curious. After he passed, he was sure he heard giggling and gossiping. Did they all know about Damian and Michelle? Was he now the laughing stock of the entire school?

Mark went to his first class – it definitely wasn't his imagination that everyone fell silent when he walked through the door.

Michelle was already there, uncharacteristically early. She briefly met his gaze, smirking, then kept her eyes firmly locked on the window. Michelle was the only student who looked directly at Mark; the rest did everything they could to avoid contact.

"Settle down class..." Mr Black's voice trailed off, as he realised he didn't have to stop the usual post-weekend gossiping. "Very well, let's crack on."

The teacher proceeded to hand out their marked sonnets, he looked unimpressed when his witty comment about Harry's sonnet barely raised a titter from the class.

The rest of the morning passed with the same awkwardness. Mark didn't have any classes with

Damian, and by dinnertime his stomach had tied up in twisted knots. Mark had thought that they were in a relationship – he most certainly saw Damian as his boyfriend - but what if Harry was right, and Damian was cheating on him? Or what if he had a different idea about dating? Mark could just imagine dating in London being a much more casual thing.

After Mark entered the food hall, and collected his plate of toad-in-the-hole, he hesitated. He couldn't sit with Harry and Sarah; Mark could feel their disapproval of him, all the way across the hall.

Mark sighed, and headed to an empty table on the other side. Those around him fell silent, whispering behind their hands after he passed. Mark couldn't understand – he had done nothing wrong; if Damian had cheated on him, why was Mark the one getting grief?

He sat down, and played with his dinner, his appetite quickly lost.

"Tut tut, all alone, Marky-boy? People will think this is a confirmation of the rumours about Friday night."

Just when Mark thought his day couldn't get any worse, of course Dean had to appear and give his unwanted opinion. "Seriously Dean, not now."

Dean took that as an invitation to sit down. "Come now, you need all the friends you can get, right now."

Mark rolled his eyes, "What I *need* is for the school to stop gossiping. I guess you're here to rub it in, that Damian might be cheating on me?"

"No, I... he's what?" Dean asked, his eyes gleaming. "Now this is juicy."

Mark paused, looking at Dean, "Wait, you mean this *isn't* why everyone is bein' weird?"

"You're the weird one. Now let's go back to Damian cheating..." Dean said with a grin, relishing the chance of dirty secrets.

"*Dean*, focus." Mark snapped. "What is wrong with everyone?"

Dean rolled his eyes, "You really are no fun anymore. *Fine*, it's no secret you're starting the witchy thing, which I think is totally hot, by the way..."

"Dean."

"What's the point in gossip, if you won't let me tell it properly?" He sighed dramatically. "All I know is that you used magic at my house on Friday night; then someone heard you get a bollocking off your Dad for doing *dark* magic. Now the whole school thinks that you caused those scary fog monsters to attack us."

"What?" Mark sat stunned that anyone could believe such a ludicrous thing. "I didn't... I *stopped* them."

Mark looked around the hall, none of the other students were meeting his eye. He honestly felt betrayed. He had tried his hardest to protect them on Friday, and now they were accusing him of being the cause of all the pain and panic. Did they really think he was capable of hurting anyone?

Mark remembered the grief he felt when he hurt the violent beasts that were attacking them; he couldn't imagine how he'd feel if he hurt someone innocent.

"Alright, I've shared, now it's your turn." Dean prompted. "Tell me all about Damian being a cheating little-"

"Dean, not now." Mark repeated, abandoning his dinner, and standing up.

He saw Damian enter the double doors, surrounded by other members of the football team, all in deep discussion. Once he saw Mark, he left his new friends and headed over.

"Are you alright? You look like you've seen a ghost." Damian remarked, his blue eyes full of concern.

Mark glanced at the students seated nearby. Even though they weren't looking at him, he was sure they were still listening. "Can we go outside?"

Mark could feel everyone watching them as they walked across the hall and out through the double-doors.

The cold hit Mark with a jolt of surprising relief, and the whispering classmates was replaced by the steady patter of rain. Stood in the shelter of the doorway, they were protected from the worst of the rain, but Mark could see Damian shivering.

"My friends said I should dump you, because *you're* the one that's dangerous." Damian said, arms crossed.

"My friends said you're cheating on me – with Michelle."

"What?" Damian asked, obviously surprised that his news wasn't the craziest revelation. "That's insane, I'm gay."

"That's what I told Harry." Mark replied immediately. "I know he's mad at me for missing his gig, but I didn't think he'd stoop this low."

"You can't think any of this is true, Mark." Damian added in a worried tone. "Even if I was interested in girls, too, I'm not... I could never be involved with more than one person. Right now, you are everything to me."

Mark felt a familiar blush creep up his neck, warmth running through every inch of him. Had he really meant that?

Damian's eyes dropped, as his brain caught up with his mouth, and his confidence wavered. "Besides, Michelle? She's not my type. And I've already decided that her group of friends will be the first in line to lynch me for being different."

Mark playfully shoved his shoulder into Damian, although his mood had barely lightened.

"So, what about your friends? Do you believe them?" He asked hesitantly.

Damian shrugged, "They don't know about 'Bob'. They haven't got a clue how dangerous I might be, but they're ready to throw you under the bus."

"That didn't answer my question."

Damian sighed, staring into the relentless grey rain. "I wasn't with you on Friday night, technically anything could have happened. This whole magic and witchcraft thing is new to me, I have no idea of what you're capable of.

"But you, Mark, I think I'm getting to know you pretty well. There's no way on earth you would do anything to hurt anyone."

"Thanks." Mark replied, not sure whether he felt any better. "Has Bob been causing you any more problems?"

"No, I've not even had any more nightmares since I told you." Damian said eagerly, "Maybe it was just my overactive imagination – maybe all I needed was to talk about it to break the cycle."

"That's good news." Mark said with a forced smile. He hadn't made any effort to stop his dreams being plagued by a handsome stranger. "I'll have to tell Nanna."

Damian seemed to sense it, and leant closer, his presence warm and grounding. "I'll talk to the football team, set them straight about Friday night. It's not the whole school, but it's a start."

"Thanks." Mark said weakly.

*****

Mark kept his head down for the rest of the day. Now that he knew the gossip of the day had nothing to do with Damian snogging Michelle, he could understand the dark looks from his fellow students.

Mark didn't need to read auras, to notice the bristling hateful energy as he walked down the corridor. He could see the stiffening muscles, and some of the lads flexed their arms; it was clearly taking all their self-control not to push and shove Mark.

Because they're afraid.

Mark realised they kept their distance, because they were afraid of him. Afraid of what he might possibly do.

Was he really that different to the clumsy, perfectly-average little boy they'd grown up with?

It was with some relief that the final bell rang, and Mark was the first on the bus, staring resolutely out the window. When Damian came on, and sat next to him, it was even easier to ignore the rest of the world.

They travelled in silence, Mark leant against Damian's arm, finding comfort in his quiet strength. Damian had been the new guy at school, the obvious outsider; something Mark was beginning to experience.

Damian gave an awkward smile when they got to his stop. And then Mark was alone, counting the minutes until he was home.

Once off the bus, Mark walked up to the old farmhouse and headed to Nanna's kitchen. Right now, he needed the comfort of normal routine – a warm Aga, a cup of tea, and a few cheeky biscuits.

As he let himself in, he was disappointed to see that Nanna didn't have everything ready, as usual. The kitchen was empty.

"Nanna?" Mark called, wondering where the daft old girl could be.

The Aga was barely warm, so Mark fed the fire, before he moved the kettle to the warming plate. It

128

seemed to take forever to boil, so Mark gave the fire a little magical kick. As the magic fed through, the kettle soon whistled and steam poured out. Mark reigned the power back and started to set out the usual tea tray.

"Michael?"

Mark turned to see Nanna standing in the doorway, frowning.

"No, it's me, Nanna." Mark replied.

It took a moment longer for the confusion to fade, and Nanna sighed. "Oh, Mark. Sorry, you do look a lot like your Dad."

Mark rolled his eyes. That was not a compliment, and he didn't really need that after the day he'd had.

"I forgot to make tea." Nanna said, still distracted, but then her usual, cheerful self returned. "At least I trained you properly. I should let you make tea more often."

Mark smiled wanly, and sat down. There was the immediate, warm weight of Tigger curling up on his lap. Mark ran his fingers through the short, ginger hair, instantly soothed.

"Alright, what's wrong now?" Nanna asked.

Mark sat for a moment, wondering how to phrase it so he didn't come off sounding like a whiny child.

"The others... at school. They think I created the monsters on Friday, and got them to attack Dean's house. Now they're all afraid of me, and treating me like..." He trailed off, failing to find a way to express himself that didn't involve vulgar language.

"I'm sorry Mark." Nanna replied, sipping at her tea. "What did they say when you told them the truth?"

Mark paused, stumped by her question. "I... didn't get round to that..."

Nanna set her mug down, regarding him carefully. "Mark... the kids at your school have grown up knowing that magic exists, but knowing it's there and actually seeing it used are two very different things. You can't expect them to automatically know what's happening, and it is part of the human condition to be afraid of what you don't know.

"And, unless you provide them with correct information, of course they're going to jump to conclusions as they try and make sense of it all."

Mark sat, stewing over what Nanna had said – it all sounded like common sense, when she put it like that.

"They won't listen to me." He protested.

"Oh, you *know* that not one single person in your entire school will listen to you?" Nanna teased. "Anyway, even when teenagers are *not* listening, it's amazing how much they hear."

Mark sighed. "But... what do I tell them? I can't tell them about Damian and his demon – he's finally fitting in. And to be honest, I don't want to tell them that I used dark magic – won't that just confirm their suspicions?"

"Firstly, we don't know for sure it was linked to Damian, so leave him out of it. I know you've got it bad, but trust me Mark, not *everything* is about that boy." Nanna said, smiling knowingly. "Second, these kids

130

don't know the first thing about magic, so don't worry about labels, just tell them you were trying to protect them."

Mark sat, staring into his cup of tea. He could sense a glimmer of hope appear, but it was too distant to reach.

"Now, are you going to tell me about the magic you used at the weekend?" Nanna asked.

Mark frowned, "We've already covered-"

"Not Friday, Saturday. I heard through the grapevine that Damian got hurt, and you helped him." Nanna said, smiling. Tell me all about it."

"Oh, that." Mark had almost forgot with everything that had gone on. He proceeded to tell Nanna all about the football game, and how well Damian had been doing; then the sickening moment when the defender collided with him.

Nanna nodded, listening with interest. "So, what spell did you use? Did you have any of the healing paste handy? I told you boys attract injuries…"

"No, I didn't have anything, and couldn't remember the formal spells. I just did that focus and intention thingy." Mark shrugged. "I didn't think it'd work, but it healed Damian enough that he could finish the game."

Nanna's eyebrows rose. "So… severe muscle damage, and you healed it without any aids?" She asked for clarification.

"Yeah, I'm sure it's no big deal. You probably could have done it better."

"Well, yes, but that's because I'm the Grand-"

"High Witch." Mark echoed, wondering if Nanna would ever get bored with rubbing in how powerful she was.

"Healing that sort of damage shouldn't be possible for you, Mark. Not yet." Nanna stated. "That was some very strong magic you produced, there."

A knowing smile crossed Nanna's face, and Mark suddenly had the impression she was making fun of him.

"What?" He demanded.

"Nowt." Nanna insisted, trying to hide her smile behind her cup of tea. "It's just that our magic is often fuelled by our emotions..."

"I know." Mark said, not grasping what she was hinting at.

Nanna chuckled. "Never mind, I'm sure you'll work it out in your own time."

Chapter Fourteen

"Mark?"

"Yeah?" Mark lifted his head from his history assignment, when he heard his teacher call his name.

"The Headmistress has asked to see you." Miss Green announced, causing a few of his classmates to snap to attention.

"It wasn't me." Mark replied out of instinct, which got a few titters of laughter.

"Not my problem." Miss Green said wearily. "Off you pop."

Mark grabbed his gear and hurried away from his seat, keen to leave the curious stares of his classmates behind.

He'd been summoned to the Headmistress' office. That had only happened once in the five years he'd been here – when they were younger, and more stupid, Harry had been quite the prankster. Most of the stuff he did was harmless, juvenile nonsense; but on occasion he did something to draw the full attention of the teachers.

A couple of years ago, after an over-zealous RE teacher had called one of their classmates ignorant for *being aware* that they were lucky to not know the hardships that went on in third world countries, Harry felt the need to get revenge.

Of course, being his best friend, and having a strong idea of what was right and wrong, Mark willingly helped. It hadn't been a *bad* act of revenge, in fact it still made Mark smile. Harry had made countless A3 posters with the dictionary definition of ignorant, and between them, they plastered them over the walls, ceiling, and every surface they could find in that teacher's classroom. At the time, Mark hadn't known that Harry had also covered the teacher's car with the same posters.

It had been inconvenient and annoying, but harmless. Still, it warranted a trip to the Headmistress. After Harry explained in his usual flamboyant way, Mark was sure the Headmistress was biting back a smile when she gave them a dressing down and detention for a week.

Now, as Mark walked there alone, he felt a stab of anxiety. He automatically knew that it wouldn't be for anything good – he wasn't academically gifted enough to warrant a positive conversation with the Headmistress.

He walked past the reception desk, and the old guy who manned it gave Mark a nod. "In you go, she's expectin' you."

Mark took a deep breath and pushed the door open. The office hadn't changed much in the years since his previous visit. The walls were still that same creamy colour as the classroom, the carpet the same tacky blueish-grey they seemed to make especially for schools. The only thing of value was the Headmistress' oak desk, which took up half the office.

The Headmistress herself stood by the window, the thickset woman with a stern expression a familiar figure in assemblies. In the office with her, sat-

"Nanna?" Mark paused. "What are you doing here?"

"The school wanted a parent or guardian to come in immediately. As your parents are *busy working*, like most folk, I came." Nanna replied, glancing at the Headmistress accusingly.

The Headmistress ignored the slight, turning to Mark. "Why don't you close the door, and sit down."

He did as he was told, sliding into the uncomfortable plastic chair, staring between his Nanna and the Headmistress.

"There have been rumblings from the other students, about events that took place on Friday night-"

"That wasn't me." Mark interrupted.

The Headmistress silenced him with a look. "Now, normally student gossip is a short-term, superficial thing; but there were *police* involved that evening."

Hardly 'involved', Mark wanted to add. They turned up after the whole drama had ended, and took witness statements, or whatever it was that police did.

The Headmistress continued. "Which naturally leads to concerned parents. I've had to field numerous calls from parents and guardians, worried that their child isn't safe in the same class as a witch. I think it would be wise if Mark continued his studies at home, with a tutor, until everything calms down."

"What?" Mark gasped.

"Of course, we will provide the tutor, there will be no expense to your family-"

"Oh, how very gracious of you." Nanna interrupted, coldly. "Now, if you've quite finished, perhaps you can tell me why you have allowed these same, gossiping students to bully and ostracise my grandson?"

"What? I..." The Headmistress looked flummoxed. "Mark is a witch, and his actions are causing distress to the masses at school, I believe that is quite sufficient-"

"You believe that, do you?" Nanna pressed. "Matilda Brace, I am ashamed of you. What would your mother have to say, if she knew you were discriminating against a witch?"

The Headmistress flushed red at the use of her full name. "It's not discri-"

"I assure you, it is. This town, these *parents*, have always been aware of witches. They have grown up with me and my coven for generations. They know the strict moral code we keep. So, for you to punish Mark, because he's joined my coven of *good* witches, is discrimination and pandering to bullies."

"Mark was seen using magic, and he was the only one to remain outside with the creatures. There were *witnesses.* I imagine it'll only be a matter of time before the police wish to speak to him." The Headmistress argued.

"Oh, and I suppose these witnesses were experts in magic, and could tell what spell he was using." Nanna huffed. "Don't be a blockhead, Matilda, he was protecting those kids. And this is how they repay him..."

Mark's attention was locked on Nanna, he was internally cheering as she bashed down the Headmistress' defence. And she called her a blockhead! He couldn't wait to tell Har-

His internal cartwheels collapsed in a heap. Harry hadn't spoken to him since yesterday morning, when they'd argued about Damian. He'd ignored all Mark's calls and texts, and Sarah had refused to answer his pleas over Facebook. What did all this matter, if he didn't get his best friend back?

"So, let us return to my previous concern." Nanna continued. "Since when have you allowed bullies to target a student so completely. Mark was miserable when he got home yesterday. Have you looked into who started these rumours? Or have you been too busy, bowing to the pressure of a mob?"

"We are looking into it." The Headmistress said through gritted teeth.

"Good. Now, I'll have no more talk of removing my grandson from classes. His exams are just around the corner, and they're too important for you to mess up."

The Headmistress looked at Nanna, completely speechless.

"Alright, I think that covers everything." Nanna said, switching back to nice mode. "It was lovely to see you again, Matilda. Say hello to your mother for me; I'll see her at Pilates on Thursday."

Nanna stood up, nodding at Mark to follow her, and went into the corridor.

"Nanna, you are awesome." Mark said, grinning. "I'm never getting on the wrong side of you."

"Hmm, just don't make me regret it. I've staked the reputation of myself and my coven, on you behaving." Nanna warned. "Don't even *think* about using dark magic."

"Don't worry, I learnt my lesson." Mark replied.

Nanna looked down at him, concern still filling her gaze, but she eventually caved, and gave him a hug. "Have to dash, I'm supposed to be going around to Denise's for tea."

Mark waited, and watched his Nanna leave the school building, before he started back towards his next class. His feet were heavy, and the anxiety was knotted anew. He had won, hadn't he? So why did Mark feel nothing but dread at the thought of the ongoing disdain of his classmates, and no Harry to lean on?

Chapter Fifteen

The next day was hardly better. Mark was starting to get used to the distrustful glances and whispering that followed him. After the Headmistress had reminded the students of the school's anti-bullying policy, everybody had backed off.

Then another day passed, and another.

Harry and Sarah were still snubbing him, ignoring Mark every time he tried to talk to them. Mark felt the only person who treated him normally was Damian. His boyfriend had been true to his word, and after some damage control with the rest of the footballers, the team had lightened up with Mark. At least now, he didn't have to sit alone during breaks. He had the football team for company, sitting next to their star striker as his official significant other.

Mark threw himself into his classwork, and his witchcraft training. It was the easiest way to distract from how shite he was feeling.

"It'll get better, trust me." Damian said for the umpteenth time.

Mark knew that he meant well, and that Damian had his own experience with bullying, but it didn't help the situation. His good intentions didn't stop the bullies. It didn't make it easier to bear.

"You know what tomorrow is?" Damian asked, with a forced casualness.

"Thursday." Mark replied quickly. "It precedes Friday and the blessed half-term; a whole week without school."

Damian punched him playfully. "I was referring to Valentine's. D'you want to go out?"

Mark stopped in his tracks. Valentine's? How had that snuck up so quickly? It suddenly occurred to him that, for the first time in his life, he had a boyfriend on the romantic holiday.

"Yes!" Mark replied in a rush.

"Good, 'cos we have a table booked at Romano's at seven."

Mark was stunned, that was the most popular Italian restaurant in the area. "How did you manage that?"

Damian shrugged. "OK, I should say that Aunt Maggie booked the table weeks ago, but her date ditched her. She asked if we wanted to go instead."

"Wow, I'm sorry for your Aunt, but yes!" Mark grinned back, feeling positive for the first time in a week.

"Alright. Meet you there?"

*****

Mark not only managed to talk his parents into suspending his being grounded, but also got his Mum to offer him a lift into Tealford. His parents had given in quickly as they acknowledged that this was his first real Valentine's. Mark didn't even need to bring up the subject of how horrible school was right now, to use as emotional blackmail.

Mark had spent an age getting ready. Jeans were a no, which left his school trousers, and his one pair of 'best' trousers, which were stiff and uncomfortable. He pulled on his favourite black shirt, but it was too much black. His white shirt was smart, but he thought he might be mistaken as a waiter. He settled for a grey shirt.

"Oh, you look lovely, dear." His Mum cooed, as he went downstairs.

Mark felt a sense of unease that was becoming commonplace, as his Dad said nothing. No humour, no whistles, their once easy relationship seemed on ice.

His Mum seemed to sense it, and hurried things along, grabbing her car keys and pushing Mark out the door.

*****

He waved to his Mum, as she drove away, leaving him alone outside the restaurant. Mark hesitated; this was his first dinner date, and he felt a stab of nerves. The nerves were replaced with something much more pleasant, as he saw Damian walking down the dark street towards him.

Damian looked like a model, his black coat flattering his athletic physique, and his hair perfectly styled.

"Hi," Mark gushed as he got closer, "Shall we go in?"

Damian gave an odd, half-smile, his eyes locked on Mark, as he opened the door.

The restaurant was packed, and the heat and noise of the crowd hit Mark, as they entered. The person on the desk took their coats, and showed them to their table for two, in the middle of the room.

As they sat down, everything else seemed to fade into the background. There was just him, Damian, and a romantic atmosphere, as music played softly. Damian looked amazing in a fitted red shirt, his golden hair shining like a crown in the candlelight. Mark wondered if it was just a trick of the low light, that made Damian's usually bright blue eyes look dark.

"Can I get you anything to drink?" The waitress asked, cutting through the mood.

"Red wine." Damian stated in a deadpan expression.

The waitress smiled at his obvious joke, "Nice try. We have Coke, Sprite, Fanta, or fresh orange juice."

"We'll both have a Coke." Mark replied, keen to get rid of the waitress, so it was just back to him and Damian.

Once she retreated to the bar, Mark leant closer to Damian, so they could talk privately in the crowded restaurant.

"You, um... you look really good, tonight." Mark stumbled over his words, and he was glad that in this low light, his trademark blushes couldn't be seen.

Damian leant in, gazing at Mark with an open curiosity. He reached across the table and gently laced his fingers between Mark's. "And I can see why Damian is so enamoured with you. Dark hair, good looks, and muscles to spare. Yes, I can definitely see the attraction."

It took a moment for the words to hit Mark, spoken with Damian's voice, but missing his soft, almost shy inflection.

Mark's eyes widened. "You..." He tried to snatch his hand away, but Damian had it in a vice-like grip.

"Me." He confirmed, his lips tilting up in an amused smile.

Mark's pulse began to race, as panic flared up, "Where's Damian?"

"He is unharmed, just dormant. I am in control this evening." He said, dismissively.

"What do you want?" Mark asked, his voice shaking.

The demon moved Damian's fingers so they stroked Mark's palm, making his skin crawl.

"Oh, I want many things, young Mark." He replied, his voice low and raspy. "Alas time is short, and I will move swiftly to my main desire. I want to employ your skills as a witch."

Mark paused, that was not what he was expecting. "Seriously?"

"Why would I jest?"

"Um, you're a demon that is possessing my boyfriend. I don't really think I can trust you." Mark hissed, trying to keep his voice down, in the full room. His mind whirred, as he tried to think what Nanna would do. A name – he needed a name. "Tell me your name, and I'll consider it."

"Well, it's certainly not 'Bob', as much as your little friend enjoyed his jokes. The full version may do – Robert. I like Robert; it was the name of a Duke I possessed once." The demon replied in a casual tone.

"Is that your real name?" Mark asked doubtfully.

"It is as real as you are going to get, young man." He replied, his dark stare making it clear he knew what Mark was trying to do.

Mark realised that it wasn't the candlelight that distorted Damian's blue eyes; they were now as black as night. A shiver ran down Mark's spine, and he struggled to pull his hand away again.

"Stop squirming, or I will break your arm." The demon, Robert, warned. "I need your magic - I don't need your body in one piece."

"I'm not gonna help you." Mark protested.

145

"Oh, you will. When the time is right, you will do everything I ask of you." Robert insisted, "You see, it is all a matter of *persuasion*. Everyone has their price, their weakness. I could give you riches beyond your wildest dreams."

Mark stared coldly at the demon wearing Damian's face. What use did he have of riches?

Robert seemed to read his mind, a knowing smile flickering across his lips. "I can give you power you never imagined."

His fingers curled deeper into Mark's flesh, and Mark could feel a sudden flood of magic. He recognised dark magic from the party; it had the same, overwhelming surge that knocked the breath out of him. But this time, the power was a deep well, a promise of endless fuel, that made Mark dizzy, and his pulse race in excitement.

Shuddering from the exertion, Mark blocked the dark magic, rejecting it firmly when its addictive tendrils sought the deepest parts of him.

"No." He grunted.

The demon withdrew the magic slowly, letting it linger along Mark's skin, hinting at the promise of power. "Ah, I see you are one of the good witches. Well... heroes are always the easiest to *persuade*."

Everything went still, and Mark wondered if it was just his stress levels blocking out everything other than this demon. A sense of dread dropped over him, and he looked around the packed restaurant. Everybody was frozen; the people at the tables, with their forks half-way to their mouths; the waiters and waitresses, mid-smile; and the barman stuck pouring a pint that was now overflowing over his frozen hand.

"Impressive." Mark conceded. "And your point is?"

"Remember, you forced my hand." Robert stated, smiling as he enjoyed the scene.

The knot of dread hardened into something painful, as Mark sent his senses out. The demon hadn't frozen the people – he had paralysed them. Mark could feel the panic rising in their unmoving bodies, their pulses racing as they struggled to breathe.

"Let them go." Mark growled.

Robert raised his free hand to stop what he had to say. "Just a moment longer, dear boy. I think the old couple in the corner will be the first to expire; or perhaps the pregnant woman by the window..." He said, conversationally, as though they were discussing options on the menu.

"Let them go." Mark repeated. "These people have never hurt you."

The demon frowned, a look of confusion crossing Damian's face. "Why should that have any bearing on the situation? I do not care if they live or die. Of course, you might. No matter the outcome, it will not benefit you."

"What do you mean?" Mark asked, another cold shiver running down his spine.

147

"I thought you were intelligent, Mark. Two weeks ago, at Imbolc, you were accused of raising hell beasts. Is it such a coincidence that you should be here, when all these innocent people have their lives stolen from them?"

"No..." Mark felt his gut wrench, as each horrid piece fell into place. "You brought the monsters."

"In a sense. They didn't approve of me breaking free of Hell on Imbolc." Robert's black eyes bore into him. "You have my thanks, Mark, for driving my jailers back."

Mark felt sick to his stomach. "That wasn't my intention."

"Your *intentions* don't hold much strength. You wanted to save people that night, but you have been cast as the villain. What will happen now, I wonder." Robert mused aloud, his fingers caressing the skin on Mark's hand, sending waves of disgust up his arm. "They know this is magic, and they know that you have a questionable reputation as a witch. This will be entertaining, I will ensure to leave a few witnesses alive."

Mark felt numb, his fear ramping up. "Luka." He murmured.

Robert snatched his hand away and scrambled out of his seat, his eyes locked on the dog that had materialised next to Mark. "How interesting that *this* spirit has chosen you." He said, sneering.

The demon's hold on the crowd disappeared, and everybody collapsed on the spot, choking and gulping down air.

Robert looked around at the barely conscious audience, before returning his gaze to Mark.

"We will speak again, soon, I promise." He said quietly, before his black eyes faded to blue, rolling back.

Damian crumpled to the ground, and Mark rushed to slow his fall, jarring his shoulder as he did. He checked his pulse and breathing, Mark felt a rushing relief that he was alive.

Damian's eyes cracked open, and Mark was relieved to see they were the usual innocent blue. Damian frowned, struggling to take in the scene. "Wha-"

"You're alright, just rest here while I sort a few things out." Mark said.

He pulled out his mobile and called for an ambulance, quickly reporting the basic facts. After sending a quick text to Nanna, Mark then headed to the other diners, keen to help.

They shrunk back from Mark, looking fearful in their weakened state.

"It wasn't what it looked like..." Mark said, his voice and his confidence fading. He sighed, speaking more firmly. "I can help."

He knelt next to the pregnant woman that had sat near them. Mark grabbed at the power that surrounded him, and pulled it towards him. He sent it out with the intention of healing the woman, but even as he did so, he knew it wouldn't work. His lack of focus made the magic scatter across the shivering woman.

Mark cast his mind back to the book of healing spells Nanna had lent him.

"Hear my will, take my strength;

"Bind the wounds, and heal the flesh;

"Honour my words;

"Secure these lives."

As Mark spoke aloud, he felt the magic around him calm, and channel into something positive and powerful. He repeated the words again, and felt the spell expand, hovering over the collapsed crowd. There were too many of them for Mark to heal alone, but he could feel the spell adapt, trying to simply *keep them alive*.

"What are you doing?" A man growled angrily, as he sensed the magic.

Mark could see the fear on his face; but couldn't allow himself to be distracted.

Damian stepped in between them. "Back off. If you want to keep your date alive, you let him do his work. Otherwise, you can explain to the ambulance why you stopped the one man who could have saved everyone."

Mark felt an extra jolt of power, along with a warm feeling, at Damian's support of him. He fed it into the spell, and repeated the words again, chanting them until they became a part of the background.

His strength was beginning to wane, when Damian shook his arm, to snap him out of it.

"Mark, the ambulances are here."

Mark looked up, his eyes unfocussed. There were bright-jacketed people threading between the tables and semi-conscious diners.

He was so tired, it took all his effort to stay awake. There was a hub of voices and activity, but Mark couldn't process it all now. He was vaguely aware of Nanna arriving with his parents in tow. They all spoke kindly to him, and bundled him away to the car.

Outside, the cold night air hit Mark, bringing his senses into sharper relief.

The road was a hive of emergency vehicles, and flashing lights. The restaurant had been cordoned off, but people of Tealford were gathering to see what was happening in their sleepy little town. A few looked at Mark with curious expressions that made his skin crawl.

They were all blocked out when the car door was slammed shut and, before the engine had even started, Mark was unconscious.

Chapter Sixteen

Mark jolted awake, finding himself in his own bed, his duvet discarded in a crumpled heap on the floor. It was still dark, and his clock glowed to show it was shortly after six in the morning. Mark groaned, having an aversion to being awake at this unnatural hour, but he could tell he wasn't going to get back to sleep.

Events from last night crashed down on him, leaving his mind spinning, and a stabbing pain in his head. It all seemed to belong to a nightmare, or a horror movie. Last night was supposed to have been a romantic night out with his boyfriend. Mark had been worried about wearing the wrong clothes, or spilling sauce on his shirt... he never imagined it could have gone so badly.

He lay in bed, his headache continuing to pound, giving him not a moment's peace. Eventually he dragged himself up, and headed downstairs.

There were voices in the living room, that stopped as Mark opened the door. His Mum and Nanna sat on the sofa, nursing steaming mugs of coffee.

"Hey sweetie, how are you feeling?" His Mum crooned.

"Alright." Mark grunted. "Do we have any paracetamol?"

Mum smiled. "Even better, Nanna brought round some of her miracle tea." She pulled out a thermos and handed it to Mark.

He felt a wave of relief, after years of various pains and illnesses, he knew that Nanna's tea was better than any medicine. Mark poured a cup and sipped slowly. "Where's Dad?"

"Out jogging, he had to clear his head." His Mum replied, not meeting Mark's eye. "You didn't have to get up, I was going to call school later and get you a day off."

"Thanks." Mark mumbled, dropping into the armchair.

His headache slowly faded, as the tea took effect, and Mark became aware of the uncomfortable silence in the living room. He glanced at his Mum and Nanna, who were both wearing identical, expectant looks.

Mark sighed. "Alright, it's open season. What do you want to ask?"

"Well, let's start with you telling us everything that happened, then we'll quiz you." Nanna suggested.

Mark went over everything he could remember from last night, his voice getting increasingly hoarse. He felt physically and emotionally exhausted.

"Does this mean the demon is at full strength?" Mark asked.

"It's hard to tell how strong he might get, without knowing which demon it is." Nanna replied, with a shrug. "But this is what we've been waiting for, Mark. He's substantial enough that we can get rid of him."

Mark leaned back in the comfy armchair, it didn't feel like they were winning. "So, all those people that got hurt last night are what, collateral damage?"

Nanna sighed. "It was unfortunate, and I wish it could have been avoided, but you did everything you could to help them."

"What do we do next?"

"I've alerted the coven," Nanna replied, "We'll marshal the troops, and kick that demon back to hell. Denise and Danny will be round later, with what they've learnt about the bugger. I know it's the last thing you want to think about, Mark, but was there anything he said that would be a clue to his identity."

"He called himself Robert, but I'm guessing that isn't his real name." Mark ran over the whole evening, his gut twisting with dread as he relived the fresh memories. "He said it was the name of a Duke he possessed once, if that narrows it down?"

"Danny would be the best person to ask – he has the head for names and histories."

Mark stewed over his thoughts, they refused to get in order, let alone make sense of anything. "What happened to Damian last night? I know he was back in control when I blacked out, but is he OK?"

"We had a chat after you left. Damian didn't remember anything after he left school, he had no memory of the demon, or what he did in the restaurant. The boy was understandably freaked out, and upset at causing more pain; but he was physically OK." Nanna answered, uncharacteristically serious. "One of my coven is good friends with his Aunt Maggie, they're staying with them, until we get all of this sorted out."

Mark sighed, his gut twisting with apprehension. The door flew open, making Mark jump, but it was just his Dad returning from his morning run. With a bunch of flowers in hand, of course.

"Oh, sweetie, you shouldn't have!" Mum cooed, smiling at her husband.

"I didn't." Dad replied, looking somewhat baffled. "I ran into old Mr Williamson outside the shop, he asked if I'd mind delivering these to Nanna, to save him a journey."

"Aw, you've got a Valentine's admirer!" Mum announced.

Rather than look happy, or flattered, Nanna snorted in a very unladylike manner. She turned away from the offered bouquet of flowers and picked up her well-thumbed paperback of 'Fifty Shades of Grey'.

155

Mum chuckled at her reaction and took the flowers on Nanna's behalf. "I'll get these in some water, they're beginning to wilt. Oh, there's a card: 'Roses are red, violets are blue, there's no girl in town, as swell as you.'"

Mark couldn't help it, despite the faint headache and all the drama of last night, it was nice to know that life went on as normal. Nanna getting a Valentine's was definitely a new development, though.

"Are you gonna reply? Will there be a date?" Mark asked, finally smiling. "Can we come along as chaperones?"

"Humph. There will be no date. That man is relentless, I've already turned him down twice." Nanna replied.

"When was that?" Dad piped up, not sounding happy about the possibility of his mother dating a man that wasn't his father.

"Oh, the first time was the summer I was eighteen. Then he asked me again, about five years after your father died."

The mood of the house lightened further, and they were all laughing at Mr Williamson's 'relentless' pursuit across the decades.

"Poor old Mr Williamson." Mum sighed, wiping tears from her eyes. "Maybe you should put him out of his misery, and go on a date."

"Why on Earth would I want to do that? That man is an absolute scrooge – he waits until after Valentine's so he can buy left-over flowers; then gets my son to deliver them for free. My heart really isn't fluttering with the romance of it all. Besides, he's so old…" Nanna shuddered.

"Nanna, he's two years younger than you." Mark argued, laughing.

"What has age got to do with how old you are?" Nanna asked. "Now, if you'll excuse me, I'll go back to my fantasies about Mr Grey and my handsome farrier."

"Too much information, Nanna." Mark and his Dad said at the same time.

*****

Just before midday, Denise and her son arrived, as Nanna had predicted. They squeezed into Nanna's cosy living room, before Nanna excused herself to make hot drinks.

Mark went to greet them, and was surprised when Denise wrapped him in a fierce hug.

"Well done, kiddo." She said, giving him a peck on the cheek.

Mark could feel the sincerity and the pride coming off her.

"Yes, not many witches could fend off a demon, alone." Danny added, sounding somewhat less sincere.

Mark shrugged, feeling uncomfortable under the praise. "Luka did most of the work."

"Right, boys, sit down. I'll help Nanna get the tea ready." Denise announced, pushing her son into the nearest seat. "Don't discuss anything important until I'm back."

157

Mark felt a lick of humour. "She knows you're a grown-up, right?"

"Sure," Danny replied, with a resigned shake of his head. "It doesn't matter what I do – degree, good job, my own house – I'm still her little boy. I don't think it helps that my mum has yet to consider herself a mature grown-up."

Mark smiled as he thought of Denise; 'mature' was the last word he'd use to describe her.

"From all the witness accounts, it sounds like you had quite the trial last night." Danny remarked, changing the topic. "This is what, the third dangerous clash involving this boy? I'm surprised you're risking so much for your new friend."

Mark stared at Danny, not sure whether to be shocked, offended, or just angry. "Because I'd like to think I'm a good person; I'm not gonna turn my back on him because a demon is involved. And, because he's my *boyfriend,* you can shove '*friend*' up your-"

"Oh! I didn't realise you were… y'know…" Danny's gaze turned curious, making Mark feel like a science project.

"Gay?" He finished. "Yeah."

"Huh. No offense, you just don't seem the type."

"And what *type* would that be?" Mark asked. "And how does that have any bloody bearing on who I'm attracted to?"

Danny was saved from digging himself deeper into his hole, by Denise and Nanna returning with tea and sandwiches.

"What's going on with you two?" Denise asked, setting the sandwiches and plates on the table.

"Danny was just about to share his learned opinion on what makes a gay man." Mark huffed.

"Oh no, I'm sorry Mark." Denise's sunny expression vanished. "Danny, as much as I love you, you are an insensitive prig sometimes."

"But-"

"He gets it from his father's side of the family." Denise added, shoving a sandwich in Danny's mouth before he could embarrass her any further.

Mark took his warm cup of tea from Nanna, and considered it a truce.

"Did you learn anything about the vision, or our demon?" Nanna asked.

Denise and Danny shared a look.

Danny swallowed his sandwich, and after he stopped choking, he replied, "We have indeed found something of interest. There are stories of a low-born man, an Eadric, who went mad and killed everyone in the area. There are different versions, where he had a separate partner in crime; or that he was possessed by a demon. In each story, the name 'Silvaticus' is used."

"You think this is the same as our demon?" Mark asked, a shiver ran up his spine as he could finally put a name to the mystery man. He wasn't particularly sold on

159

the idea that Eadric's demon was the same as his – they *felt* different, in his dreams at least.

"There are a lot of demons in this world." Denise said, "But it's too much of a coincidence that your demon disturbed the scars of the past. We think it's very likely they are one and the same. Demons are creatures of habit, they like to return to the same areas, the same bloodlines."

"It if it true, then this is what we've been looking for," Mark replied, trying to feel more optimistic. "We needed his identity, didn't we? You said that names have power."

Nanna nodded, keeping uncharacteristically quiet, and to the background. "Yes," she answered, but there was no victory in her voice. "I don't think it'll be enough, we need to call the whole coven."

Denise looked at her curiously. "The *whole* coven for expelling a demon? It seemed a little extreme at the Winter Solstice; now you want to do it again?"

"It didn't *work* at the Winter Solstice." Nanna pointed out, then sighed. "I have a bad feeling about this one, I'd rather have the other witches behind me, in case it goes wrong again. When's the next night of power?"

Denise bit her lip, staring into space for a moment. "Ostara is in a month's time, if you're willing to wait..." She caught Nanna's eye, and got a nonverbal answer for that one. "OK... the quicker the better. There's a full moon tomorrow, we should be able to channel plenty of energy from that."

Nanna sighed, "It will have to do. The longer the demon is in this boy, the more trouble he's going to cause. I get the feeling that last night was merely the warm-up act."

Mark sat watching the exchange, it was rare that he saw his Nanna look worried. He was used to her being the confident, all-knowing, slightly-crazy witch. Right now, she refused to even meet his gaze.

"Denise, Danny, round up the troops. Get them here for five o'clock tomorrow, we can start as soon as the moon rises." Nanna dictated.

"What about Damian?" Mark asked.

"You are not to tell that boy anything, do you understand?"

Mark was rattled by Nanna's strict tone. "Yes."

"Good. The last thing we need is his demon to find out what we're planning." Nanna replied, a little gentler. "He can stay where he is, we don't want him to suspect anything is happening."

Mark chewed over everything. "Can I at least see him."

Nanna nodded, "Yes, if you promise not to say a word about this."

Chapter Seventeen

Mark tried calling Damian, but he got no reply. He wondered if his boyfriend was ignoring him; not that Mark could blame him. As much as Mark didn't want to think about it right now, his reputation had only worsened in the last twenty-four hours.

Or, more worryingly, was Damian blaming himself again. The last time he'd done that, and pulled away from those he loved, he'd nearly died.

It was mid-afternoon, and Mark knew he still had a couple of hours of daylight left. He grabbed his bike and set off down the drive.

Damian's house was only a couple of miles away, amongst a cluster of cottages near the village church. They were all old, stone buildings, that looked a natural part of the rugged land around them.

Mark propped his bike up in Aunt Maggie's tiny front garden and rang the doorbell.

His hands were sweating, and his nerves were running high. What would he do if Damian refused to see him? What would he do if Aunt Maggie had him pegged as a trouble-maker? What if-

The front door opened, and Mark was greeted by the witch in charge of watching Maggie and Damian.

"Miriam, how's it going?"

"Good... great..." The witch looked sheepish, motioning for Mark to come inside. "They're in the living room."

Mark squeezed past Miriam and headed into the house. He walked into the living room, which suddenly felt cramped with so many people in it. Aunt Maggie sat on the sofa, curled up with a book; and Damian sat on the floor, his legs crossed, as he played a computer game.

Damian looked up, and nervously smiled when he saw Mark. "Hey." He managed to say.

"Hey." Mark said back.

Aunt Maggie hit Damian with her book, giving him a meaningful look.

"C'mon, we'll go to my room." Damian said, clicking the controller off, and standing up. "It's way too crowded in here."

Mark followed him, hesitating at the doorway. He'd never been in Damian's room. He wasn't sure what he was expecting, but it was a cosy room, with light blue walls and mismatched blue carpet and curtains. The bedding was also blue, and in the same mess that Damian had left it this morning. There were some boxes in the corner, Mark guessed Damian hadn't finished unpacking – he seriously hoped he wasn't *re*packing.

"So, um... you like blue?" Mark asked, not sure what to say.

Damian shrugged. "I prefer red. But blue is good and, y'know, Aunt Maggie made such an effort to make me feel at home."

"So... how do you feel?" Mark asked, after an uncomfortably long silence.

"I'm fine. I feel absolutely fine, and that scares the crap out of me." Damian's words came out in one continuous rush of anxiety. "If you hadn't been there, and witnessed it, I wouldn't have known that *he* had taken over."

"Well, that's a good thing." Mark argued. "You don't want the demon to hurt you?"

"You don't understand." Damian snapped, dropping down onto his untidy bed. "There weren't any signs that he had been there, I just came out of a daze, with no idea he'd controlled me. How do I know that hasn't happened before?"

Mark tried to come up with a reassuring answer, but he failed. There was no way of telling Damian and Robert apart, they looked the same, even if they acted differently. Even in this town that accepted witches, they wouldn't think to look closer, to see if Damian or his demon was in control.

A thought occurred to Mark, and he sat on the bed next to Damian. "I guess we know who was kissing Michelle, the night of the party..."

"Oh!" Damian groaned, his blue eyes filled with guilt. "That just feels so wrong, what else is he doing with my body."

Mark shuddered. "That means I owe Harry a huge apology."

Damian leant his head back against the headrest. "I want him out of me. We can do it now, what else are we waiting for?"

Mark bit his tongue. "Nanna's looking into it." He said vaguely.

Damian grunted, unconvinced.

"Have you told your Aunt, yet?"

Damian chewed on his lip. "No," he eventually admitted.

"You know you have to" Mark sighed.

"It's not that simple." Damian argued. "Besides, if we're getting rid of the demon, there's no real reason for her to know."

"Isn't she suspicious about what happened last night? About having a witch on guard duty?"

Damian rolled his eyes. "Ugh, no. Turns out that Miriam has had a crush on Aunt Maggie for years, and in the spirit of Valentine's she confessed everything last night. Then stayed *all night*, if you know what I mean. Aunt Maggie has been sufficiently distracted."

"Huh." Mark didn't think that was what Nanna intended when she sent her coven to guard this house. No wonder Miriam looked sheepish. "I didn't realise Aunt Maggie swung that way. Didn't she just break up with a guy?"

"Yeah, I think this is her first girl." Damian said with a shrug. "I hope she doesn't start asking me about the gay thing, I don't think I'm ready for that talk."

"Well, I'll talk to her, if she wants. It's the least I can do after she sorted us out with that romantic meal last night." Mark mused aloud. "Shame about the outcome."

"I'm sorry I ruined our big date." Damian said, sincerely.

Mark nudged him with his shoulder. "It's fine, we'll take turns trashing dates. Maybe one day we can have one that doesn't involve the emergency services."

"How about now? Can you stay and watch a film?"

"Yeah." Mark had barely spoken, when Damian jumped off the bed and dashed out.

He returned a few minutes later with a bag of popcorn and a DVD. "Time for your Van Wilder introduction." He said, grinning.

*****

Mark didn't know when they'd fallen asleep, but he awoke to Damian curled up to his chest, fitting snugly under the crook of his arm. Mark lay there, watching him sleep, marvelling at how relaxed Damian looked, without the stress and constant worry eating away at him.

Mark could stay there forever, but his arm was going dead, and as soon as the realisation struck him, he couldn't ignore how uncomfortable he was. Trying not to wake Damian, he slipped out of bed. He checked his phone, finding a couple of texts from Nanna.

'*Where r u?*' Followed by '*Miriam txtd me. Nvrmind.*'

Mark cringed, wondering what Miriam had said; and what Nanna must think of him having an impromptu sleepover.

Mark sighed to himself, walking around Damian's small room. He switched off the TV, the glowing screen fading to black, the room darkening along with it. The only light was the almost-full moon outside, and the stars shining brightly.

Mark hovered by the window, letting the moonlight wash over him. He'd never noticed how refreshing it was, and how it connected with his magic, boosting his strength. He couldn't wait to see what would happen with a full coven and a full moon, the idea set off a rush of adrenaline.

Mark's train of thought was broken by a lone light bobbing about, with the rise and fall of the land. Someone was wandering outside, in the middle of the night. It could be someone perfectly innocent, perhaps heading back from the pub, but Mark felt a niggle of doubt.

He turned back to get his phone and jumped. Damian was stood merely inches away, silent and waiting.

Damian's dark eyes locked onto Mark's, and he gave a confident smile. "Why, hello Mark."

"Robert."

Before Mark could react, Robert swung his fist. Pain briefly blossomed in his jaw, before it was swallowed in blackness.

Chapter Eighteen

Mark woke up shivering. He was lying on a cold, hard surface, with a thin blanket that did nothing to keep the cold seeping into his bones.

Mark slowly sat up, aching all over, and especially sore around his jaw area. He rubbed it, wincing as he touched the burgeoning bruise. He looked about, though there wasn't much to see. It was pitch black, and Mark shuffled around with his hands outstretched. He could just make out the stonework that made up the floor and walls of his current location, but no door or window.

He ventured further from his blanket, hoping to find something, anything; but the rough-hewn stone continued without any change. Mark crawled on, with nothing better to do, when he suddenly hit a soft, warm lump.

"Mmm... five more minutes..." It mumbled in a familiar voice, before rolling away from him.

"Harry?" Mark gasped, his panic increasing. "What are you doing here?"

"Mark?" Harry's groggy voice came out of the darkness. "W-where's here?"

"Dunno." Mark replied honestly.

He needed to see where they were, and how to get out. Mark crawled back to the thin blanket he'd been wrapped in, and bundled it up. He called the corners and, despite the terrible situation he found himself in, Mark felt a calmness thread through him. He pulled on his need for fire, imagined it sparking to life on the bundle of material.

Magic flowed through his veins and focussed on the blanket. An orange ember curled in the darkness, and as Mark concentrated, it spread and took hold, a red flame flickering up weakly.

In its light, Mark could see Harry, looking pale and dirty, but uninjured. The room they were in was an imperfect rectangle with a sloping floor. The rough stone walls continued up and across the ceiling. As far as Mark could see, there was no door, and no windows. He got to his feet, he had to hunch over to stop his head hitting the roof. Mark stamped down the panic, as he raised the burning rag to every corner, to check how dire the situation was.

"I wouldn't do that, if I were you."

Mark spun round to see Damian lounging in the corner. Not Damian, Robert. He could see the cocky smile, and the confidence he exuded.

"Do what?" Mark asked through gritted teeth.

"This room is sealed, and I would estimate that the two of you have enough air for a day. Although that..." Robert nodded to the home-made torch in his hand. "...is likely to burn through it quicker. I would advise you to put it out."

"And I would advise you to *let us go*." Mark growled.

Robert raised his hand, to signal he should stop. "Now Mark, I do not want to keep you here. In fact, I want you to get out."

"What do you mean?"

"There is a door, and but one way to use it." Robert leant forward and grabbed Mark's free hand, sending shivering tendrils of addictive power licking along his flesh. "It is unlocked by dark magic. All you have to do is access it."

Robert released him, and Mark felt dizzy as the power receded from him, leaving him feeling strangely empty.

"You have one day to submit, or you both shall die." Robert's dark eyes fixed Mark to the spot. "*Dworestu*."

Daylight cracked open overhead, and the stones in the wall started to move, forming uneven steps. Robert snapped to his feet, and waved. "I wonder what will last longer; the air, or your stubbornness..."

He skipped lightly up the steps and vanished. The door closed with a sickening thud, coupled with a gust of air that blew out the flame in Mark's hand.

171

"What the hell is happening?" Harry hissed. "Why has Damian shut us in here?"

"That wasn't Damian, that was Robert."

"Who's Robert?"

"The demon possessing Damian's body." Mark explained with a sigh. "He didn't approve of Bob."

Mark could hear Harry snort in the darkness.

"Robert wants to enlist my help for... something. Not sure what, but it involves me using dark magic." Mark continued. "But I can't use it again, I've never felt anything so *wrong*."

"Again?" Harry echoed.

"At Dean's party, I tapped into dark magic to repel the monsters." Mark confessed, a sick feeling in his stomach. "I, um... I owe you an apology."

"Y'think?" Harry snapped. "I can't believe I'm stuck in this freezing box of a room with you; buried alive and running out of air. To say I'm pissed off is an understatement."

"I'm sorry, I shouldn't have doubted you and Sarah when you tried to warn me about Damian."

There was a strangled laugh from Harry. "You think that's why I'm annoyed?"

"Erm..." Mark's confidence wavered. "No?"

There was a long silence, and Mark began to wonder if the conversation was over. Eventually, Harry spoke again, his voice unusually cold.

"So, what now, how do we escape?"

"I don't-" Mark broke off. "Can you hear that?"

172

There was a pause, followed by a sullen, "No."

Mark could hear a voice, faint and barely audible, he couldn't work out what they were saying. He was overwhelmed by a rush of a foreboding, but familiar power.

"I... think I know where we are..." He ventured. "We're near the river, where I fell off the horse. There must be a room underneath the ruins."

"That's great. How does that help us get out?" Harry asked, unconvinced.

Mark shrugged, realising as he did so, that Harry couldn't see the gesture. "Dunno." A spark of hope lit within him, as he remembered his protective spirit.

"Luka?" he murmured. Mark could feel the soft, warm fur of the dog leaning against his leg in the darkness. "Please, help us."

Mark's hope faded, as Luka simply licked his hand, and curled up, as useless as a real dog.

"What's 'appening?" Harry asked from the darkness. "Has he gone to save us?"

"No, I think he's gone to sleep." Mark replied, bitterly.

"Fat lotta good that is." Harry grumbled.

Mark sighed, trying to shut out his best friend's negativity, whilst he tried to work some other spells. He tried traditional spells, chants, and focussing his intentions. Mark had to admit that his knowledge of spells was pretty narrow, and it didn't take long to exhaust everything he knew.

173

It was so frustrating, as he could connect to the magic, and some spells worked within the room, but Mark couldn't send anything outside. Obviously, the only thing that could penetrate these walls was dark magic. Well, that and the creepy voice that drifted in and out of focus.

Mark sat down, meditating on the idea. The voice seemed so real, someone within reach; this was the second time that it had awoken in the presence of the demon, Robert. Mark didn't think it was coincidence; he also didn't think that it was Robert in another life.

Time was slowly running out. Mark had no idea how late it was, but he knew that every minute took them closer to death. Maybe it was time for something drastic.

"I have an idea, but it's crazy, and I don't know if it will even work." Mark confessed. "And if it does, it may put us in even more danger."

"Well, anything is better than sitting here, doing nothing. Do your voodoo stuff."

Mark crossed his legs, trying to feel balanced in the disorientating black room with the sloping floor. He called the corners, settling his mind, and letting his body relax.

Mark started to draw the magic towards himself, surprised by how different it felt. He was tapping directly into the magic that naturally occurred on this site, feeling a deep well of power. It was ancient and untouched; strong but unstable.

"Through the mists of time and space;

"Through locks and walls, to this set place.

"We call upon the ancient power;

"Greeted at the darkest hour.

"Link our hopes and hearts as one;

"Til our intentions be done."

Mark chanted the verse, until he felt the foundations of the spell was laid. Tonight was a full moon, it might not have risen yet, but it was fuelling the rest of his coven. Would they feel his little spell, drawing on them, seeking their help?

He repeated the words, feeling comfort in the strength of the magic that was being woven.

"Silvaticus, I invoke you." He said firmly. "Eadric, come to my aid."

There was a shimmer in the air, and Mark looked up. The dark was receding, there was a lamp burning in the furthest corner, and daylight coming through the windows that appeared on the long side.

There was a smashing noise, and Mark noticed someone else in the room, fragments of pottery at his feet. It was the same young man he had seen before, with broad handsome features, long dark hair, and startlingly green eyes. He stared at Mark in surprise.

"Who are ye?" The young man demanded, picking up a scythe that was propped against the wall.

"My name is Mark, I'm not here to hurt you." Mark said, eyeing the sharp tool warily. "I need your help."

"Are ye demon?" He asked, his voice low and rough.

"No, I'm a witch." Mark felt his concentration wavering, and he fought to stay in the spell. "Eadric, I need your help."

"Witches." The young man spat. "How do ye know my name?"

"It's a long story. I'm from a long way in the future, and I'm trapped. I need someone to provide demonic power to release me."

"Ahhh, ye kennan Silvaticus."

Mark frowned, not understanding him, but latching onto one word. "Yes, Silvaticus!

The young man shook his head. "Dafte lad, do ye ken what ye axe?"

"Please, there's a demon that has taken over my friend. I think you have a history with him, why else would your power stir when he was around?" Mark begged. "I can't use dark magic to get us out, but Silvaticus could save us."

"That's a hefty lot o' trust ye puttin' in Silvaticus. Mayhaps he's anutha demon – worse than yer beast." Eadric said, his smile jarring with his warning words.

"I trust you." Mark said firmly, meeting Eadric's green eyes unflinchingly.

Eadric looked back, with a keen intelligence that Mark did not expect, and a sorry understanding.

"I cannae fathom how dire it is for ye." He said, quietly, his voice full of compassion, "Yf what ye say is trew..."

Mark watched as Eadric knelt in the middle of the room, and pushed a brown pelt rug out of the way. With his strong and nimble fingers, he pulled up one of the stone slabs, to reveal a small hidden hole, lined with stone and pottery to keep the wet earth at bay. Inside there were bundles wrapped in rags, and a few glimpses of shining coins.

"Non but me an' thee ken aboute this." Eadric stated, as he pulled a knife from his belt. It was a short, stubby blade, but looked sharp in the daylight. He dropped it in the hiding place, then moved the stone and rug back into place. He fixed Mark with a meaningful gaze, "Call him, if ye most. He'll be waiten."

As Eadric stood looking at him, Mark became aware of the scene fading. As the spell reached completion, the dark and the cold of his current predicament returned like a flood. Eadric, and his light and warm house, became a fading memory, until all that lingered with Mark were those knowing green eyes.

He took a deep breath, starting to feel around the floor. "Where's that blanket?" He asked.

"Are you... talking to me now? Or are you still in your crazy-psycho-trance?" Harry asked in a bored tone, as though he'd already asked this a few times.

"I'm talking to you, Harry." Mark confirmed.

"Well, you might have been talking to that Eddy person. Although it was weird, only hearing your side of the conversation. I didn't realise how whiny you could sound."

"Thanks, Harry, that's awesome." Mark grumbled. "Now, if we can put insults and the fact that you're still pissed at me aside, we might have a way out."

Mark felt some coarse material, and bundled it up, getting it to spark to life again. He set the make-shift torch on the ground, and ran his fingers over the stone floor, until he traced the right panel. He grunted as he tried to lift the slab, but it stayed reluctantly in place.

"Can you give me a hand wi' this?" He asked, trying to not sound too annoyed with his best friend.

Harry shuffled round next to him, grabbing at a gap in the stonework. Together, they heaved the slab out of the ground. There was a hiss as stale air was released from the hiding spot.

Mark looked down, he could see that it was a warped version of what he had seen mere minutes ago. The shiny brass coins had been reduced to rusty dull circles, and the precious items wrapped in rags were now damp and filthy. Mark leant forward, and gingerly picked up the knife that Eadric had dropped, the leather handle had perished and become a thick black stain around the body of the knife, whilst the blade still held the promise of sharpness.

"*That's* supposed to save us?" Harry said, unimpressed. "We'll run out of air before we cut through these bloody stone walls."

"It's not for cutting walls." Mark replied quietly.

He rolled up the sleeve on his left arm, and held the blade over his smooth and unmarked flesh.

Chapter Nineteen

"No!" Harry leapt to his feet, yelping as his head hit the low ceiling.

Mark hesitated, a coward in the face of causing himself pain.

"Mark, are you mad?" Harry said, hovering next to him, his eyes fixed on the knife. "You won't use dark magic, but you'll summon a demon? Have you lost the bleedin' plot?"

Mark shivered at the enormity of what he was doing. Then he thought again of Eadric, of his dreams, of every instinct that was screaming at him. "I can't explain it," he admitted, "but I think we can trust him."

"Oh, you *think* you can trust him!" Harry mocked, "Well that makes me feel loads better. You might be ready to risk damning yourself, but I don't want to die in this pit! Or release another demon into this world!"

"Harry..." Mark trailed off. There was nothing he could say that would make this any easier.

Before his best friend could argue any further, Mark cut the sign of Silvaticus in his arm in three sure strikes. It hadn't hurt as much as he had expected, but Mark still shuddered as blood pearled out of his wounds and slowly dripped to the floor.

"Silvaticas, I summon thee." Mark said faintly.

Within a heartbeat Mark could feel the presence of something else in the small room. He got the impression it was old, so very old; and more powerful than Mark had anticipated. It wrapped around Mark's arm with a cold touch, and he noted that his cuts had healed to angry red marks.

Icy tendrils ran across his body, and though it repulsed him, he couldn't sense the anger and violence that emanated from Robert. Mark could feel this demon seeking ownership of his body, and he gave it a mental shove. "No."

There was a pause, another heartbeat, and the presence withdrew.

"Please, Silvaticus, release us from this room." Mark begged.

The essence of the demon curled indistinctly, making no attempt to obey. Mark could almost see the demon sitting back and waiting until it benefitted him.

"Eadric said you would help." Mark insisted, pushing away the first niggle of doubt.

Still, nothing happened.

"There's another demon involved, he goes by the name of Robert, the same name of a Duke he once possessed." Mark added in a mad gamble. "I know he's connected to you."

The demonic energy in the room started to swell, finally excited by the prospect.

"I'll take you to him." Mark promised, "Just get us out of here."

'Dworestu.'

The single word came out like a whisper. There was the grinding of old stone, and a crack of light pierced the darkness; cold, fresh air hit them. The slabs shifted, and a set of rough steps staggered up the wall.

Mark stood, hunched in the small room, and started to move towards the light.

"Mark-"

"Harry, escape now; argue later." Mark cut off the inevitable, and grabbed his best friend be the arm, dragging him to the exit.

They stumbled up the uneven steps, and Mark collapsed on the grass, breathing in the air, the clean damp scent of the hills in spring. He'd never took such pleasure in something so simple, after the dark, dank nothingness of that room.

"Mark, it might be a good time for something witchy..." Harry said, giving him a kick in the shins to get his attention.

Mark dragged his gaze up from the ground to see a gathering of people, surrounding his prison. They just

182

stood there, watching silently, eerie witnesses to their escape. Most held something that could be turned into a weapon – thick lumps of wood, or gardening implements with sharp attachments. Mark shivered as he noticed their auras, all browns and blacks and coiling with pain and anger.

"He's out." A familiar female voice said.

Mark turned to see Michelle putting away her phone. He felt a stab of betrayal that one of his classmates would stand alongside Robert.

Mark's own phone buzzed with messages flooding in, now that he was out of that black hole. He took it out of his pocket, and saw messages from his family rushing in. The latest one from Nanna glowed on his screen: *'You're back on the grid. We're coming.'*

Mark felt hope stir in his chest. Whatever was going to happen, Nanna was on her way; the bad guys stood no chance.

"Is there a party invitation we missed?" Harry asked loudly.

There was silence in return, as everybody continued to stand and stare.

There was movement on the horizon, and a figure crested the hill on horseback. They cantered down the gentle slope, and Mark felt a stab of surprise as he recognised the horse. It was Lulu, the feisty brown mare his Nanna owned. He couldn't believe that she was behaving so sedately for the demon; Mark sent his senses out. He could read her straining against the dark magic controlling her.

As he drew near, Mark could see Robert smiling in victory.

"I knew you would break, you just needed the right incentive." Robert said, halting the horse inside the circle of his servants. "Now, there is a full moon tonight. If you obey me, I will see that you will be rewarded; you will be the most powerful witch in Britain."

"Oh Robert, it really didn't go the way you planned." Mark replied, crossing his arms. "Sorry."

As Robert looked over him, trying to find out what he'd missed, Mark summoned Luka for extra protection. He didn't even have to look down to see the dog beside him, to feel the warmth of his presence rush through him.

Mark rolled up his sleeve to show the bright red marks he'd cut into his skin, and he saw Robert's confidence waver.

"Silvaticus, he's all yours." Mark said.

The ground began to rumble, and Mark could see that Robert's servants finally took a step back, cowed by what they were witnessing.

Slabs of stone pounded together to make the body and limbs of a giant beast, which towered over Mark and Harry. On its ugly head, it had a row of great, uneven teeth; and black eyes that absorbed all light. It began to move, and dust filled the air. The ground shook again as its four feet planted, ready to pounce.

"Silvaticus, so good to see you again, even if it is in this dismal form. Couldn't bring yourself to take a human host, again?" Robert sneered, but Mark could tell his cockiness had faded.

The giant beast opened its mouth, giving a guttural roar, with a great gust of foul breath. It stamped its front legs deeper into the earth, claws forming at the end of the limbs.

Mark felt two hands dragging him back, he looked over his shoulder to see Harry looking justifiably worried.

"I think we should run now." He hissed.

Mark didn't argue, and they both set off running across the uneven ground. Mark's legs were screaming with pain, after being cramped in that prison for hours.

Behind him, Mark felt dark magic accumulate, and he dared to glance over his shoulder to see Robert unleash what looked like a black cloud towards the creature. There was a resounding crack, and the stone shoulder crumbled to dust.

Another roar followed, and Silvaticus lashed back.

Harry had stopped in his tracks, causing Mark to collide into him with a grunt of pain. Mark lost his balance, falling to his knees. He looked up to see what was wrong.

Robert's servants were converging in front of them, blocking their escape.

Mark took a deep breath, these were people, just people. He couldn't fight them, he could only keep them off until the cavalry arrived.

"Luka." Mark commanded.

The dog jumped in front of them, its usual friendliness replaced by pinned-back ears and sharp teeth bared. A low growl was coming from his throat, as he warned the enemy to stay away.

Mark got to his feet, and tried to connect to the magic around him, but he found it jumping around and agitated by the presence of the demons. He tried again, forcing himself to be patient, even as Harry tugged annoyingly on his sleeve. He finally latched on, and let his intentions carry out with the magic, to protect, to keep the enemy at bay.

The servants looked confused, as they were repelled by something unseen, and they couldn't gain any more ground. Mark felt their repeated attempts at getting through, and it reminded him of Dean's party, with the snarling beasts trying to rip into the house. This time it would end differently, this time he would continue to channel light magic; he would do what he was trained to do.

The experience was quickly draining him, as the servants hammered relentlessly on his shields, he could feel his spell start to falter.

And then hope came again.

Mark felt a blaze of power light up the horizon, like the rising of a new sun. The witches had arrived.

Nanna was in front, her power so bright that Mark couldn't look directly at it; she ran down the grassy slope with the speed and grace of someone a third her age.

Behind her the rest of the coven followed. Mark could spot Danny and Denise, close to Nanna's heels. Even now, faced with demons and their supporters, Denise still wore a carefree smile. Danny, on the other hand, was looking more serious than ever.

The human servants split, half of them turning to face the witches' magic. They wielded clubs and sticks and some only their bare hands, but it didn't weaken their resolve.

Chaos was unleashed. All around them, there was fighting. Witches and humans and demons all piled into the mess of spells and violence.

The servants blocking Mark and Harry shifted to help their friends, and there was finally an exit.

"Go." Mark ordered Harry, "Go now, you can't help, but I can."

Harry hesitated, clearly not happy about retreating without his best friend.

"Go, I promise we'll argue more later." Mark repeated.

He watched long enough to see Harry start to run away from the fight, before Mark turned to face it. He couldn't fight, he didn't know the first thing about offensive spells – well, the first thing about *good* offensive spells. He wasn't about to unleash dark magic again. But, he could protect his coven.

He stood, pulling at the magic again. It was easier to craft the spell now, without anyone attacking him. He sent the protective spell into the battlefield, he could see it weave between the fighters, and curl at the feet of the witches. A couple looked over at him in surprise, but most kept their focus on the enemy.

It was becoming obvious that Robert's people were quickly becoming subdued. A few tried to run away, but most were submitting to the coven.

Mark looked up at the demons. Silvaticus and Robert were still circling, both looking worse for wear.

Robert tore his attention away from his opponent, noticing that his side had lost.

"No." He snarled.

There was a flood of dark magic, which rushed towards the demons. An explosion followed, that rocked the ground they were standing on. Mark stumbled back as debris and stone whistled through the air. His eyes were filled with stars, as the sudden bright light faded.

He couldn't see Silvaticus, only a pile of rubble.

Galloping towards him on his Nanna's horse, Robert leant down and pulled him up with an inhuman strength, dragging him up in front of him.

Mark was disorientated for a moment, he could smell the sweat of the horse, and there was the constant discomfort of the horse's bony withers digging into his gut with every stride. When Mark tried to push himself away, a strong hand held him in place.

"We're not done yet." Robert snarled, as he pushed the horse on, forcing her to race away from the scene of his defeat.

Laying over the front of the horse, Mark could feel all the blood rushing to his head. He couldn't think, he couldn't fight, he... smiled.

"You should have picked a different horse."

Mark put all his remaining energy into one intent - to give Lulu her freedom from the demon.

It was almost too easy, her wild spirit was already straining against the spell of submission that had been placed on her, and when Mark's magic opened the gate for her, everything exploded.

Lulu gave an equine scream of fury, slamming on the brakes. Mark jolted forward, and felt the air leave his lungs as he was jerked around like a ragdoll, before being thrown unceremoniously on the ground.

Mark scrambled back, away from the flying hooves of the broncing horse. Robert was clinging on for dear life, and it was mere moments later when he too was falling through the air.

Having got rid of her riders, Lulu spun to face Robert. Her ears were flat back, and the whites of her eyes shone. She placed herself firmly between Mark and the demon, her tail flicking sharply in agitation.

Clearly, Mark was *her* human, and she was going to protect him.

Trying to see between the shifting legs of the tall horse, Mark could see Robert back away. A moment later, he was gone.

Chapter Twenty

There was the sound of footsteps, as people ran in his direction.

Nanna and Harry were the first to reach him, and as Mark got to his feet he was pulled into a fierce hug.

"I'm alright." He protested.

Nanna wasn't satisfied, and checked every inch of him, pausing as she found the demon's mark cut into Mark's arm.

"You didn't..." Nanna gasped. "You stupid boy, how could you let a demon in? When we're working so bloody hard to get that one out of your boyfriend!"

"I didn't let him in. We agreed to help each other." Mark sighed.

He wasn't surprised that Nanna was upset, and he didn't object when she checked him over again. She grabbed his head whilst she looked deep into his eyes, searching his soul for that hidden darkness.

Eventually Nanna let him go, stepping back. She still looked less-than-pleased, and Mark guessed he was in for an ear bashing when he got home.

"Right, let's get you boys home." She announced, grabbing her horse's reins, and proceeding to lead the way back over the moors.

The thick cloud veiled the sunset, and it was getting dark by the time they reached the yard where Nanna kept her horses. The car park was full of vehicles, abandoned by the witches as they raced to save the boys. Nanna insisted that Mark and Harry sit in her Land Rover, whilst she put Lulu away, and saw to the horse's needs.

Once the car door closed, Mark was aware of the awkward silence.

"So... that was wild." Mark said.

His attempt to start a conversation was met with stony silence.

Mark sighed, "C'mon Harry, are you not gonna talk to me? At least give me a hint at what's wrong with you?"

"Sorry, I thought everything had to be about you." Harry replied, coldly.

That wasn't the response Mark was expecting. "What?"

"You seriously don't get it?" Harry snorted, facing away from Mark. "All my life, I have gone out of my way to support you. I was there when you came out; I was there when you decided to be a witch; and I've been there through all this crap with Damian."

"I know, you're my best friend." Mark replied, wondering where this was going.

"Yes, but lately, I don't think you're mine... You're never there for me, when I need you; you missed my first gig; ignore what I say 'cos it doesn't suit you..." Harry took a deep breath, "And today? I'm stuck in that hole *because of you*, and you dare to summon a demon? Even when I begged you not to. Clearly, you don't give a shit about me."

Mark was lost for words, had he really been such a bad friend? He felt his emotions rush into his throat, and Mark bailed from the car before he could break.

Outside, it was getting colder, and a breeze was picking up. Mark crossed his arms, wishing he had a coat. Even more, he wished he could fix things with Harry. He wandered over to the well-lit barn, in time to see Nanna throw a rug on Lulu.

"How is she?" Mark asked, his voice cracking.

"Tired, possibly lame. Your demon didn't have the decency to put boots on her." Nanna replied, with half-hearted humour. "She'll be fine in a few days."

"Is there any news on Damian? Or Robert?"

Nanna shook her head. "He disappeared, along with one of his servants – we've accounted for everyone except one girl...."

Mark felt his stomach drop, and he didn't need two guesses as to who, "Michelle?"

"Yeah. They'll surface soon enough, I've got people looking out for them." Nanna said. "The coven is dealing with the rest of the servants, taking them to the police for processing. The best thing you boys can do right now, is go home and sleep."

"We will, just waiting on our designated driver."

Nanna smiled, and cuffed him playfully. Taking the hint, she said goodnight to her horses, and grabbed her keys.

*****

As soon as Mark got home, negotiated two very worried parents, and dodged some prying questions from Nanna; his head hit the pillow and he was unconscious.

The following day, he was finally awoken by his phone. His ringtone blared out, rudely interrupting his dreamless sleep. Mark jerked fully awake when he saw Damian's name flash up.

"Hello?"

"Hi, it's me."

"Which 'you' am I talking to?" In a few short words, Mark could hear the guilt in his voice, and could already guess; but he had to know for sure.

"The real me: Damian. I think last night really took it out of Robert – I've never known him to be so dormant." Damian replied, sounding exhausted.

"How are you? Where are you, I'll come meet you?" Mark said, getting out of bed, and rummaging around for some clean jeans.

There was a pause on the other end of the line, and Mark started to think that Damian had hung up.

"I'm fine, all things considered." He said with a sigh, "I'm... not coming back to Tealford."

Mark felt a cold chill down his spine, "What?"

"I can't put you in danger anymore. You, Aunt Maggie, Harry and everybody else. I can't risk Robert getting to any of you. He's shown what he's capable of, and there's no stopping him."

"There is, I promise there is a way. The witches were going to expel him last night..." Mark argued.

Damian gave a humourless laugh. "Thank you for trying to give me hope, but I know, this is for the best now."

"You're leaving me?" Mark asked, his voice cracking up.

"It's for the best. You..." Damian broke off, struggling for words.

"W-what about Aunt Maggie, what did she have to say?" Mark asked, realising the answer, even as he said it. "You haven't told her."

"No, I did, I... left her a letter. She's done so much for me lately, I couldn't just leave her without a word." Damian said, trying to reclaim some dignity. "I didn't tell her *why*, of course."

"Damian, you belong *here*." Mark said firmly, knowing that his pleas were falling upon deaf ears.

"These last few weeks have been amazing, they have been perfect, and I have loved every minute. Well,

195

except for the sixty minutes you forced me to sit on a horse." Damian commented, failing to hit the right note for humour. "Don't you see, that's why I have to leave. I don't want Robert to tarnish the only good things I have left in my life. I'll take him far away, and hopefully he won't return to Tealford."

"You can't run away from this."

"Thank you Mark, but we have to end this." Damian said firmly, and cut the call.

Mark was left, staring at his phone in disbelief, his thoughts sluggishly catching up with what had been said. Damian had broken up with him... that couldn't be the whole story. Mark would demand to at least speak face-to-face.

He called Damian back, but the phone kept going straight to voicemail.

Mark took a deep breath, suddenly his room felt too hot and claustrophobic. Without thinking, he grabbed his coat and headed out the house. He marched up into the moors, walking for miles, waiting for his thoughts to work properly again. His feet took him back towards the river, towards the site of the battle last night.

There were signs of destruction everywhere, but Mark knew they'd soon fade. The grass would regrow, and soon there would be no sign that anything had happened.

Mark took a deep breath. He'd lost both Harry and Damian in the last twenty-four hours. It didn't seem possible, they had both been such strong and certain

196

parts of Mark's life, it hadn't occurred to him that they'd leave him. What was he supposed to do now? Carry on with his life? Go back to school and pretend everything was fine? That was, if his school would still have him, after all this extra drama...

He felt like he was crumbling from within, his heart aching with every beat, pushing pain down every vein and artery. He loved Damian, the revelation came swiftly, along with the knowledge that everything was broken and beyond repair.

Mark saw movement near the stone ruins, and initially dismissed it as a fox or rabbit. Until it moved again.

"Damian?" Mark called out, feeling hope stir in his chest.

A familiar someone stood up, turning to face Mark, with a gentle smile on his broad face. His bright green eyes stood out against the dull background.

"Eadric... how?"

"Ye summoned us." He smiled, as his green eyes shifted to black.

Other books by K.S. Marsden:

Northern Witch

Winter Trials (Northern Witch #1)

Awaken (Northern Witch #2)

Witch-Hunter

The Shadow Rises (Witch-Hunter #1)

The Shadow Reigns (Witch-Hunter #2)

The Shadow Falls (With-Hunter #3)

Witch-Hunter Prequels

James: Witch-Hunter

Sophie: Witch-Hunter ~ *coming soon*

Kristen: Witch-Hunter ~ *coming soon*

Enchena

The Lost Soul: Book 1 of Enchena

The Oracle: Book 2 of Enchena

Printed in Great Britain
by Amazon